IMAGES
of America

TRACY

IMAGES
of America

TRACY

Tracy Historical Society

ARCADIA
PUBLISHING

ISBN 978-0-7385-2872-4

Published by Arcadia Publishing
Charleston, South Carolina

Printed in the United States of America

Library of Congress Catalog Card Number: 2004104917

For all general information contact Arcadia Publishing at:
Telephone 843-853-2070
Fax 843-853-0044
E-mail sales@arcadiapublishing.com
For customer service and orders:
Toll-Free 1-888-313-2665

Visit us on the Internet at www.arcadiapublishing.com

Contents

ACKNOWLEDGMENTS

Over the years many artifacts, photographs, postcards, documents, and maps have been donated or loaned to the West Side Pioneer Association/Tracy Historical Museum by people interested in preserving the history of Tracy and Tulare Township. Many of these items are on display in the museum, while others are stored in the museum's library and archives. This book, created by members of the West Side Pioneer Association/Tracy Historical Museum, showcases some of the photographs and postcards from the organization's collection. We would like to thank those who have given us permission to include photographs and documents from their private collections: Paul Andersen, Kate DeLap, Clifford W. Koster, Dennis Maddix, Al Rinaldo, and First Presbyterian Church.

The intent of this book is not to represent every segment of Tracy's history but to try to capture the essence of the town and the people who created the area's history. Some areas of Tracy's history are not included in this book because the museum does not own any photographs of these subjects. The number of photographs also had to be limited in order to meet the publisher's guidelines for the book's format.

The following people, under the direction of Onalee Koster, chairperson of the Tracy Historical Museum, put in many hours in the development of this book: Darlene Bonbrake, Dennis Maddix, Jeanie Karas, Onalee Koster, Ellen Opie, and Virginia Mynatt in selecting the photographs; Ellen Opie and Virginia Mynatt in researching and writing the text; Sam Matthews in researching and naming people in the photographs; and William "Bill" Carter and Steven Greiner in scanning the photographs.

—Onalee Koster, Chairperson
Tracy Historical Museum

INTRODUCTION

On reaching Tracy we found . . . evidence of thrift and enterprise; several new buildings being in process of erection, and considerable life and activity.
—*Stockton Daily Independent*, August 5, 1879

Tracy's history follows much of California's history. First inhabited by Native Americans, by the early 1800s much of the land around Tracy was part of Spanish and Mexican haciendas, and then, later in the century, railroad land grants. As parcels were sold and the remaining land homesteaded, farmers and ranchers, many of them immigrants, set up stake in the area.

The Yokuts were the Native Americans who lived in the San Joaquin Valley around Tracy. Their lives revolved around the wet and dry seasons, relying on food and water from the rivers, acorns from the valley oaks, and small wild game. As with other native Californians, the Yokuts were displaced by the settlers and fell victim to their diseases.

In the late 1860s railroad ties used to build the first tracks in the valley arrived at Mohr's Landing on Old River aboard the *Salana*. The *Salana*'s captain, John Collins, was the father-in-law of Adolph Linne and grandfather of Wilma Linne Frydendahl, dry land farmers south of town near present-day Linne Road.

In the 1870s two railroads companies—Southern Pacific and Central Pacific—merged to become the Southern Pacific Company. On September 8, 1878, the railroad town of Tracy, believed to have been named after Ohio grain merchant Lathrop J. Tracy, was founded. The buildings at Ellis, a coaling station at the foot of the Altamont hills, were moved three miles to the east at the point where the rail lines connected, and they became the first buildings in the new town of Tracy. Jim Eagan, a railroader who originally worked at the Ellis stop before it was moved to the Tracy junction, was probably Tracy's first resident. His sons are buried in the Tracy Public Cemetery, and his descendants still live in the area.

Tracy was the hub for three main railroad lines built between 1869 and the late 1880s—Central Pacific's route from Sacramento over the Altamont, through Niles, and then by ferry to San Francisco; Southern Pacific's line from Oakland around the bay through Martinez; and Southern Pacific's line through Los Banos to Los Angeles. By 1894, Southern Pacific railroad headquarters were moved from Lathrop to Tracy. The railroads brought a rough transient lifestyle, including bordellos and gambling, that lasted into the late 1950s.

The early settlers in the Tracy area were pioneers scraping an existence from the land. In the latter part of the 19th century, agriculture took hold, first with sheep grazing, moving flocks between the hills and valley, then with farming as the Delta levees were built and river irrigation was established. Sheep ranches largely gave way to cattle ranches around World War I. Even on the drier west side of the valley, farming flourished with varied crops such as barley, tomatoes, and nuts, and large processing plants. By the 1950s, agriculture was Tracy's main industry.

Life in the town of Tracy was focused on commerce to support the surrounding farms and ranches, as well as the railroads. Schools, churches, and community organizations provided stability for the residents.

As in all communities, Tracy's prominent citizens helped shape the community. The Tracy Historical Museum has artifacts from many of those citizens, including a writing box carried by farmer Martin Lammers, who was Tracy's first state assemblyman in 1875 and the namesake for Lammers Road and Lammersville School.

Growing from its beginnings as a town created by the railroad to a community of about 2,000 by the time it was incorporated as a city in 1910, Tracy remained a regional railroad town and local commerce center for surrounding farms and ranches into the late 1970s, when growth in the Bay Area started to spill over the Altamont and turn the small town of Tracy into the city of today.

The photographs and postcards we have selected for inclusion in this book cover the time period from 1878, when Tracy was founded, to approximately 1950. We hope you enjoy this photographic journey into Tracy's past.

One

The Railroad

Founded in 1878 by the Central Pacific Railroad, at the junction of the Central Pacific's Altamont line and the San Pablo and Tulare line, Tracy's growth for many years followed that of the railroad. The earliest residents of the town were railroad workers and their families and the businesses that provided needed services for them. Each spurt or decline in railroad activity affected growth and activity in Tracy. Increased rail traffic through Tracy resulted from the merger of Central Pacific into Southern Pacific and was further increased in 1894 when Southern Pacific decided to move its headquarters, including the repair shops, switching yards, and employees and their families, from Lathrop to Tracy. In 1910 railroad activity again increased when Tracy was named a Southern Pacific division point in the Stockton Division. Tracy's importance as a railroad center diminished when the steam era came to an end in the 1950s.

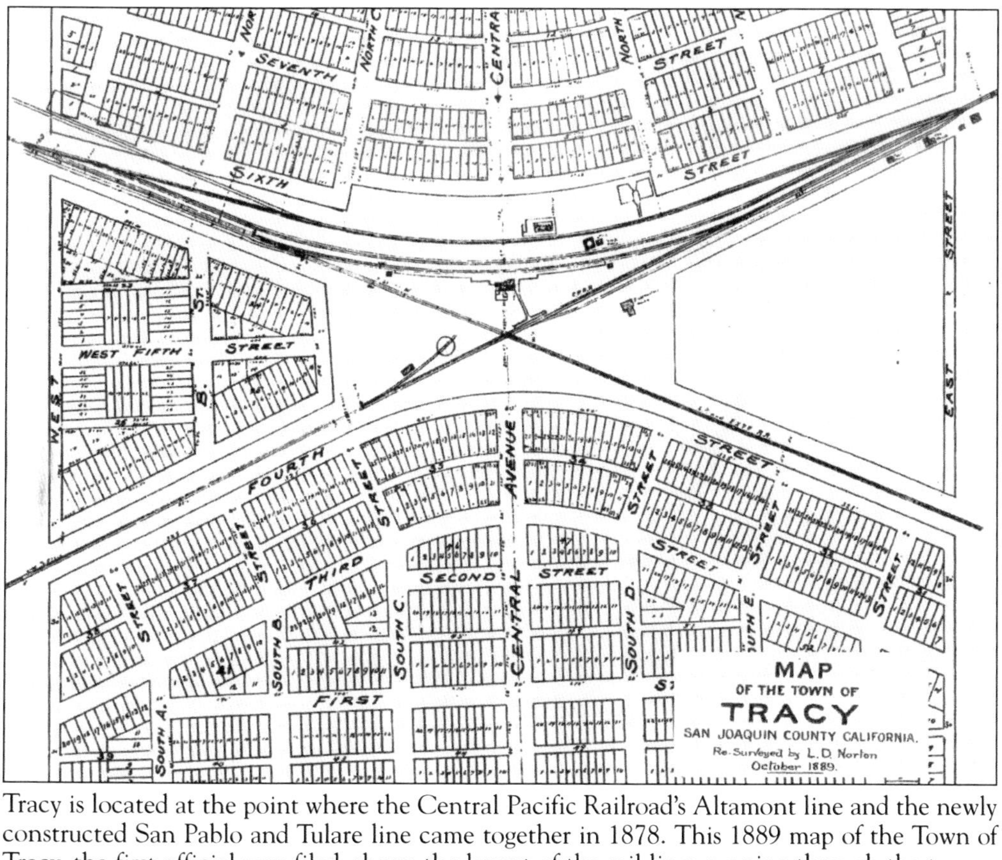

Tracy is located at the point where the Central Pacific Railroad's Altamont line and the newly constructed San Pablo and Tulare line came together in 1878. This 1889 map of the Town of Tracy, the first official map filed, shows the layout of the rail lines running through the town.

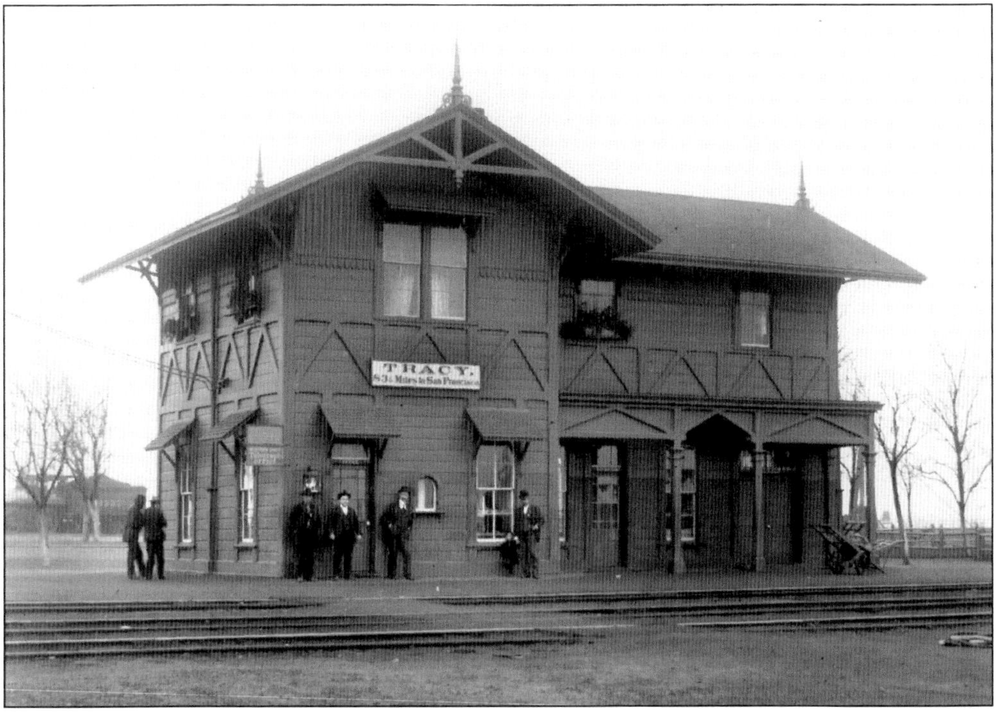

Standing in front of Tracy's Southern Pacific passenger depot in the early 1900s are, from left to right, Henry Turner, Dave Welch, agent Dave Pontius, young Charlie Payne, and his father, Dave Payne. The two-story building had two rooms on the lower level and living quarters for the station master's family upstairs. After a new depot was built, this building was moved to the east side of C Street, facing south toward Fourth Street.

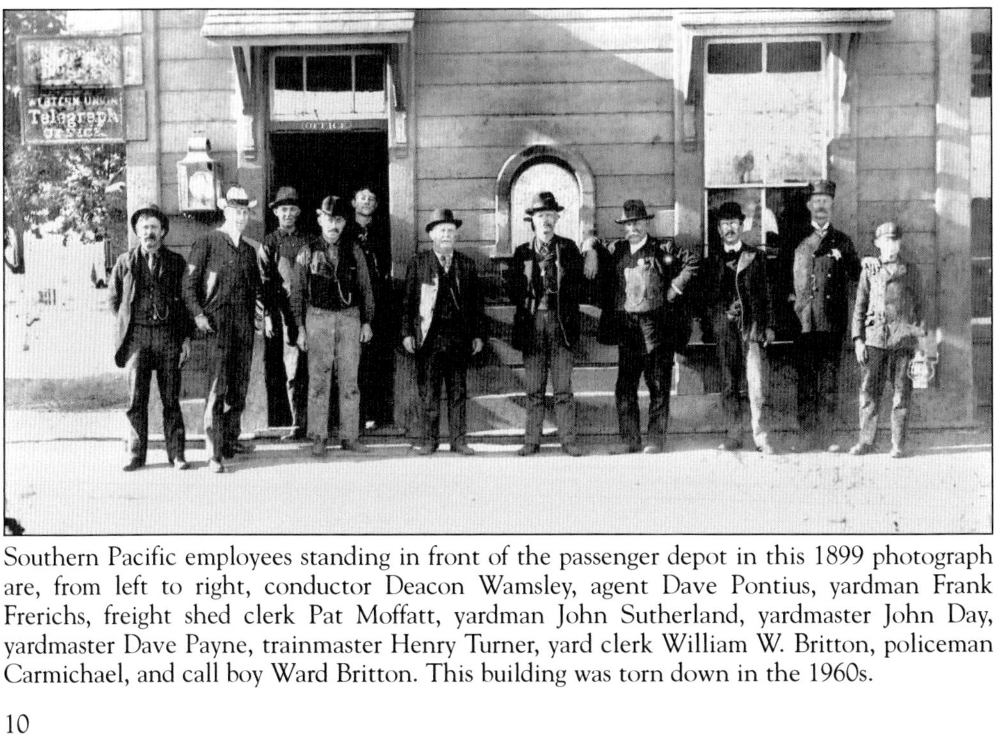

Southern Pacific employees standing in front of the passenger depot in this 1899 photograph are, from left to right, conductor Deacon Wamsley, agent Dave Pontius, yardman Frank Frerichs, freight shed clerk Pat Moffatt, yardman John Sutherland, yardmaster John Day, yardmaster Dave Payne, trainmaster Henry Turner, yard clerk William W. Britton, policeman Carmichael, and call boy Ward Britton. This building was torn down in the 1960s.

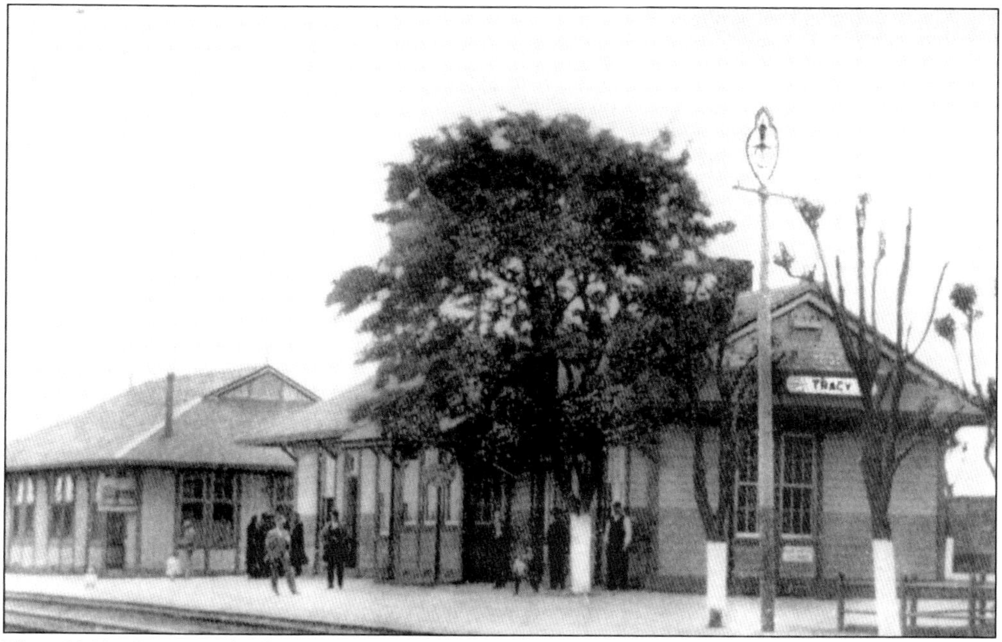

This 1918 photograph shows the new Southern Pacific Railroad depot and grill, located at the south end of Central Avenue. Built around 1903, the depot was painted a medium yellow with brown trim, Southern Pacific's colors for all stations. A few trees on the west side of the building offered some relief from the hot afternoon sun and were referred to as the depot's "air conditioner."

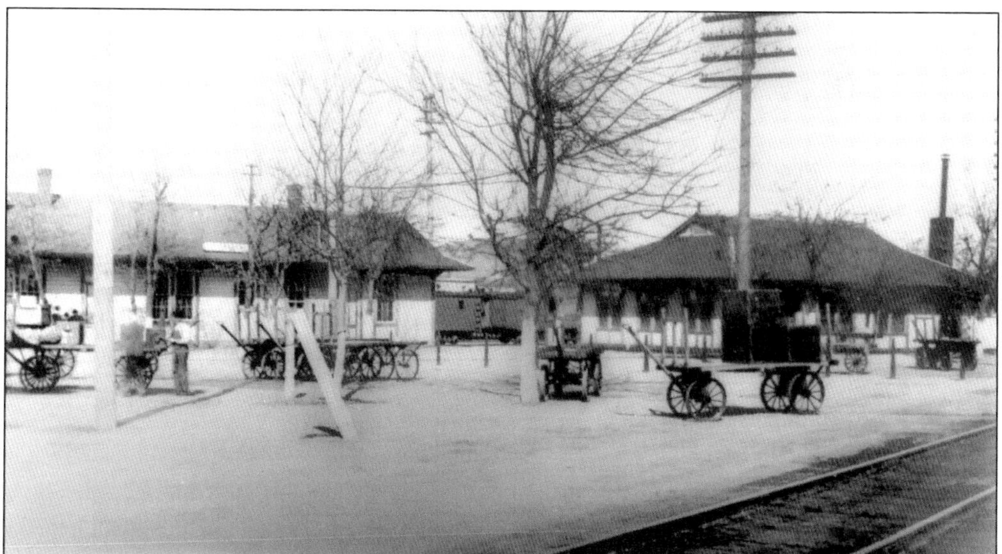

This photo shows another view of the depot and grill. The depot housed the local offices of the railroad, the yard master, the crew dispatcher, and Western Union. The waiting room was on the far left. The building to the left of the depot contained the baggage room and a small restaurant called a grill because most of the food was fried on a grill.

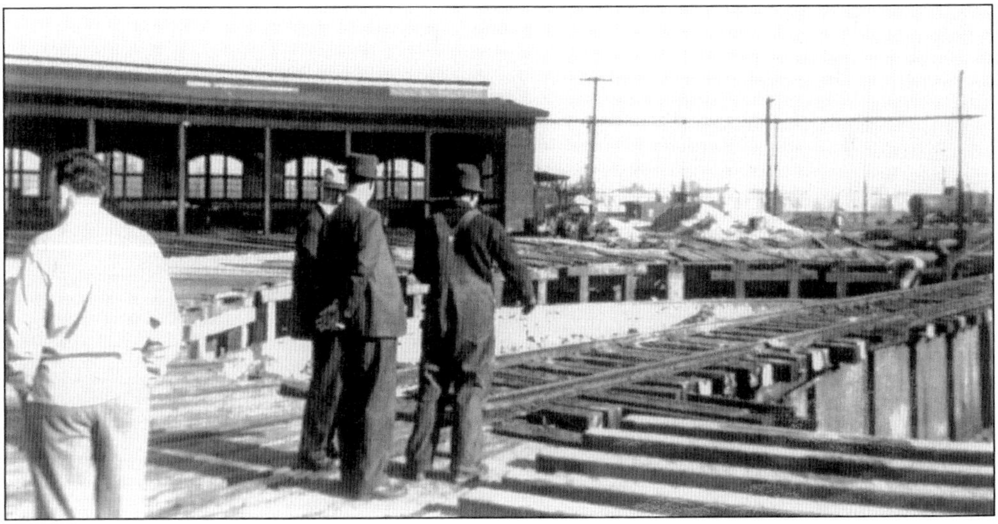

Southern Pacific's headquarters were moved from Lathrop to Tracy in 1894. Construction of the first unit of the Southern Pacific roundhouse was started in 1896. After the brick walls were completed and the roof was ready to be installed, a strong wind bearing down from the Altamont blew the walls down and construction had to be started over.

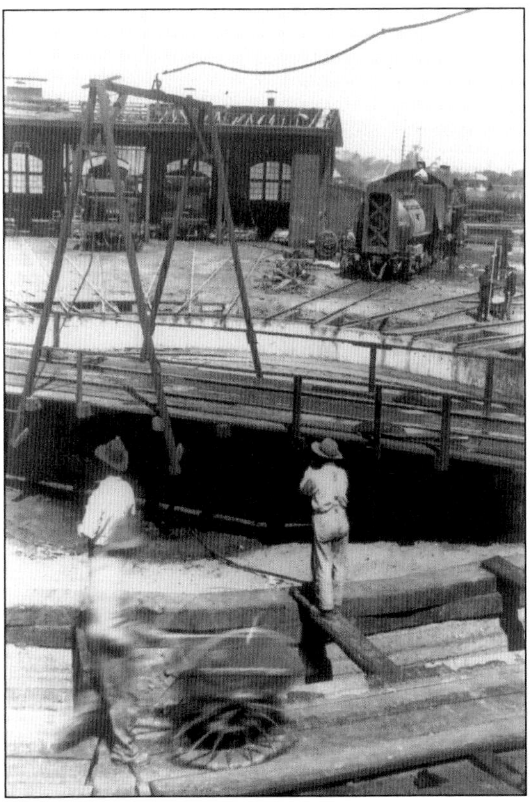

To meet increased activity in the Tracy roundhouse, construction on a second unit, built of more durable concrete, began in August 1918 and more than doubled the original capacity. It was not uncommon to service 35 to 40 engines daily in the roundhouse. This photograph shows the roundhouse in 1920.

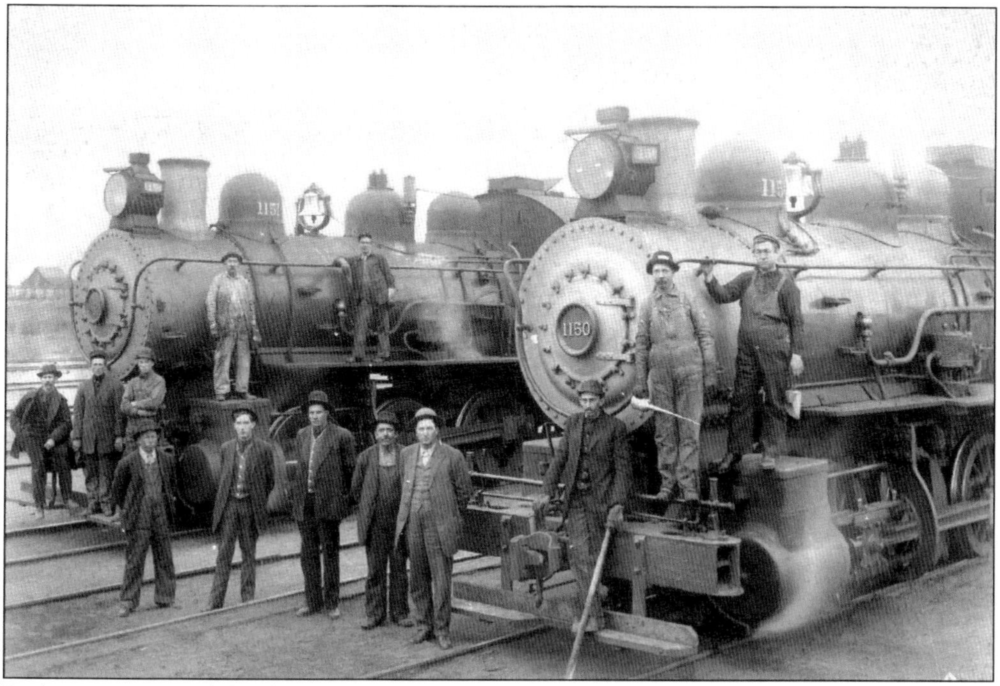

Both passenger and freight trains passed through Tracy. This photograph shows two steam engines and their crews ready to head out on their routes after being serviced in the Southern Pacific roundhouse in the Tracy yard in the early 1900s.

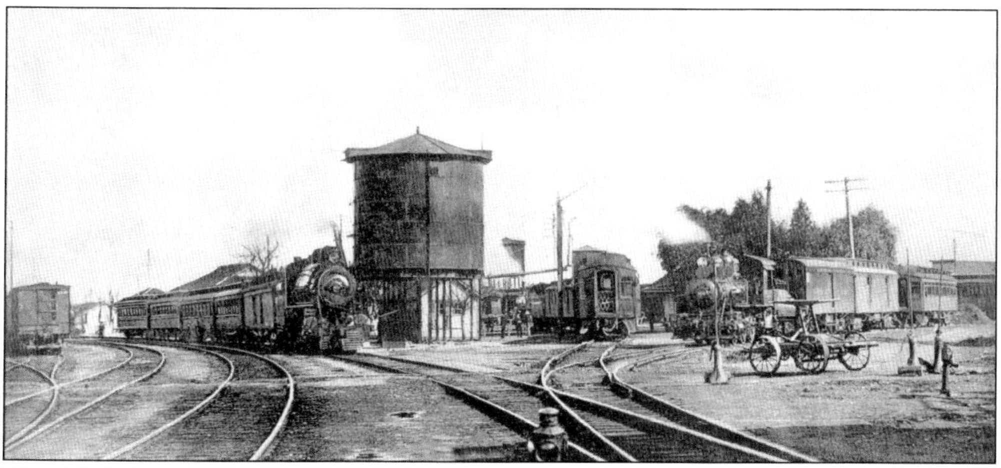

This 1908 photograph of passenger trains near Tracy's Southern Pacific depot shows the rail lines converging near the water tank. After the rail line along the west side of the San Joaquin Valley had been completed between Tracy and Fresno in the 1890s, trains arriving from all four directions made the local yard a very busy place.

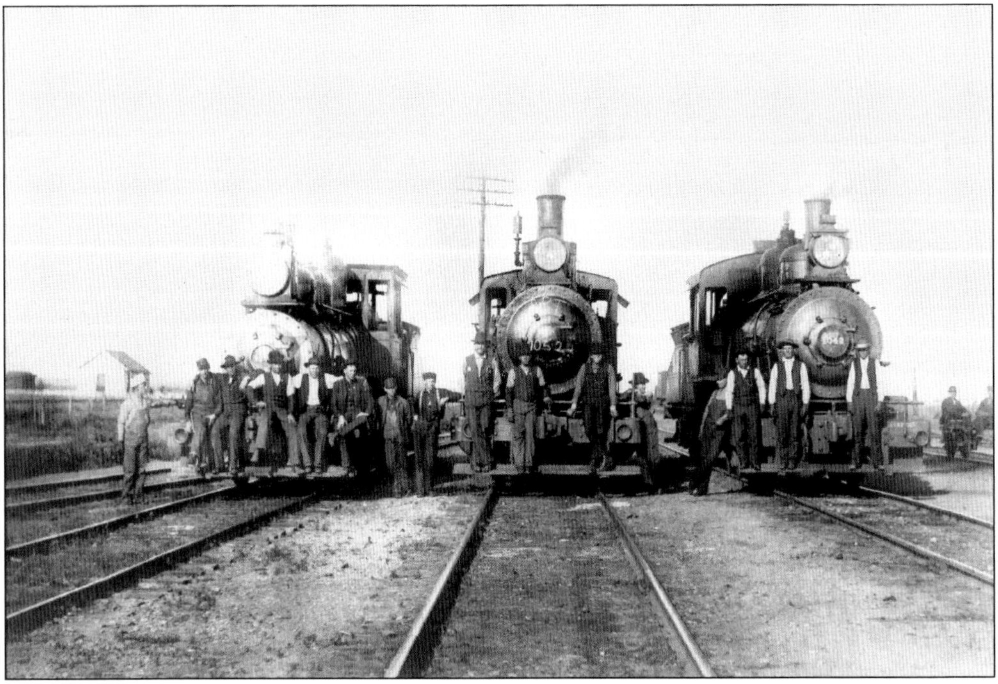

Switch engines, working 24 hours a day in the Southern Pacific yard in 1902, moved cars around in the yard until trains made up of many cars were formed. Switch engines didn't leave the yard. Once a train was formed, a larger steam engine was attached to the train to pull it to the next stop after Tracy.

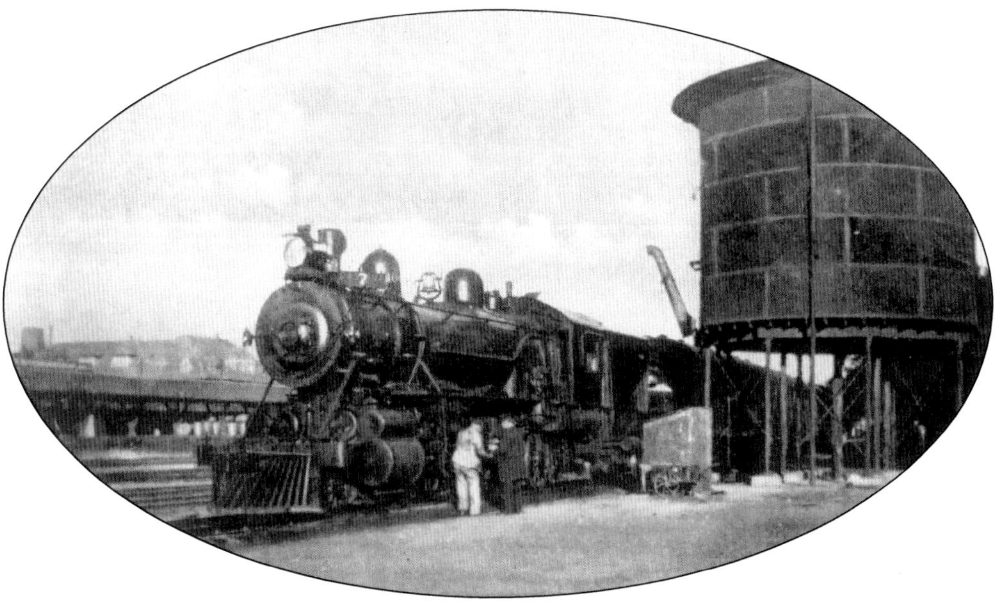

"The Owl," the steam engine shown in this photograph taken c. 1908, began operation on December 19, 1898. Because it ran an overnight schedule from Oakland to Los Angeles, the engine was named "The Owl." It followed the west side of the valley, stopping at various towns along the way—including Tracy—to take on water for the engine.

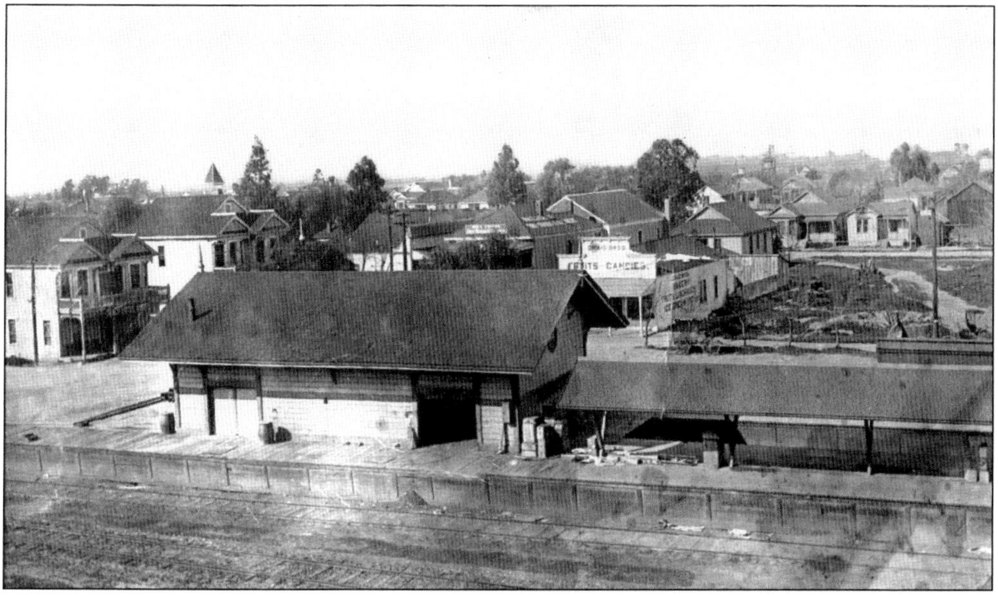

This 1909 photograph of the Southern Pacific freight depot, located on the south side of West Sixth Street, shows a portion of the city of Tracy in the background. Note the residential area, the steeple of the Methodist Episcopal Church located at the corner of Seventh and B Streets, and Craig Bros. Fruits and Candies to the north of the freight depot.

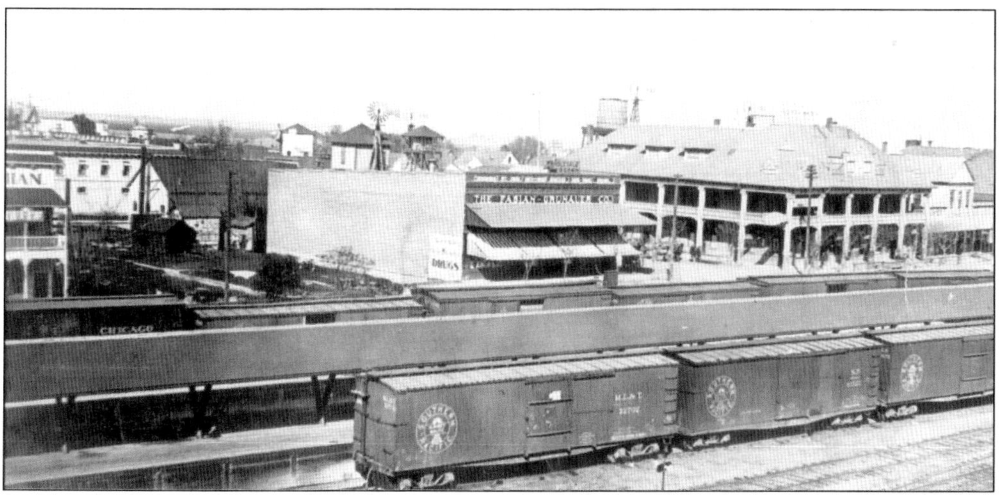

Some Tracy businesses are seen in this photograph showing the freight docks bordering Sixth Street in the early 1900s. The large-columned building on the right is the Tracy Hotel. To the left of the hotel is the Fabian-Grunauer Co., a general merchandise store. The Bohemian Saloon and Hotel is on the far left in the picture. Note the water tanks and windmills.

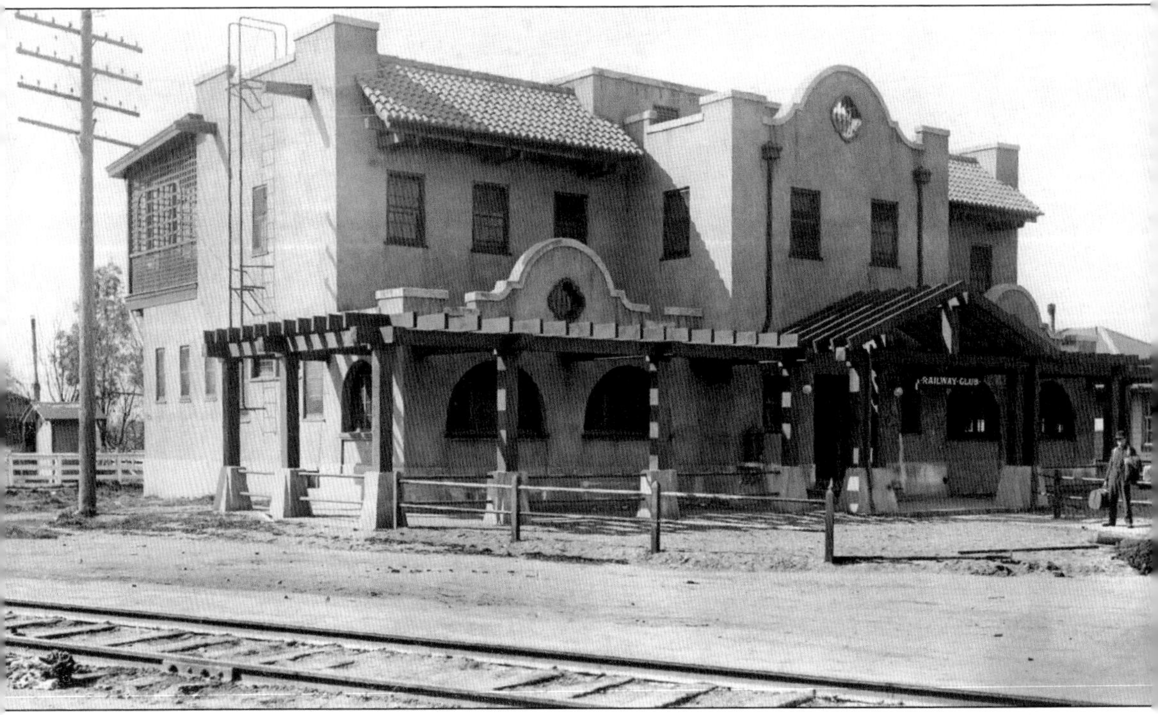

The Southern Pacific Clubhouse, a two-story structure built in the modified Mission style, was located near the tracks along C Street. The 72-by-47-foot building was constructed with money given by Mrs. Edward Henry Harriman, wife of a deceased railroad magnate. The clubhouse, which opened November 3, 1909, served as a hotel and recreation center for railroad employees. The main entrance to the steam-heated and electrically lighted building was lined with two palm trees and a carefully groomed garden of shrubs and flowers; ivy grew along a covered patio. The lower floor contained the recreation area, which had a reception room, a billiard room, a library, a barbershop, the office, and a baggage room. The sleeping quarters, located upstairs, were comprised of 17 bedrooms, each containing 2 single beds, and a screened sleeping porch with 25 beds. The beds were rented by the "sleep," not to exceed 12 hours. There were also 3 separate rooms containing bathtubs and 5 separate showers in the building. The building was torn down in the 1960s.

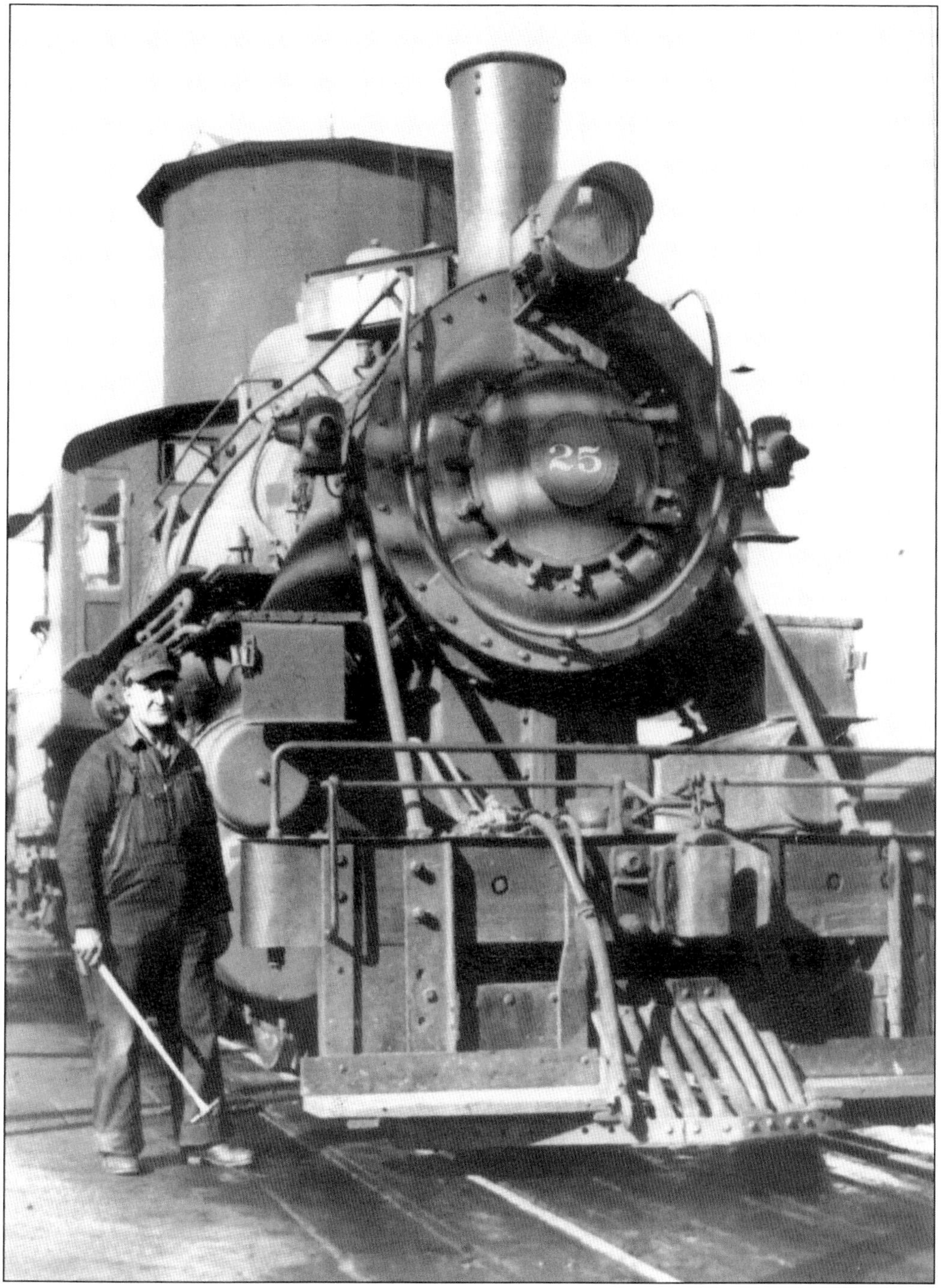

Following a common pattern, the sons of many "rails" followed in their fathers' footsteps and also worked for the railroad. Edwin "Eddie" Shelton, pictured here standing by a steam engine, worked for the Southern Pacific Railroad for 42 years. Like his father, Stanley, Eddie was also a machinist in the Tracy roundhouse. Eddie, a Montana native who came to Tracy in 1922, lived here for 27 years before moving to Manteca, where he lived for 21 years before his death in 1971.

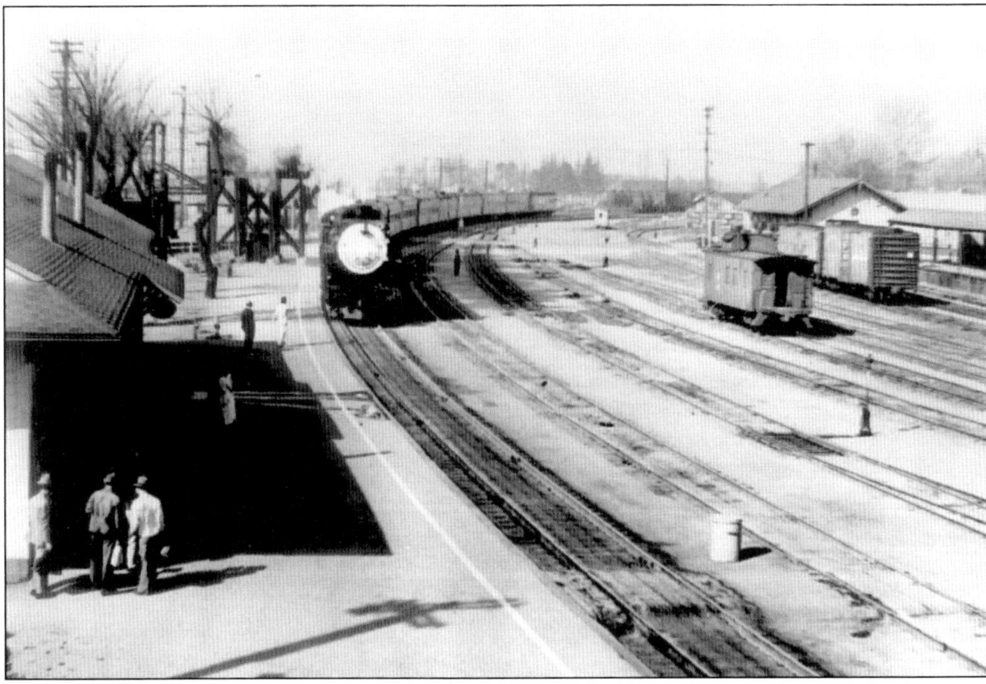

This photograph of the Southern Pacific yard in Tracy shows the area in 1948. Southern Pacific's peak activity here was reached in the 1940s during the years of World War II; around 1,000 railroad workers were employed in Tracy during that time. Trains carrying troops and war equipment and supplies passed through the local yard at all hours of the day and night.

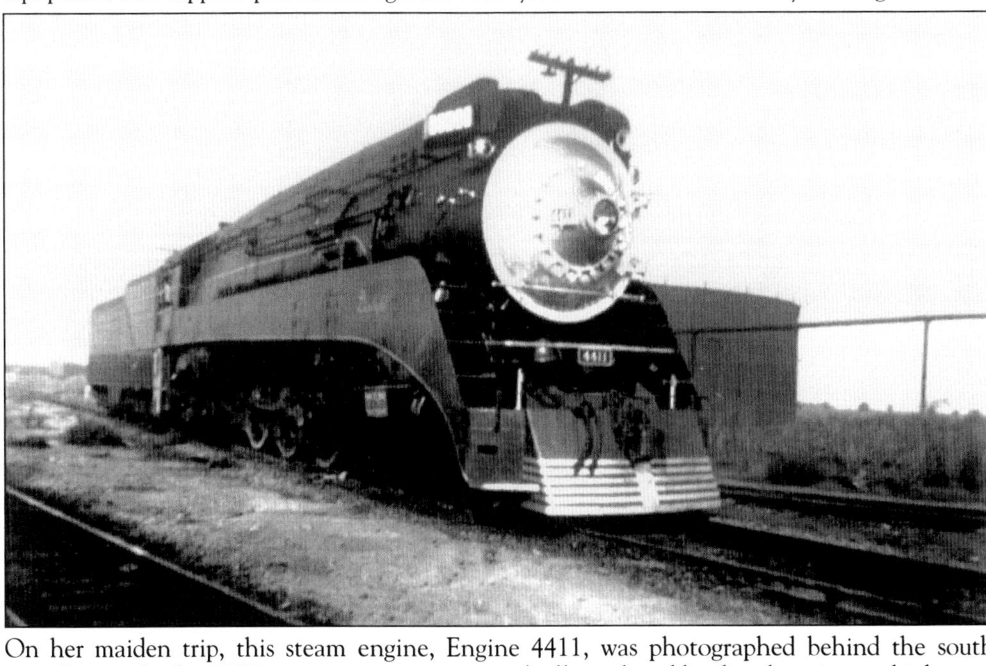

On her maiden trip, this steam engine, Engine 4411, was photographed behind the south roundhouse. In the 1950s steam engines were gradually replaced by diesel engines, which were more powerful and more efficient. With the passing of the steam era, the importance of Tracy as a railroad center began to decline.

Two

AGRICULTURE

The history of dry land agriculture on Tracy's West Side rested on the use of the plow. Experimental plowing and seeding showed that grain production was risky, dependent on seasonal rainfall on the virgin land. Because of the risk, farmers developed the multiple gang plow. In the beginning, plowing was just deep enough (two inches) to kill wild oats and weeds. Wheat for bread was needed, and for awhile the land withstood cropping every year. When yields dropped, hardier barley was planted. The method of "summer fallowing," which idled the land to store that year's moisture and hold the wild oats in check, was initiated. In spite of that, the oats took over when the farmer switched from six-inch-depth plowing to disking. The wild oats survived and crowded out the grain. In retrospect, those that stayed with the Stockton Gang Plow, religiously practiced summer fallowing, maintained a small band of livestock and chickens to help weather the dry years, and saved their money had the best chance of being "dry land survivors."

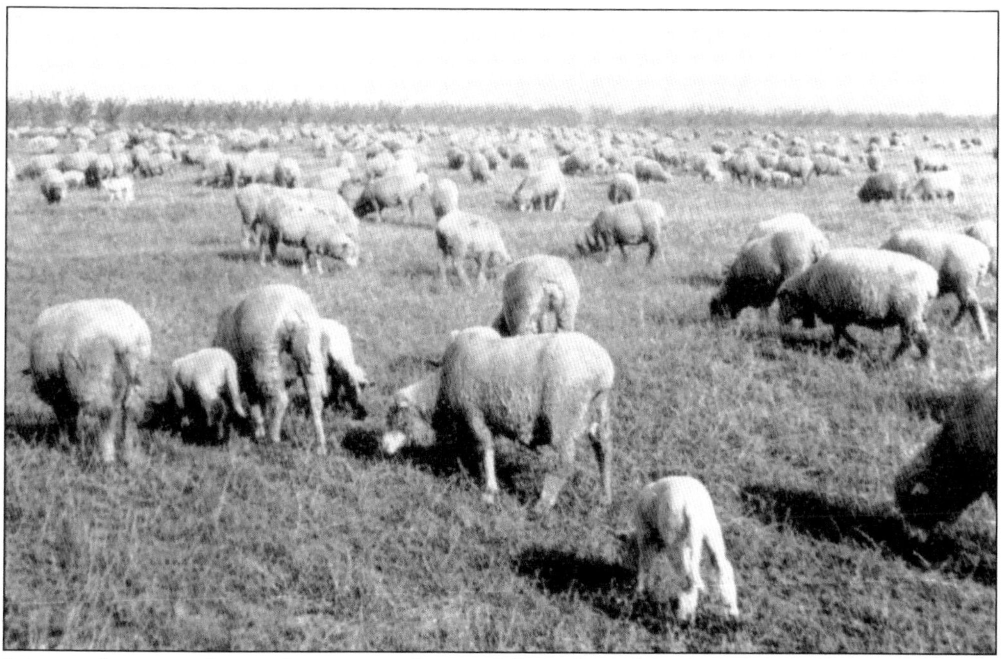

Prior to plowing and grain farming, settlers used the unfenced land for grazing sheep. Shropshire and French Merino sheep were raised mainly for their wool. Fences were built later for raising cattle, horses, and mules.

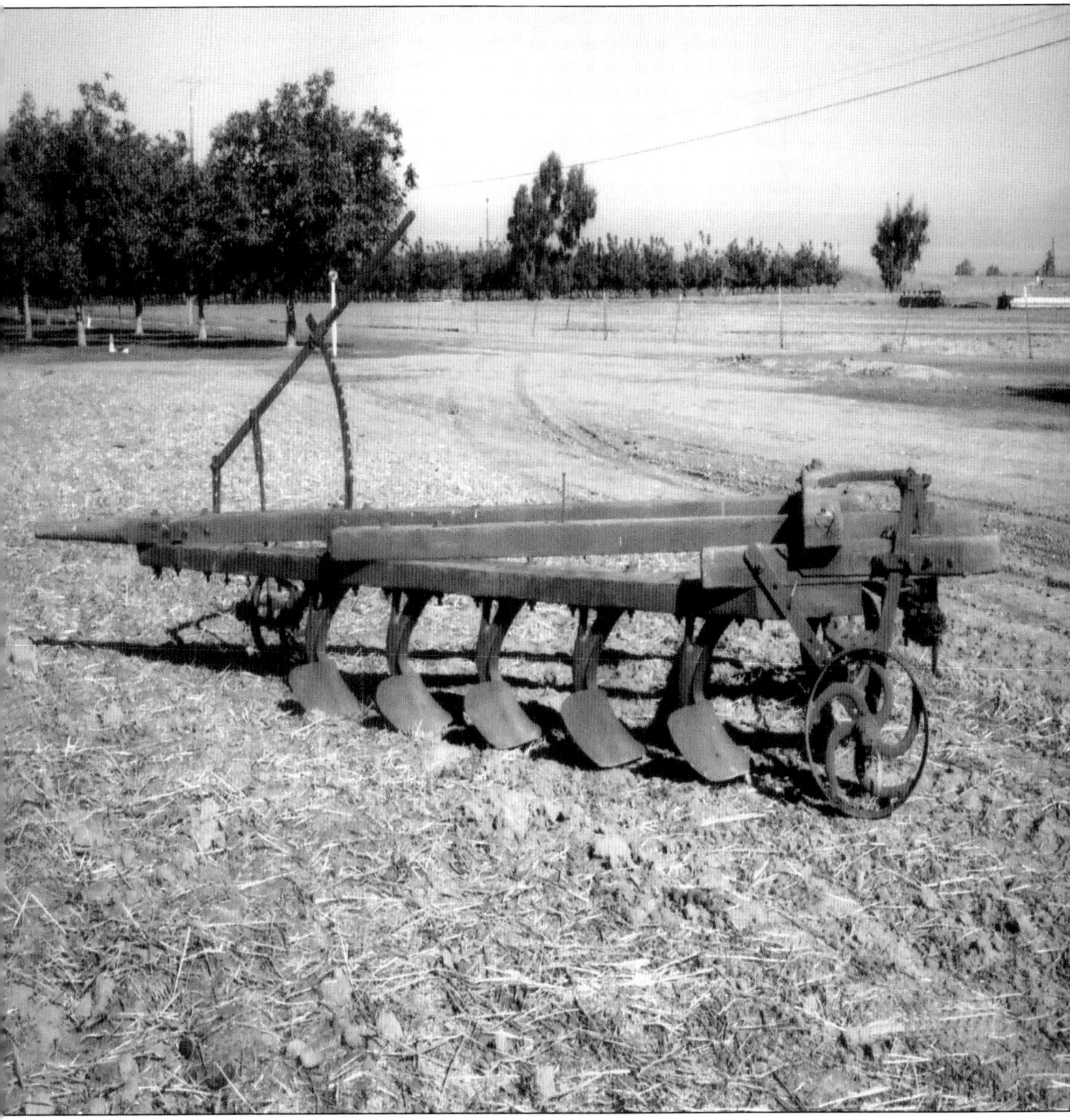

The Stockton Gang Plow, with the plowshare sharpened on both top and bottom, used one edge at a time to invert the soil. With this plow, a man could plow 10 to 15 acres a day. Plowing was no easy task, especially in the early years on the unbroken land; it required an experienced man with weight and strength in his back and arms and knowledge of the land and mules. Once the land was plowed, the farmer strapped half a sack of seed grain on his back, broadcasting the seed by hand as he walked back and forth across the field. One sack of seed would last half a day and sow 10 acres or more. The seed was then covered using either willow branches or a harrow. With the introduction of mule- or horse-powered seeders that planted and covered the seed in one operation, planting took less time and more acreage was covered.

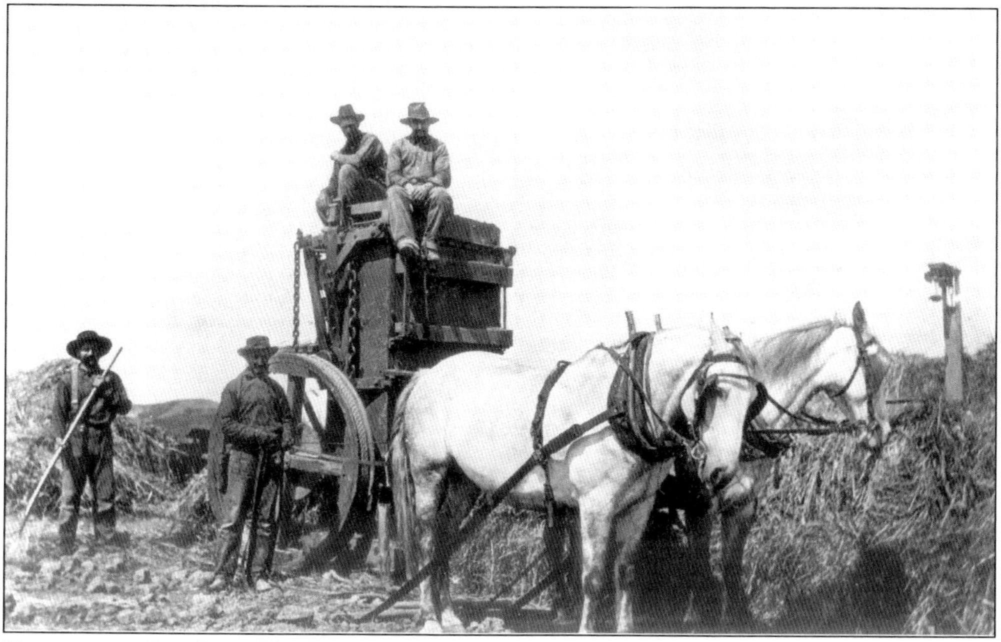

To operate a Petaluma Hay Press, an operator opened the top doors, hand packed the hay over the bottom plunger, and then closed the doors when full. The horses then pulled forward, winding up the chain on the windlass, which compressed the hay. Once the hay was compressed, the operator opened the side doors, punched six wires, and tied them around the bale. Lastly, the door was opened and out rolled the finished bale. (Courtesy of Clifford W. Koster.)

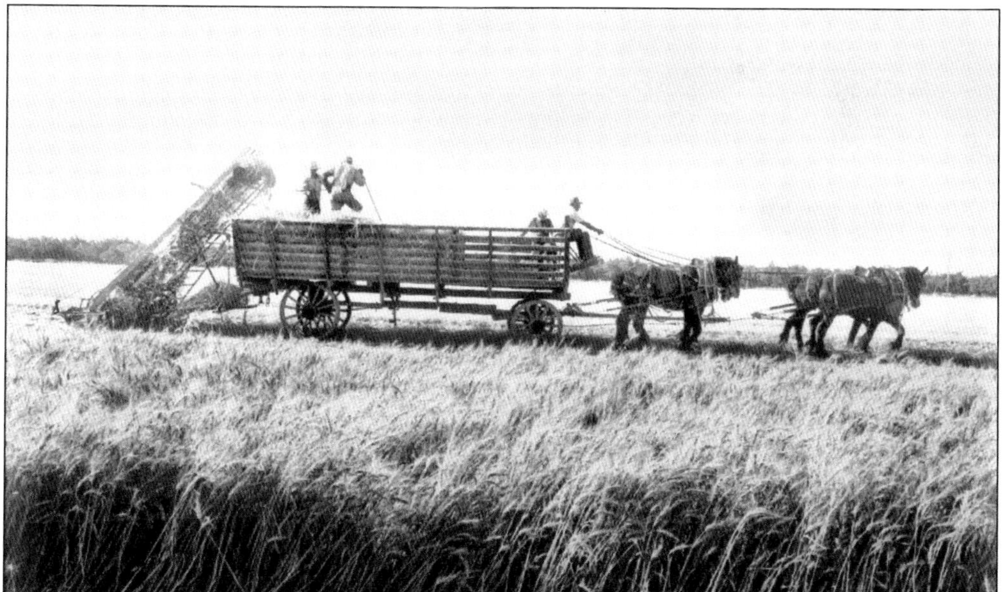

Four black Percherons pull a 20-foot wagon with compartments for 3 hay nets. The hay loader on back of the wagon loaded the windrow—a long row of cut hay or grain left to dry in a field—into the wagon. Nets were unloaded by means of a pole derrick or an A-frame hoist. A trip, when pulled, allowed the nets to split, dumping the hay. (Courtesy of Clifford W. Koster.)

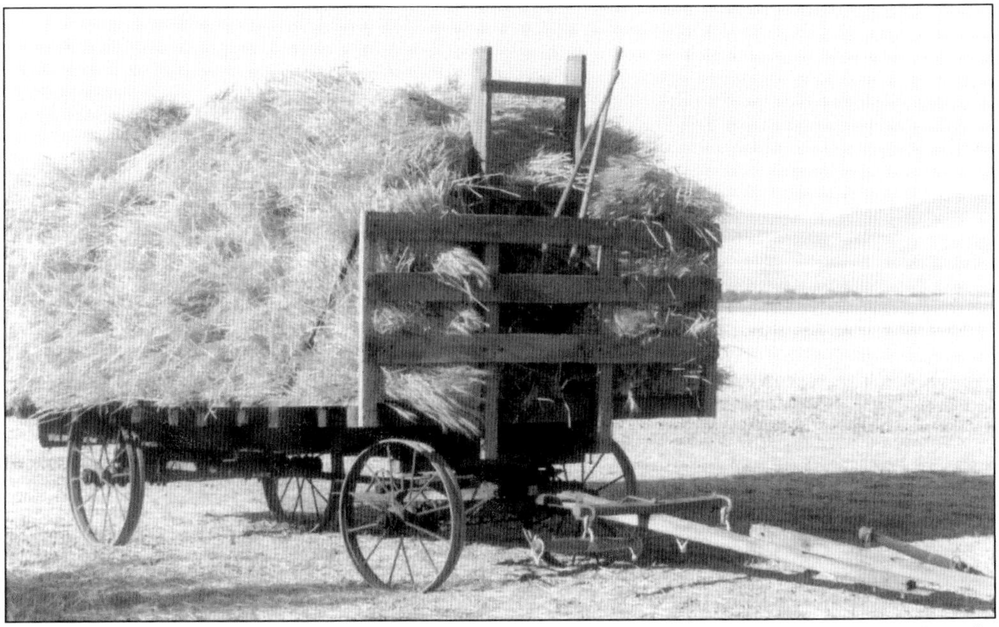

The following four photographs show the process by which hay was transferred from bundle wagons to a stationary threshing machine. A horse-drawn bundle wagon, loaded with bundles of grain, is ready to move to a stationary thresher, set up on a site determined by wind direction as a precaution against the danger of fire. (Courtesy of Clifford W. Koster.)

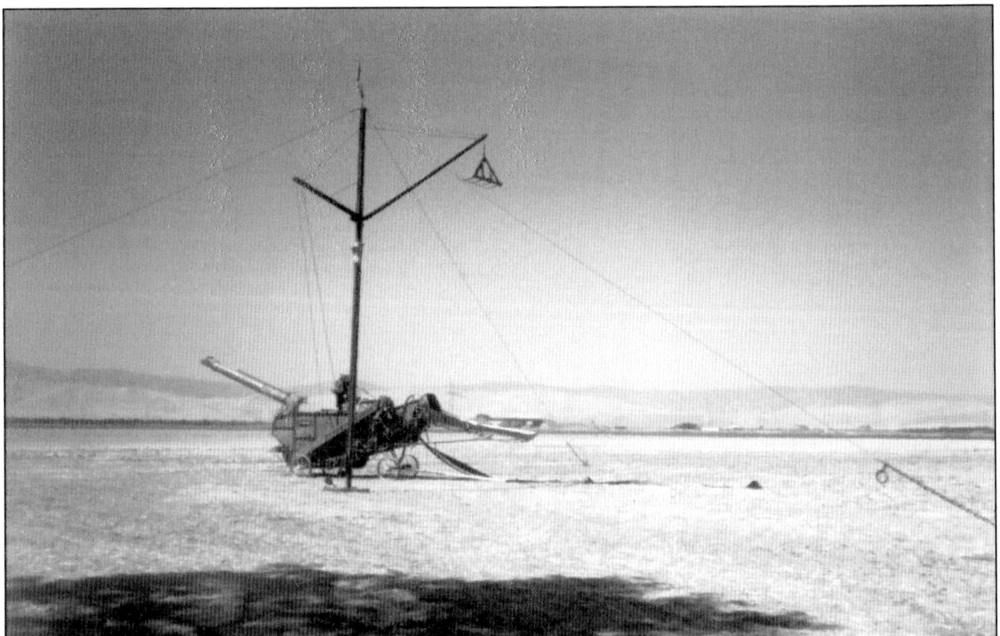

A pole derrick is in position to use a Jackson Fork to transfer bundles from the wagon to a stationary thresher. The Jackson Fork was made with a trip release, which released the load. The trip rope was also used to pull the forks back to the beginning to be reset for the next load. (Courtesy of Clifford W. Koster.)

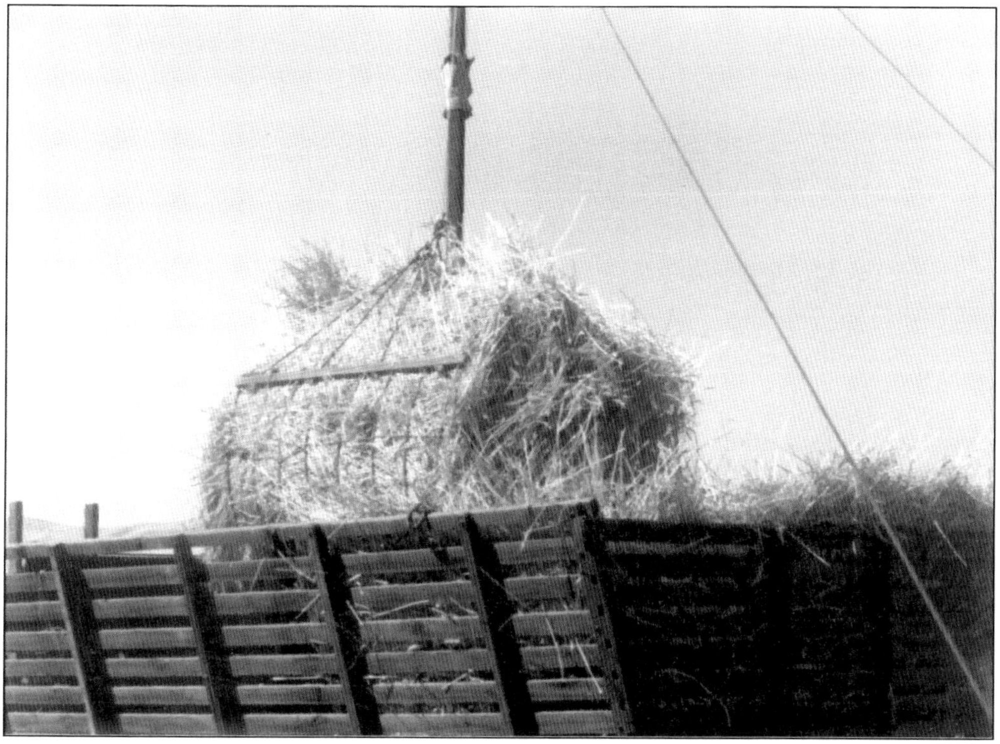

A pole derrick starts to hoist the hay nets out of the wagon. The pole is guy wired so it has a slight lean toward the dump site. As the load leaves the wagon, it swings toward the dump site, rotating the pole. The nets open on the bottom when the trip rope is pulled. (Courtesy of Clifford W. Koster.)

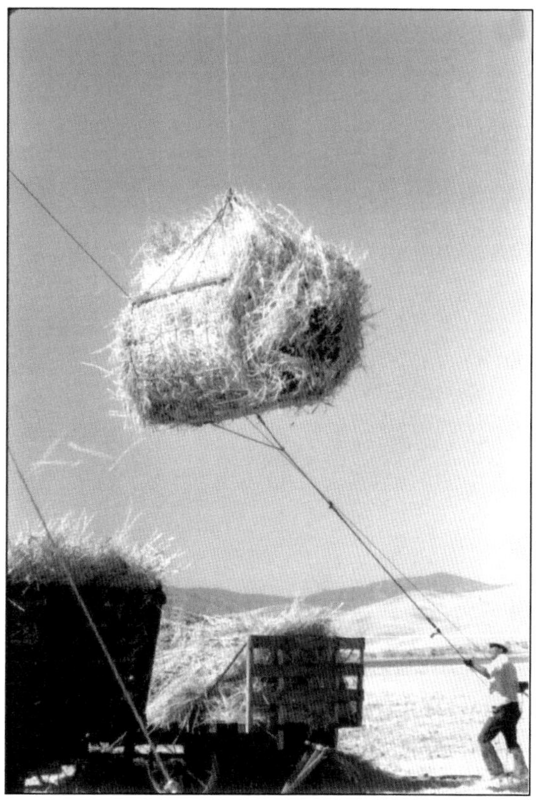

The pole derrick rotates on its base. When the derrick is in position to dump, the man trips the catch with the trip rope, the nets split, and the hay falls. The man rotates the pole to start the process again. The pole and arms are a unit and rotate as a unit with the load. A horse or mule powers the derrick lifting cable. (Courtesy of Clifford W. Koster.)

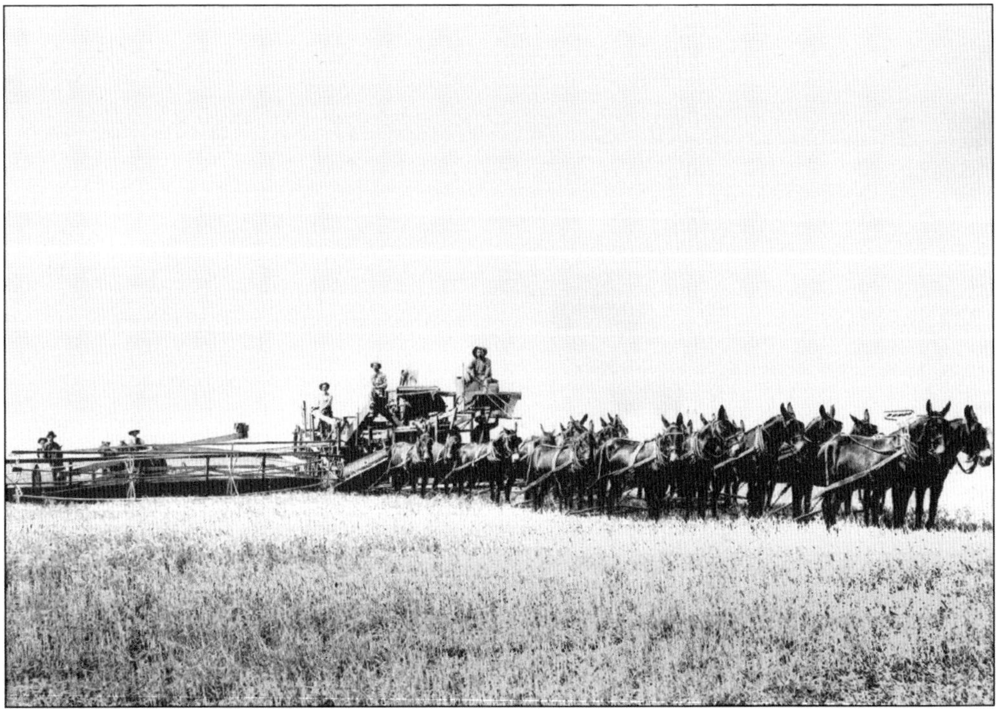

This Daniel Best ground-powered combine, c. 1900, was operated by a mule skinner who controlled the mules with jerk lines to the leaders. Bells on the hames—the curved pieces of a harness that fit around the neck of a draft animal—of the leaders kept the walking cadence. Under the skinner are the sack sewer and the separator man (the "boss" and head mechanic), the header tender on a pole regulating the height of the cut, and the owner and a "gofer" on the left. (Courtesy of Clifford W. Koster.)

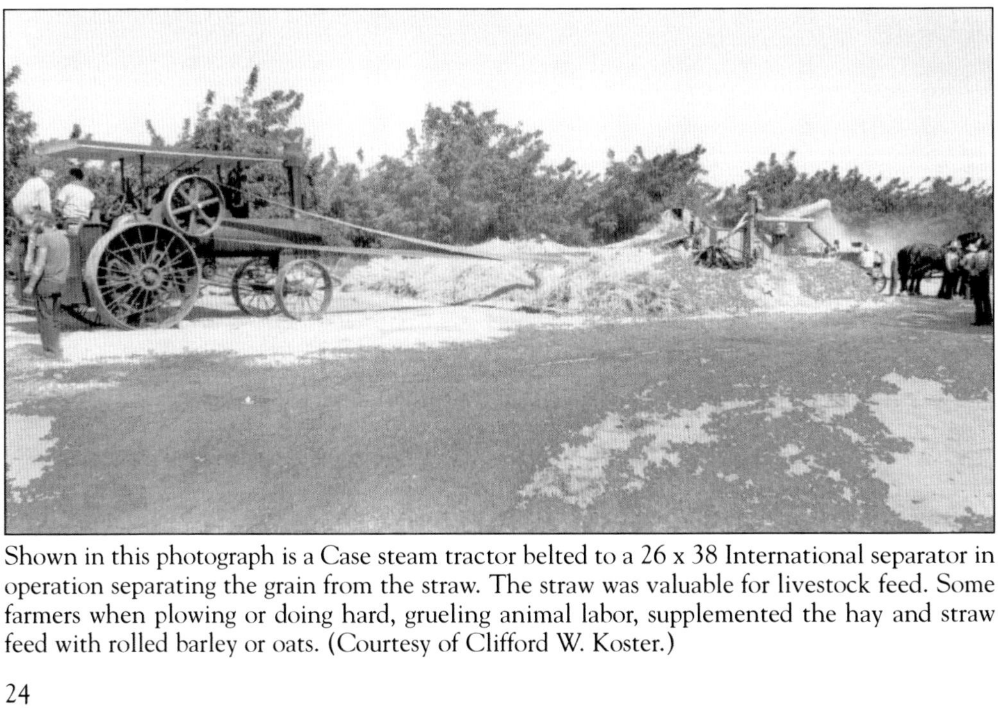

Shown in this photograph is a Case steam tractor belted to a 26 x 38 International separator in operation separating the grain from the straw. The straw was valuable for livestock feed. Some farmers when plowing or doing hard, grueling animal labor, supplemented the hay and straw feed with rolled barley or oats. (Courtesy of Clifford W. Koster.)

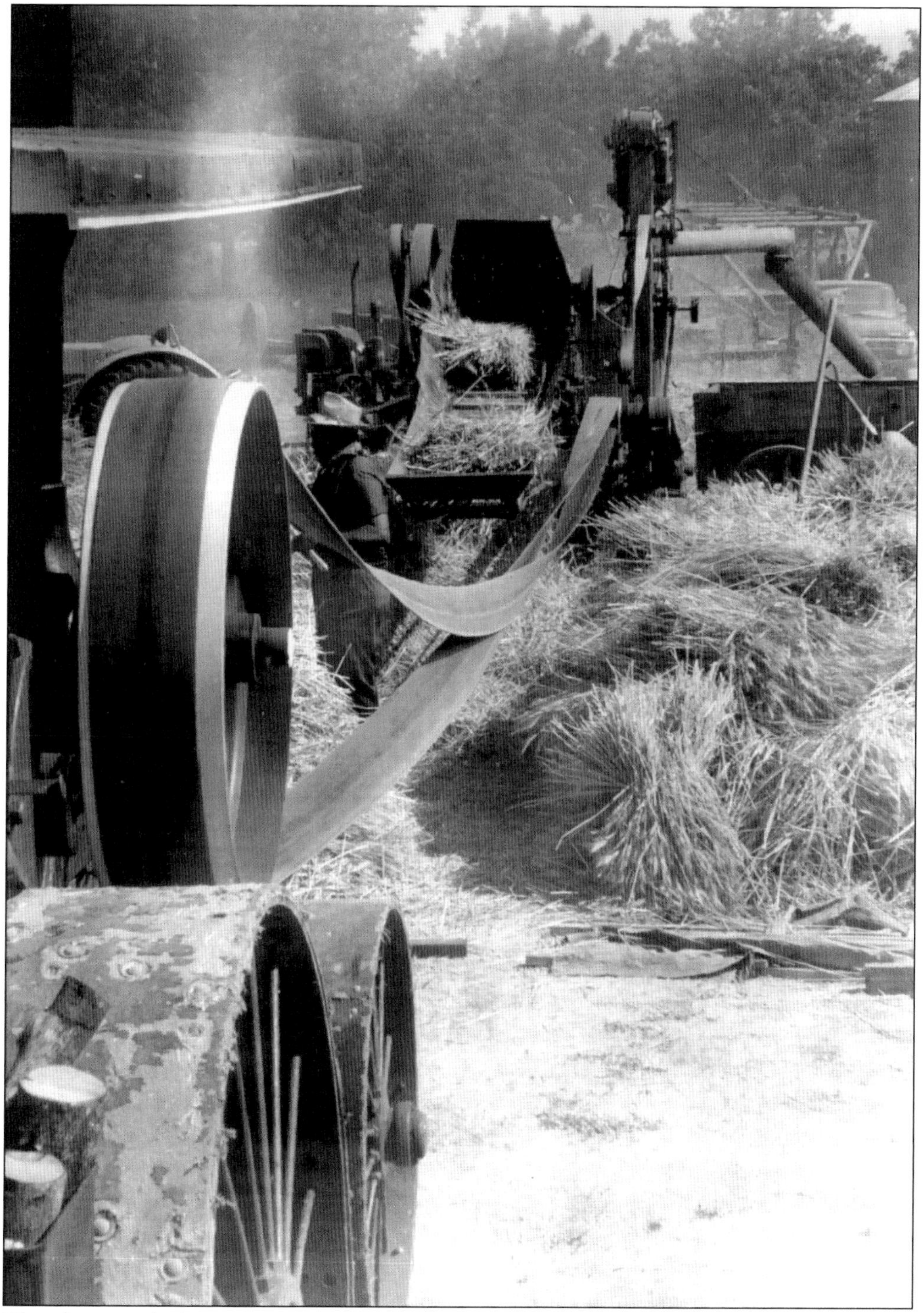

This photograph shows a Case steamer belted to an International-Harvester thresher, *c.* 1936. The belt length got the steamer away from the grain bundles. It was necessary to have the steamer away from the grain bundles in order to prevent the possibility of setting the bundles on fire. (Courtesy of Clifford W. Koster.)

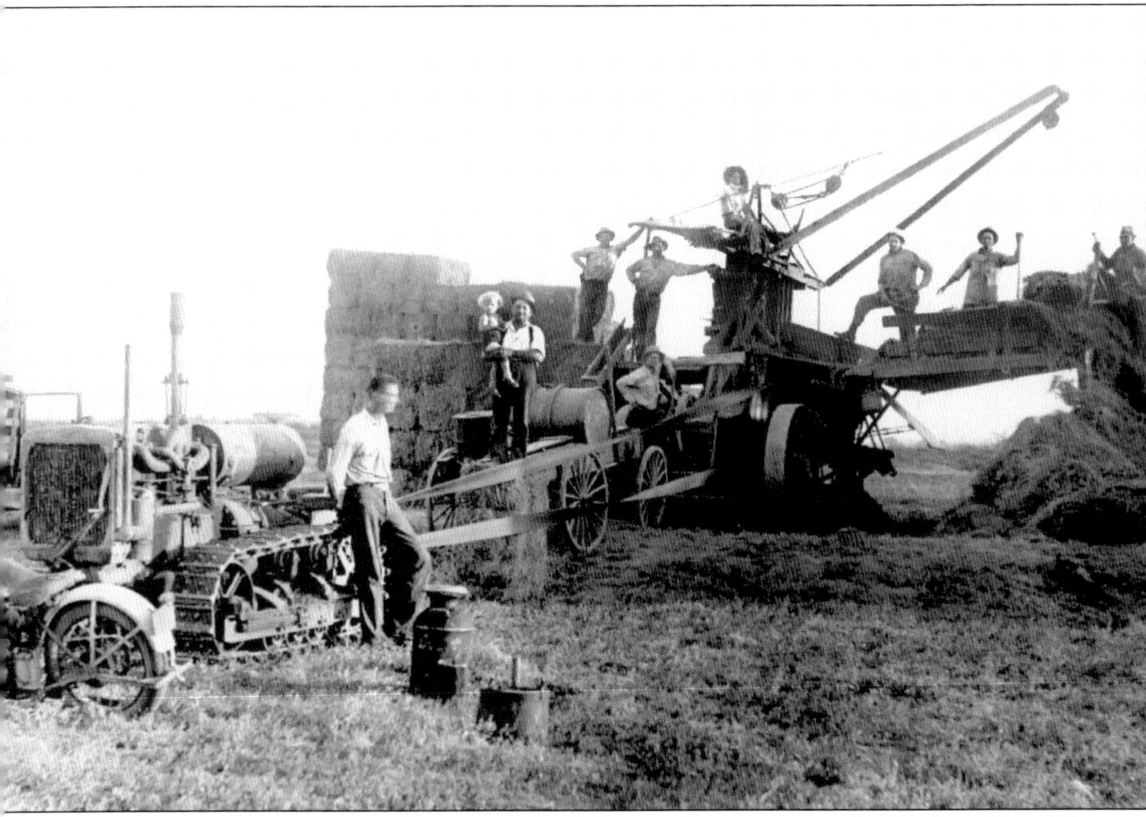

The five-wire Junior Monarch stationary hay baler was the successor to the Petaluma Press. The bale was tied with five wires under tension. The tractor on the belt is a Best '30' or a Caterpillar '30.' The daily goal was 100 tons of hay compressed into 275-pound bales. Men operated the baler by feeding hay into it, with one man on the spool, one man punching wires, one man tying wires and weighing bales, one man as the bale roller, and one man operating the clutch for the belt. The tall man on the left side of this photograph is Mr. Cordes. The appearance of the one-man automatic wire-tie baler in 1948 signaled a change away from the large crew on the Junior Monarch stationary baler.

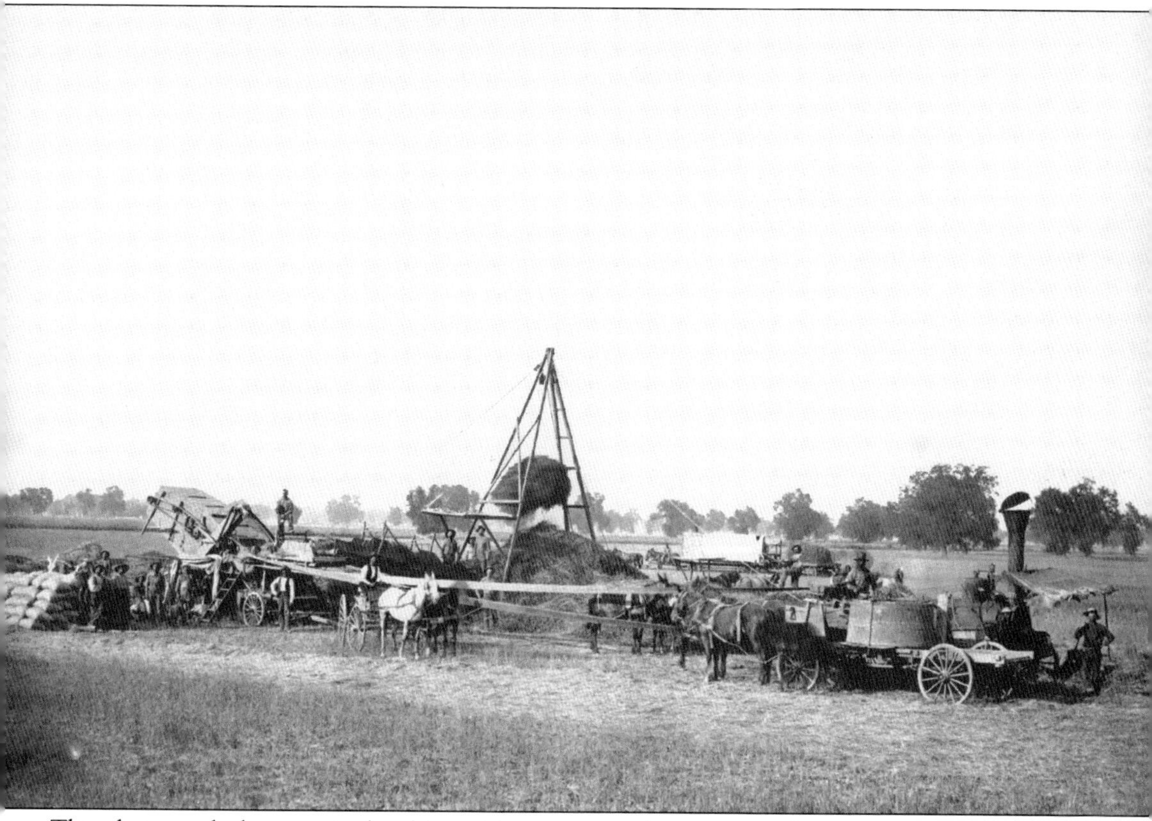

This photograph shows grain threshing with a stationary harvester run by a steam engine fueled by grain straw. A water tank, ready to supply water to the steam tractor, was placed in front of the steamer. A derrick supplied unthreshed grain to the harvester. Both horses and mules were employed in this harvesting process. The man in the two-horse buggy was ready to go for supplies. The chuck wagon, in the back with a white canvas covering, was the "kitchen" for feeding the crew of 19 men and 1 boy.

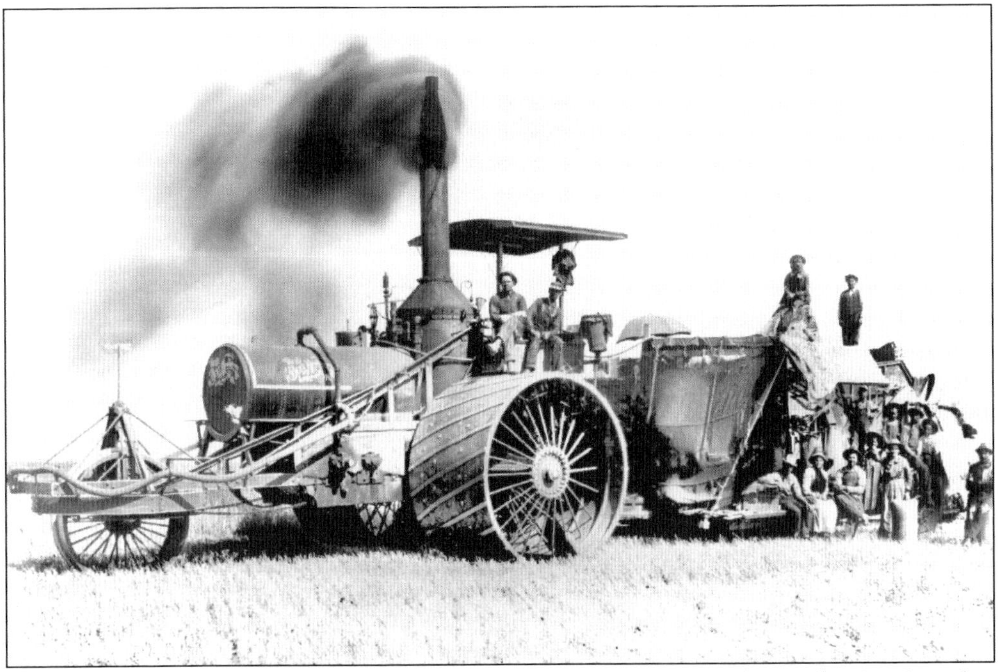

This is a 1910 Best steam tractor and combined header-thresher. Manufactured in San Leandro, Best steam tractors were not very popular because of the constant threat of grain fires ignited by sparks from the smoke stack. This combined harvester was unsurpassed in harvesting capacity, turning out as much as 2,700 sacks (600 bushels) in a day.

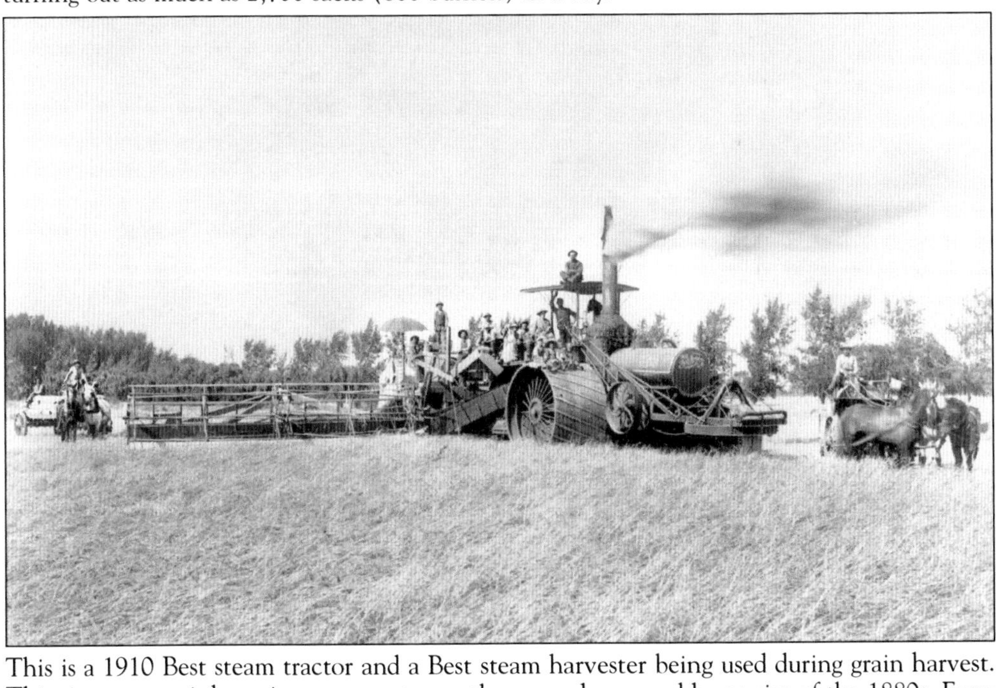

This is a 1910 Best steam tractor and a Best steam harvester being used during grain harvest. This rig was certainly an improvement over the ground-powered horse rigs of the 1880s. Even though the Best '75' gas tractor was introduced in 1912, steam tractors continued to be used in the Tracy area until the 1920s. (Courtesy of Clifford W. Koster.)

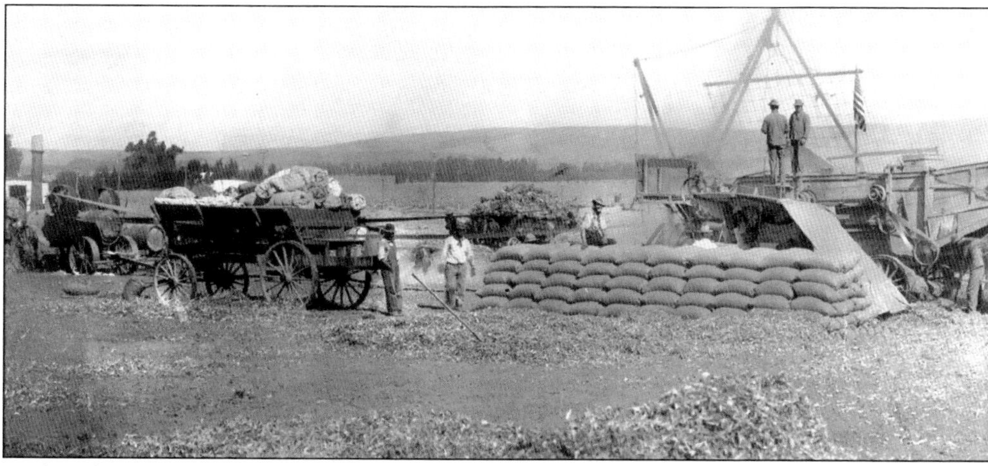

In this photograph, a portable steam engine is belted to a stationary grain thresher. The sack sewers are under the shade between the sack pile and the threshing machine. A sack of wheat would take 11 or 12 stitches to close, and barley took 9 stitches. Sacks were made in either Calcutta, India, or at San Quentin Prison in California. (Courtesy of Clifford W. Koster.)

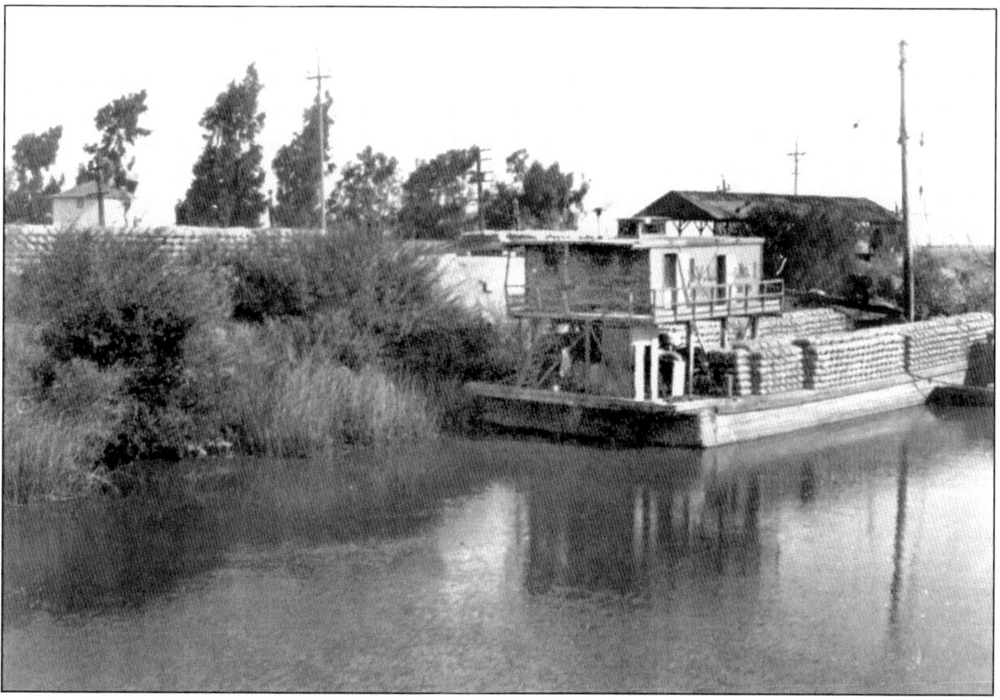

After harvest, sacks of grain were hauled to the river by wagon and loaded on barges to be shipped to flour mills in Stockton or San Francisco. When filled with 60-pound bushels, a 2.25 bushel sack of wheat weighed 135 pounds. There are stories of old timers who could carry a sack under each arm. The writer favored two arms for one sack; even then it put him in Dameron Hospital in Stockton, ruptured!

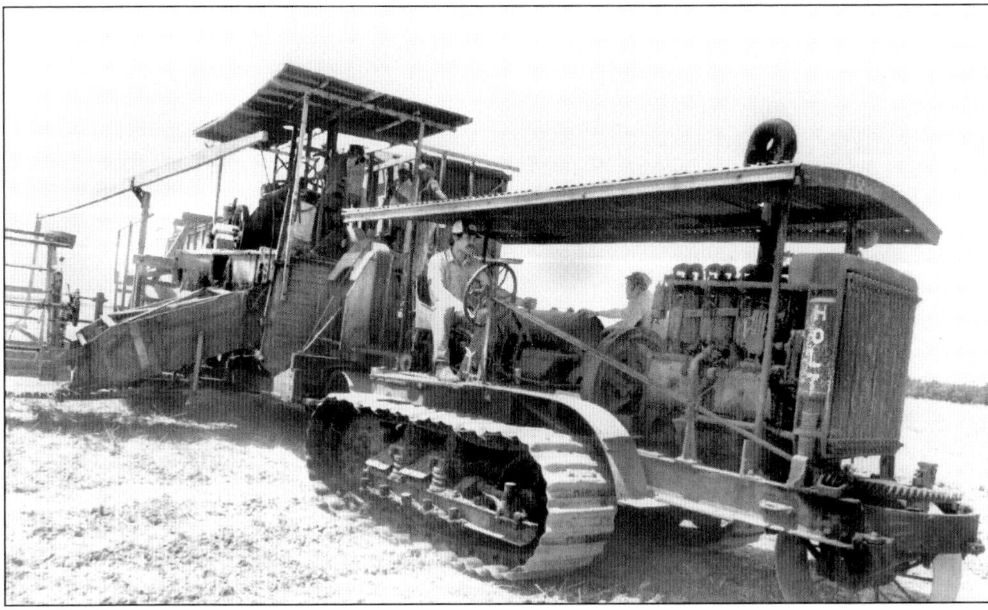

This 1914 Harris Combined Harvester pulled by a 1923 Holt '75' Caterpillar tractor, was the largest Harris built. This was the last model of Holt's '75.' When C.L. Best merged with Holt's Caterpillar in 1925, the '75' was discontinued in favor of Best's '60' tracklayer, a more advanced design. (Courtesy of Clifford W. Koster.)

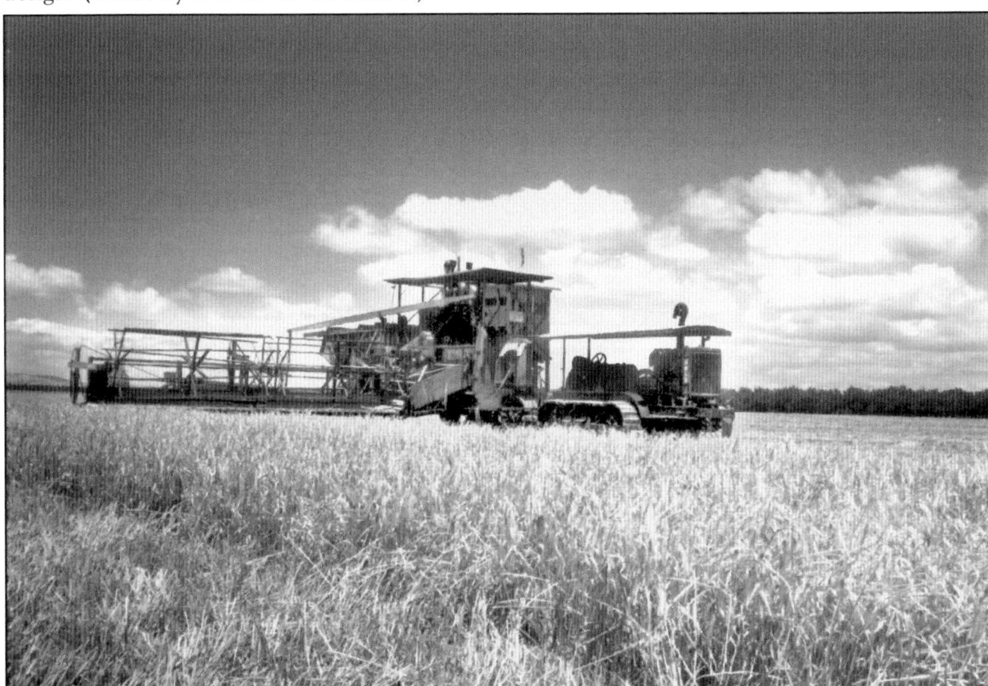

This Holt '75' and Harris combine, built in 1914, was used to harvest wheat in the Vernalis area. Harris built five sizes of combined harvesters in the first half of the 20th century in Stockton and Walla Walla, Washington. Powered by a 50-horsepower Atlas engine, the header cut 24 feet wide and could cut 60 tons or more of grain per day. (Courtesy of Clifford W. Koster.)

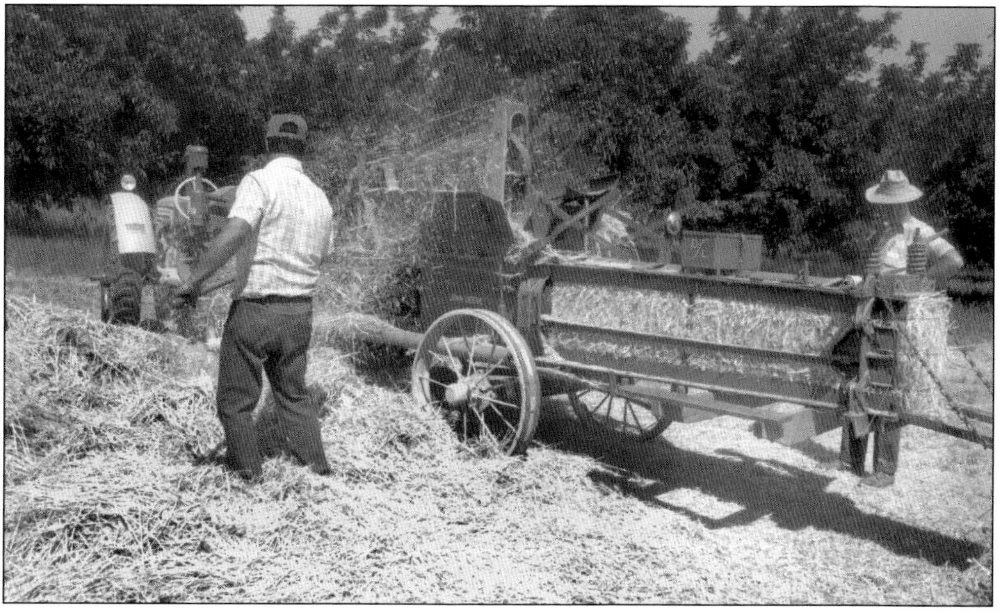

A John Deere 'pitch in' hay baler, in use prior to Case's 'pick up' baler, baled hay that had been cured in shocks while the Case 'pick up' baler took hay continuously from cured windrows. There were old timers who swore that hay cured in a shock was better quality than windrowed hay, but reducing labor costs favored baling hay out of the windrow. (Courtesy of Clifford W. Koster.)

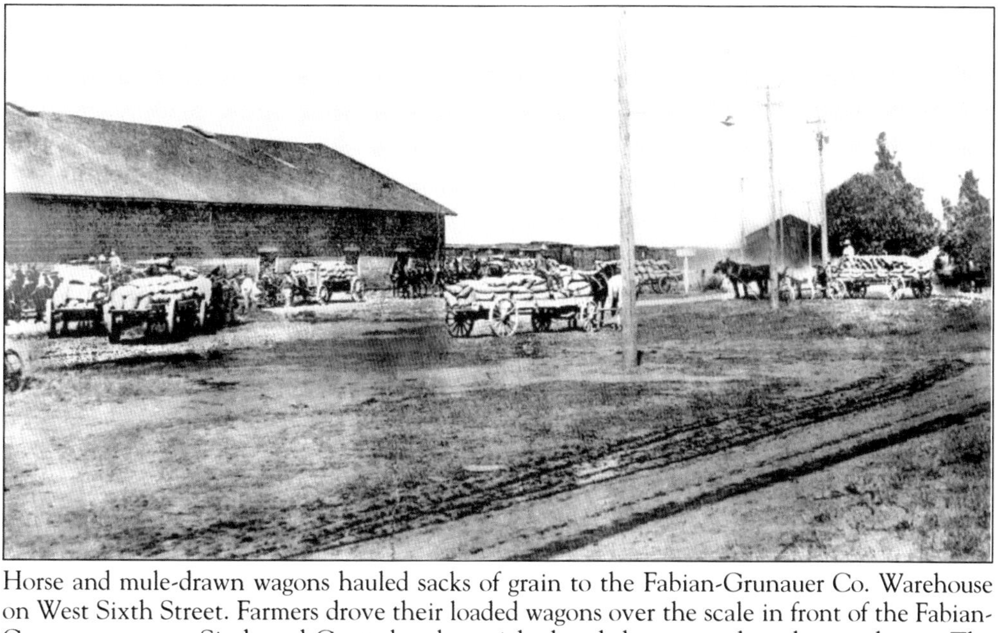

Horse and mule-drawn wagons hauled sacks of grain to the Fabian-Grunauer Co. Warehouse on West Sixth Street. Farmers drove their loaded wagons over the scale in front of the Fabian-Grunauer store at Sixth and Central to be weighed and then moved to the warehouse. The Fabian-Grunauer Co. was one of the principal grain merchants on the West Side and had several warehouses in and around Tracy.

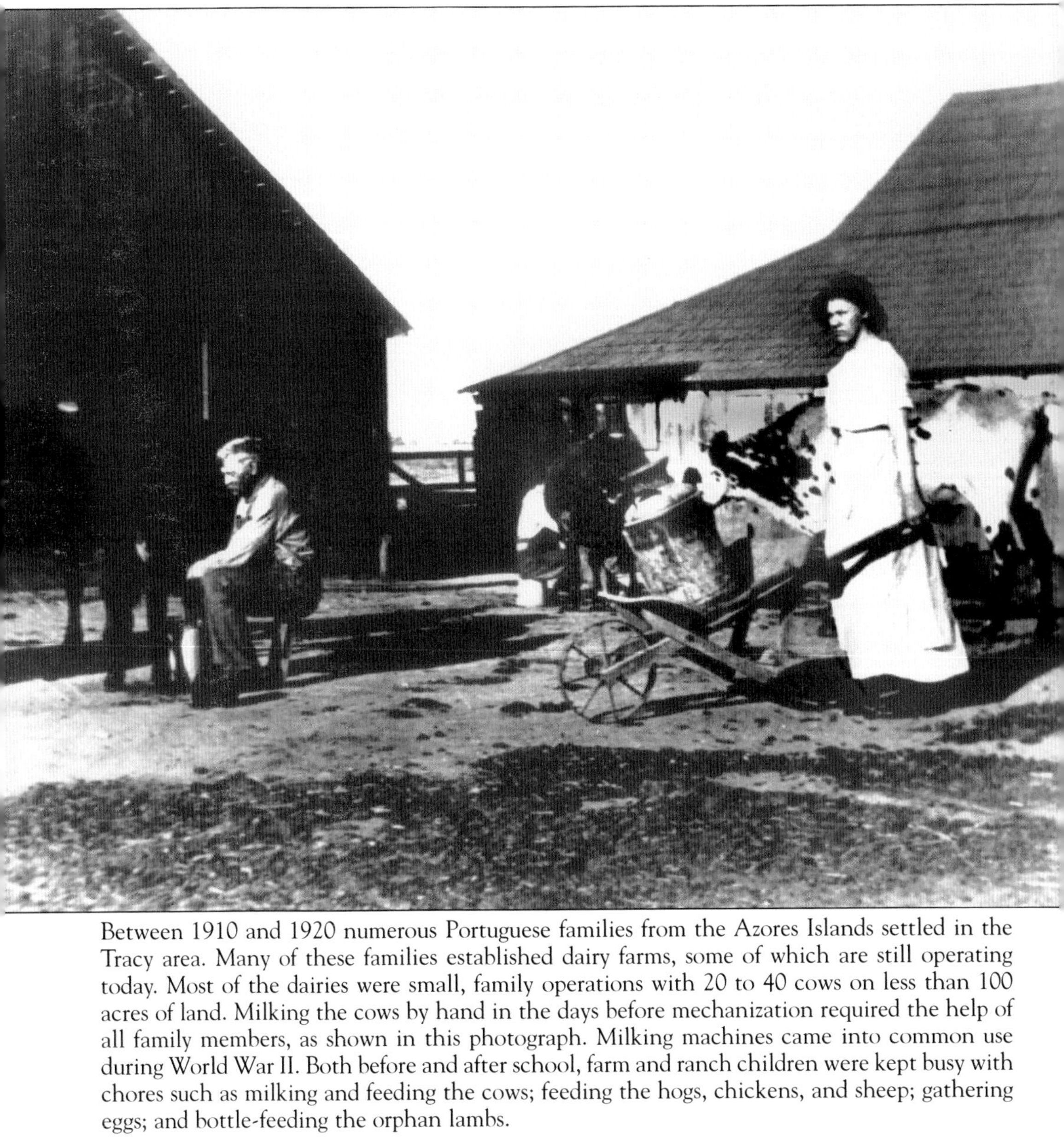

Between 1910 and 1920 numerous Portuguese families from the Azores Islands settled in the Tracy area. Many of these families established dairy farms, some of which are still operating today. Most of the dairies were small, family operations with 20 to 40 cows on less than 100 acres of land. Milking the cows by hand in the days before mechanization required the help of all family members, as shown in this photograph. Milking machines came into common use during World War II. Both before and after school, farm and ranch children were kept busy with chores such as milking and feeding the cows; feeding the hogs, chickens, and sheep; gathering eggs; and bottle-feeding the orphan lambs.

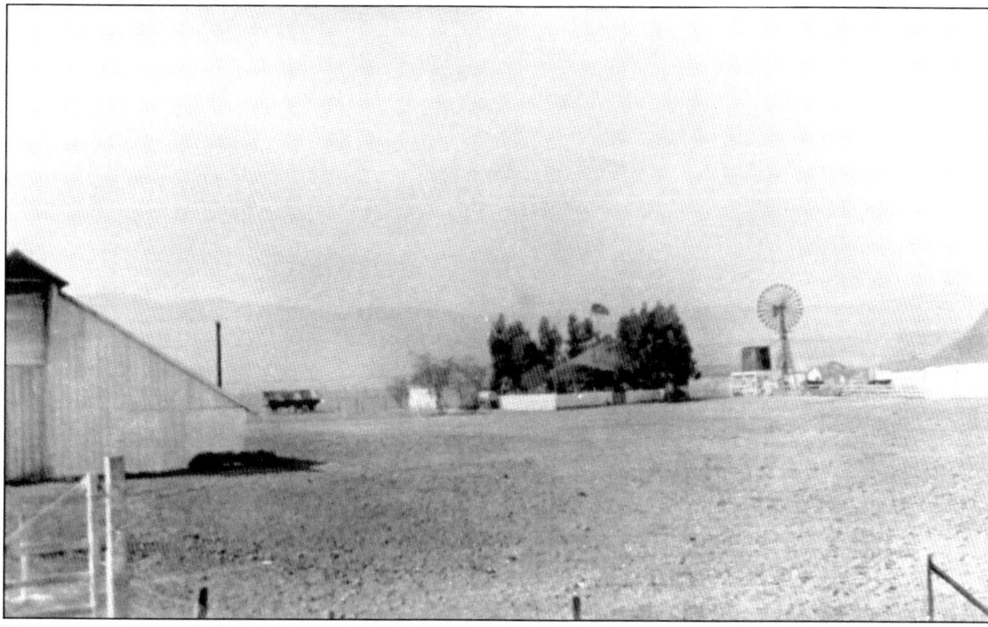

The remoteness of the Messer ranch, located near Vernalis southeast of Tracy, was typical for this area. Surrounded by trees to help keep it cool in summer, the two-story, wooden house had a white fence. The outbuildings housed hay, straw, livestock, poultry, and a garage for repairing machinery. The wooden windmill supplied water for the house, the vegetable garden, and the livestock.

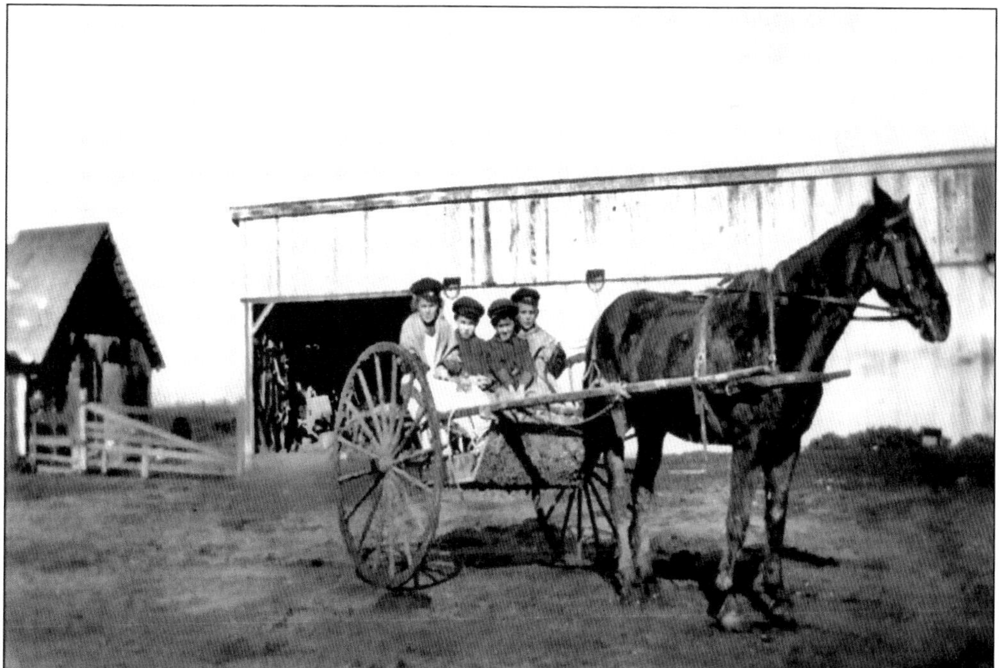

Four young boys were photographed in 1909 in a single-horse buggy on the Cordes ranch west of Tracy. The two boys in the center, Charlie and Julius Cordes, were ready to leave for Lammersville School, a one-room, country school. (Courtesy of Paul Andersen.)

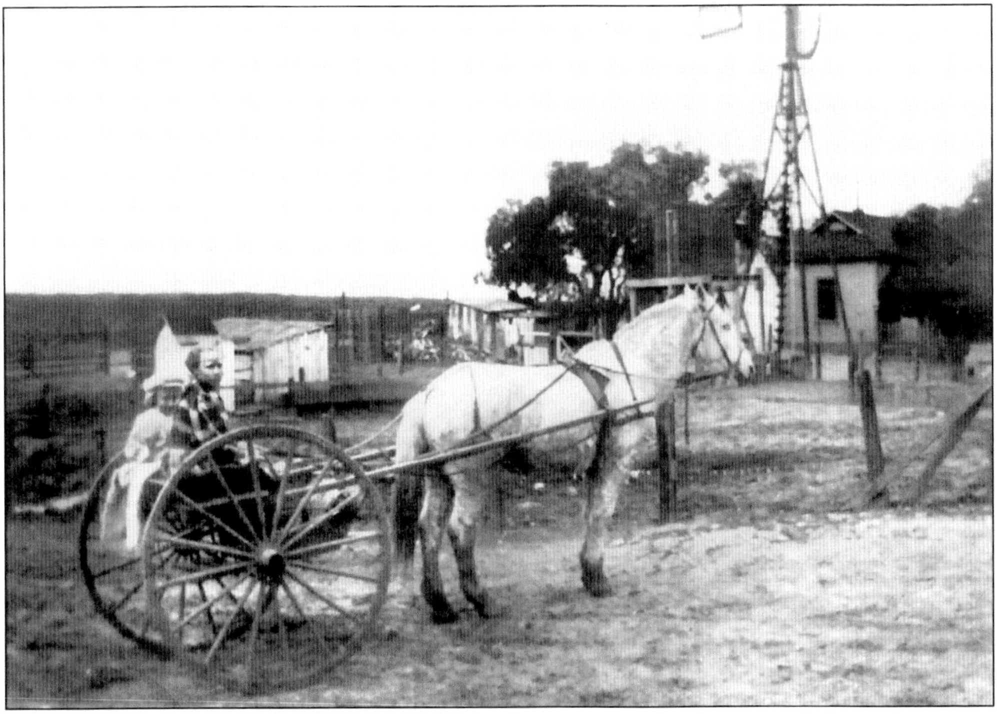

Also pictured on the Cordes ranch in 1909, on their way to school in a single-horse buggy, are Elsa and Edna Cordes, John Cordes's daughters. Children attending country schools walked, rode horses, or went by buggy. (Courtesy of Paul Andersen.)

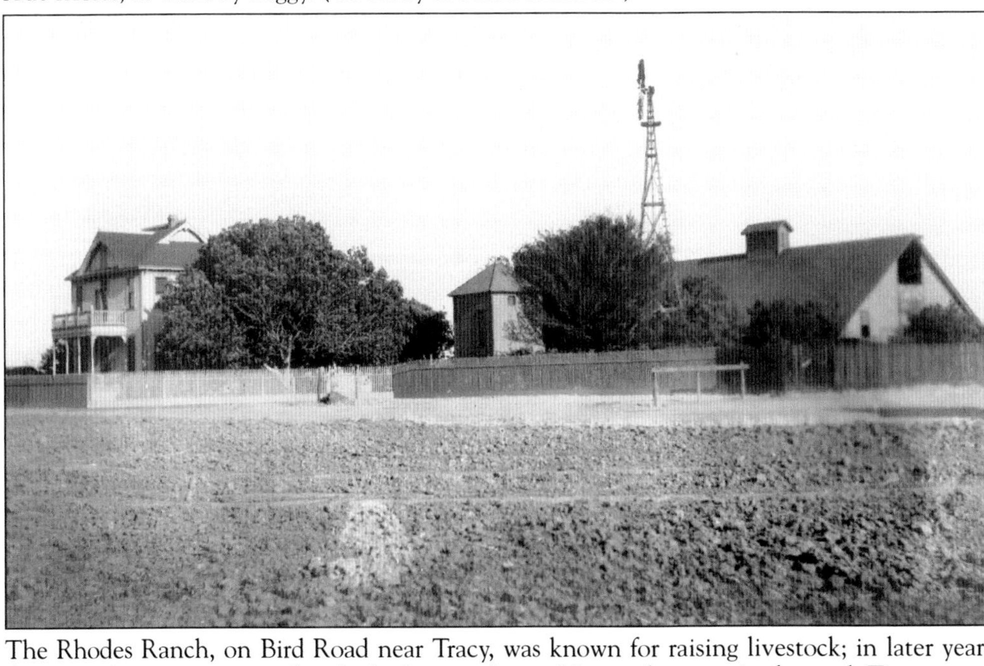

The Rhodes Ranch, on Bird Road near Tracy, was known for raising livestock; in later years the name became associated with the bean industry. Notice the trees in the yard. Trees grown on the West Side before the establishment of irrigation districts were usually types that could survive against strong winds and low rainfall, such as pepper, olive, and eucalyptus trees.

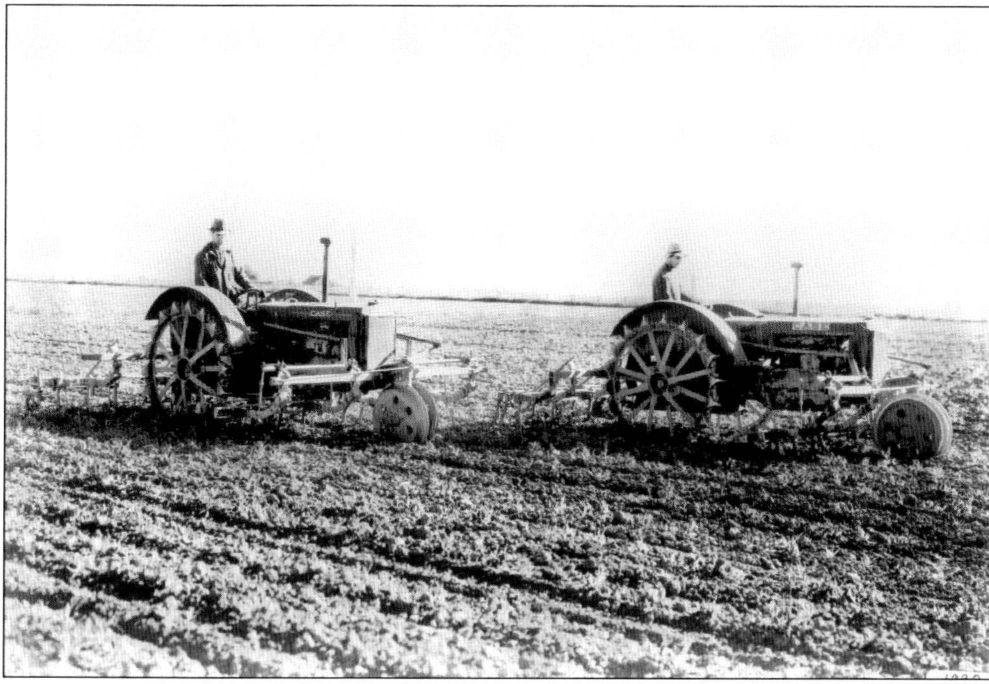

The two photographs on this page show the Alfred Pereira farm near Carbona in the late 1930s. In this photograph, two farm workers are cultivating a row crop. The coming of irrigation to this area made it possible for the cultivation of different types of crops, including beans, sugar beets, asparagus, and other vegetable crops, as well as the planting of orchards.

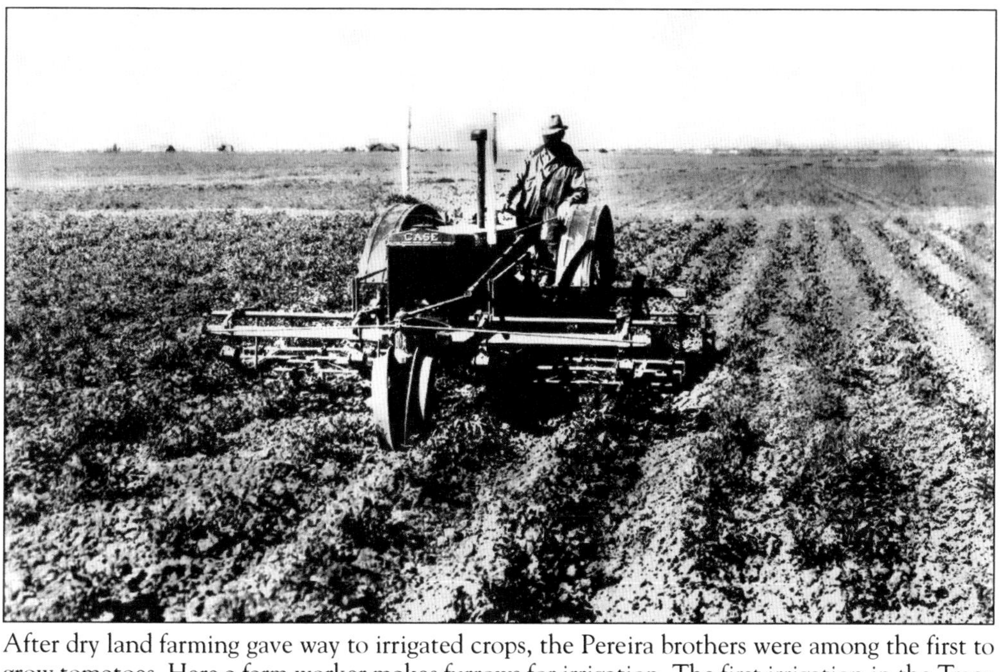

After dry land farming gave way to irrigated crops, the Pereira brothers were among the first to grow tomatoes. Here a farm worker makes furrows for irrigation. The first irrigation in the Tracy area was in the Naglee-Burk Tract in 1912 and was soon followed by the West Side Irrigation District in 1918 and the Banta-Carbona Irrigation District in 1926.

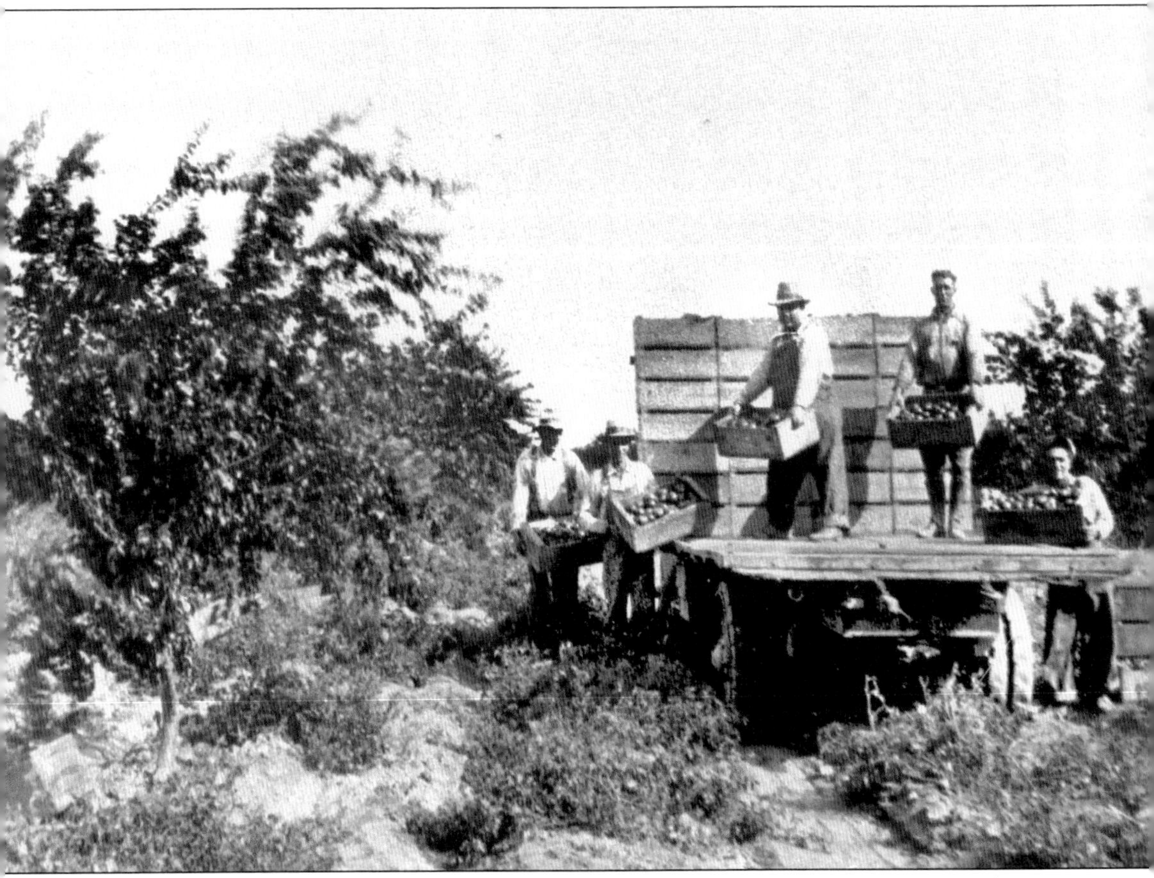

Grown for both canneries and the fresh market, tomatoes became a major Tracy crop beginning in the 1930s. A group of workers are shown here harvesting tomatoes, which had been planted in a young orchard. All the harvesting was done by hand. The growth of the tomato industry led to Heinz opening a processing plant in Tracy after World War II.

Three

CHURCHES

In the little railroad town where numerous saloons flourished, traveling ministers and priests provided spiritual stability to the early residents until they were able to organize congregations and build their own churches. Not only were the churches the center of the community's spiritual life, but the buildings also served secular purposes. The Presbyterian Church's bell served as the city's fire bell for a number of years. The Methodist church annex was used as a school classroom when Willow School became too small for the growing community and was also used as an emergency ward during the 1918 flu epidemic. In an ironic twist, after years of various ministers speaking out against the "evil" influence of local pool halls and saloons, some of the pool halls closed on February 22, 1921, to join other community businessmen, farmers, railroad workers, Boy Scouts, Catholics, Lutherans, Methodists, and Presbyterians on a trip to the old Carnegie brick plant in Corral Hollow to collect 25,000 to 30,000 white bricks to be used in the construction of a new Presbyterian Church building.

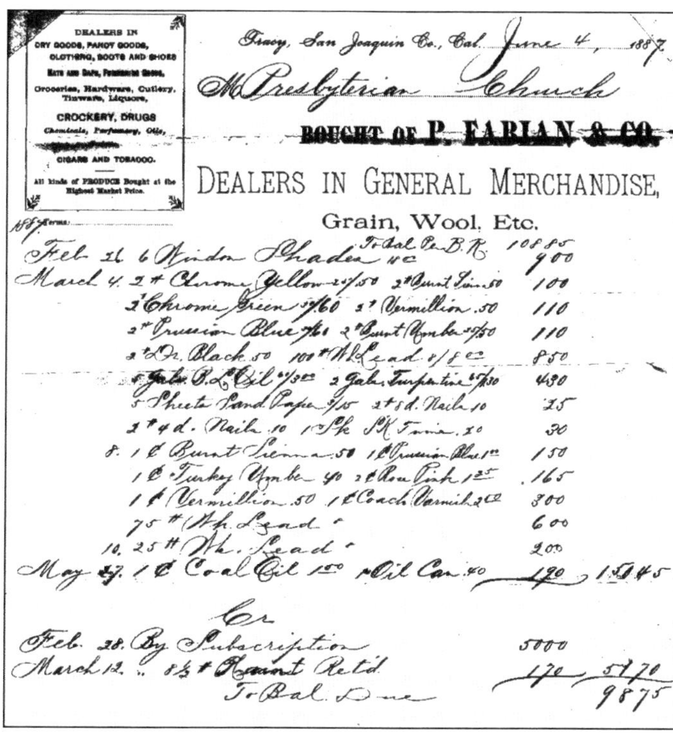

DEALERS IN
DRY GOODS, FANCY GOODS,
CLOTHING, BOOTS AND SHOES
CROCKERY, DRUGS
CIGARS AND TOBACCO.

Tracy, San Joaquin Co., Cal. June 4, 1887

M Presbyterian Church

BOUGHT OF P. FABIAN & CO.

DEALERS IN GENERAL MERCHANDISE,

Grain, Wool, Etc.

Terms:

Feb. 28. By Subscription 5000

To Bal. Due 9875

When looking at old photographs, we tend to "see" only black, white, and gray and forget how colorful the landscape, buildings, and people were. This bill from P. Fabian and Co. for paint used on the original Presbyterian Church includes colors of the era: chrome yellow, burnt sienna, chrome green, vermilion, Prussian blue, burnt umber, turkey umber, and rose pink. (Courtesy of First Presbyterian Church.)

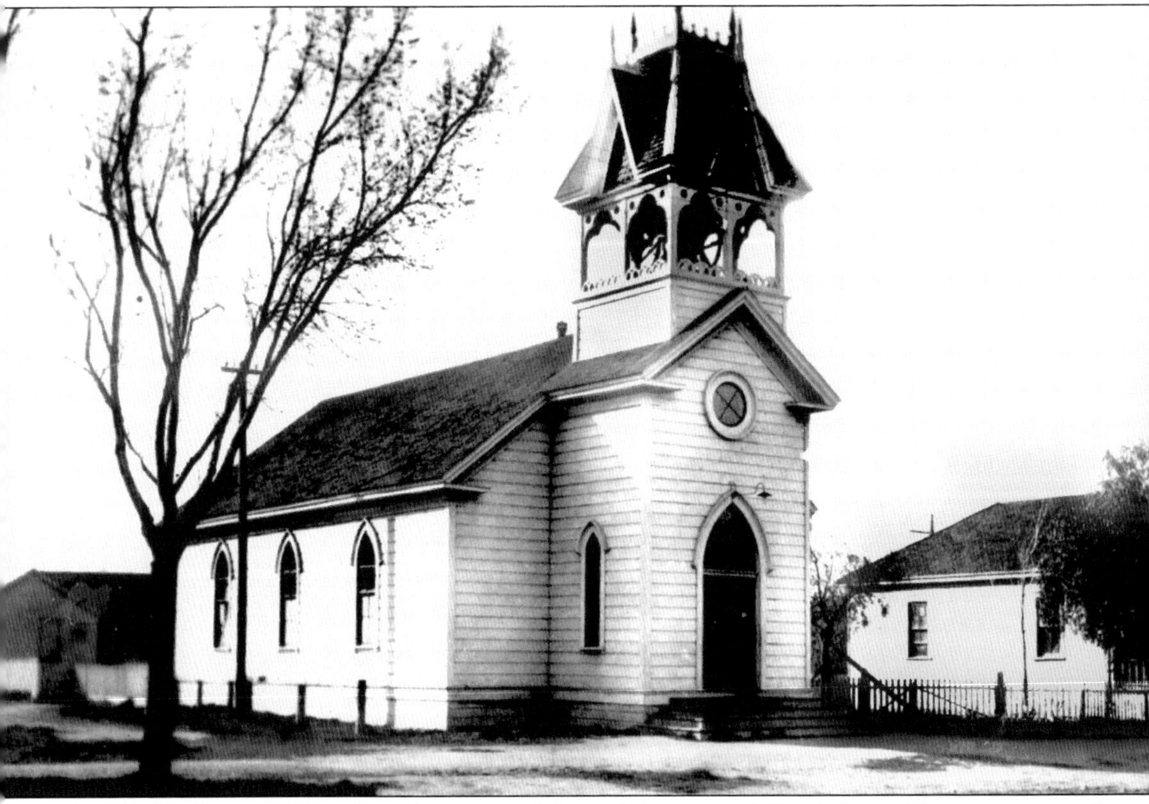

The Presbyterian Church, at the corner of Central Avenue and Ninth Street (the present site of the Tracy Fire Station), was the first church building erected in Tracy. Founded in Ellis in April 1876, the Presbyterian Church held services in Willow School until this building was erected in 1886–1887 and dedicated October 2, 1887. Built on lots donated by Charles Crocker of Southern Pacific Railroad, the building cost $2,400 and was funded with subscription donations from many Tracy residents. Serving as a community church, the building was shared with German Lutherans and German Methodists, who both held services in the building several Sunday afternoons each month. The church building and manse were moved to Tenth Street near B Street (the present site of Bank of America) in 1917 when the City of Tracy wanted the lots on Central and Ninth to build a new city hall. (This building is now the Abundant Life Church located at the corner of West Ninth Street and Metcalf Court.)

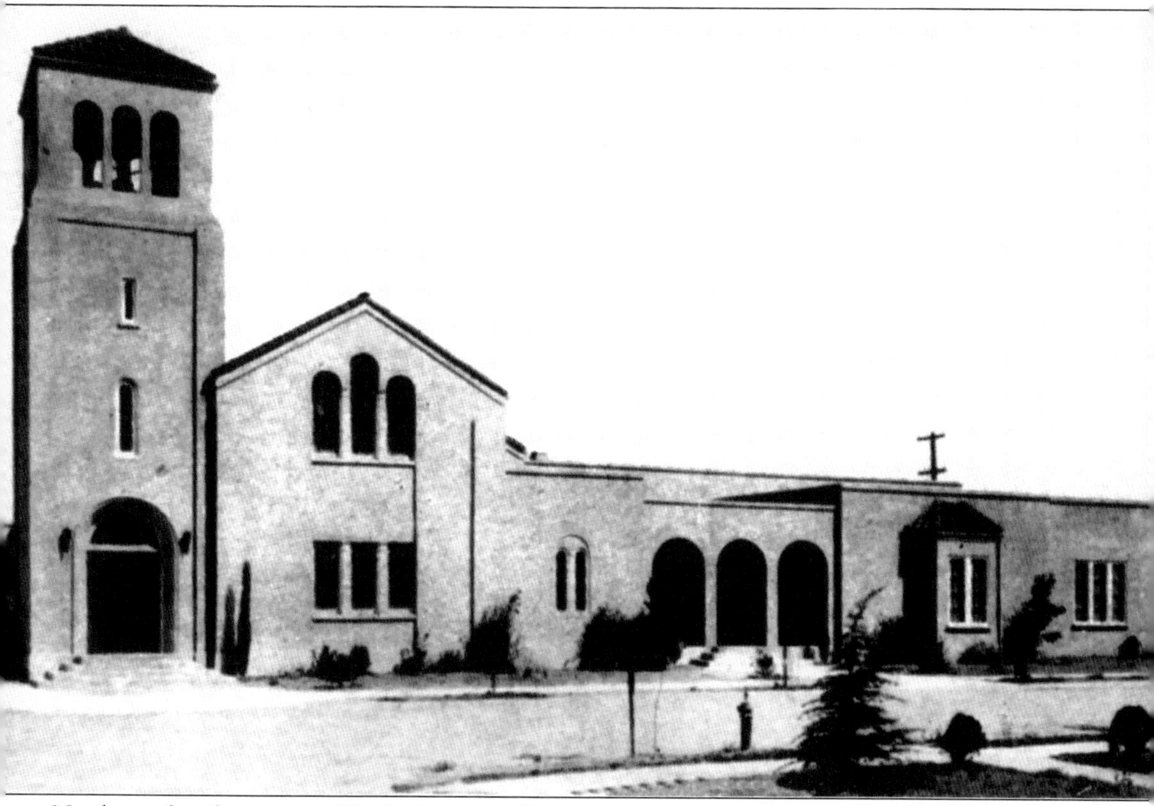

Not long after the move to Tenth Street, the Presbyterians outgrew their small, wooden church building and made plans in 1920 to erect a new building on the same location. Even though members of the church and the entire community had spent a day salvaging Carnegie bricks at the old plant in Corral Hollow, those building plans didn't succeed because of a lack of funds to proceed with the construction. Several years later, land was donated for the new church by two of Edward Wacksmuth's daughters and their husbands, Elda and Charles Slack and Mae and Abe Grunauer. This land, which had been part of Edward Wacksmuth's estate, was ideal for the new church building designed in the Romanesque style by Rollin S. Tuttle of Oakland. At a cost of almost $40,000, the church, located at 101 Berverdor Avenue, was dedicated on March 14, 1926, and is still home to the First Presbyterian Church.

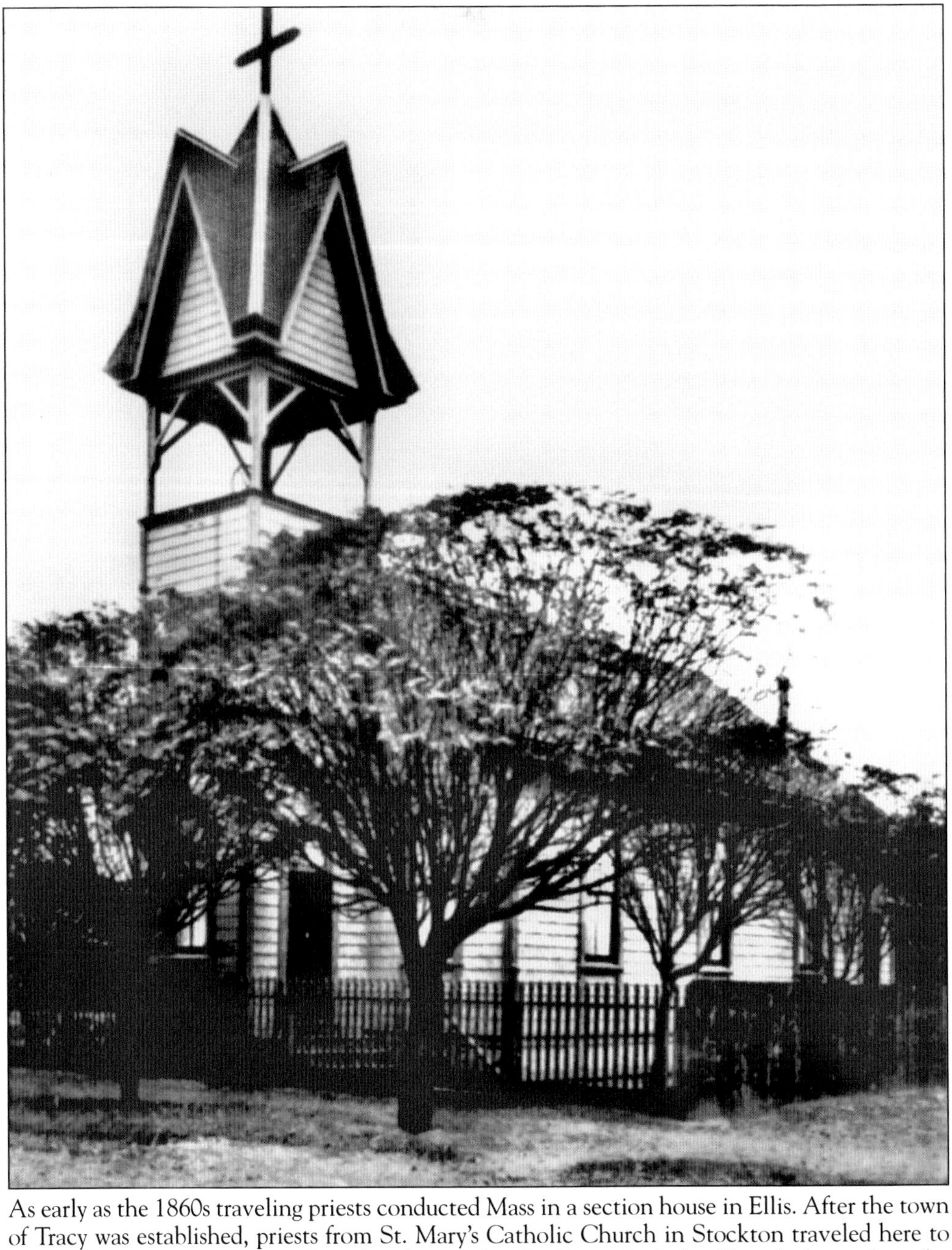

As early as the 1860s traveling priests conducted Mass in a section house in Ellis. After the town of Tracy was established, priests from St. Mary's Catholic Church in Stockton traveled here to conduct Mass on the last Sunday of each month. The Tracy Catholic Church, located on the northeast corner of Central Avenue and Eighth Street (currently the site of a city parking lot), was built for about $1,800 in 1887–1888 on lots donated by Charles Crocker of Southern Pacific Railroad. The church was named St. Bernard's after St. Bernard of Clairvaux, who was chosen as the patron saint when the Tracy congregation became a parish in 1908. The small, wooden structure, which had seating for about 100 worshippers, soon became too small for the rapidly growing congregation. Beginning in 1910, many fund-raisers were held in order to raise money to enlarge the building. A parish house was completed north of the church in 1912.

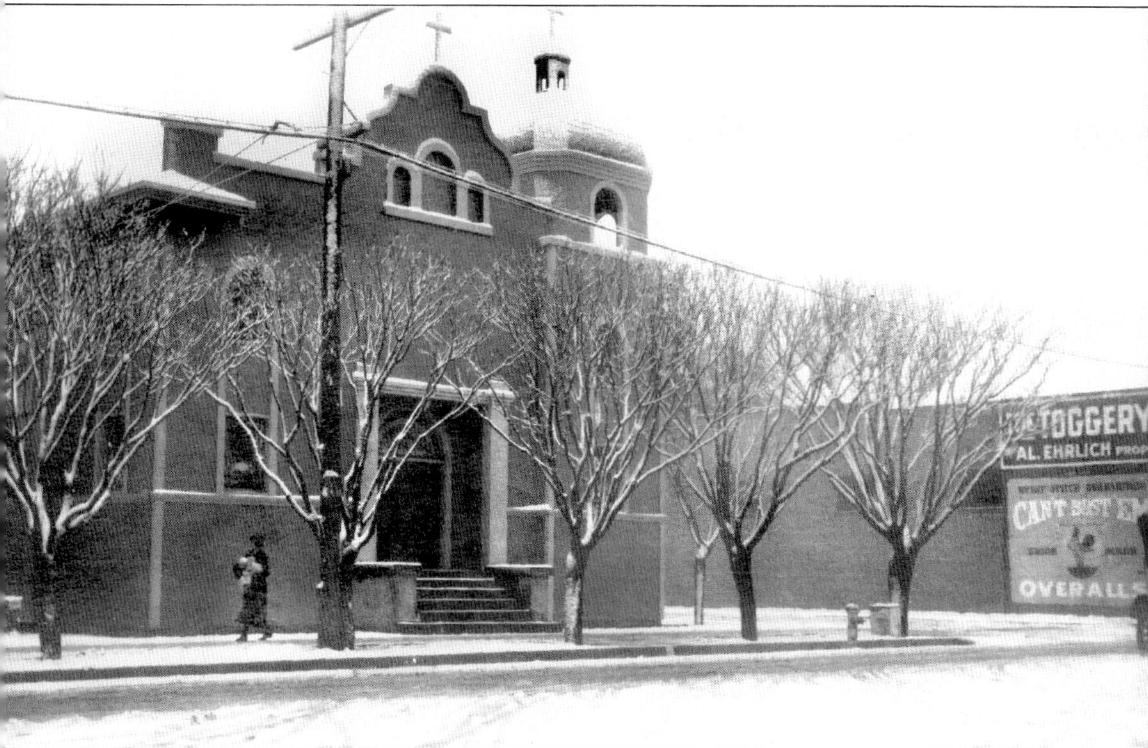

In response to the need for more room at St. Bernard's Catholic Church, a larger stucco building, which had seating for 260 people, was dedicated on June 15, 1913. This photograph of the snow-covered church was taken in 1921 after a rare snowfall. Built in the same location as the original church building at the northeast corner of Eighth and Central, this Mission-style building served St. Bernard's parish until they moved to their present location on West Eaton Avenue in 1951. Originally the interior was finished in large panels of elm veneer. It also had golden oak pews and electric lighting consisting of two large grape-like clusters hanging from the ceiling. In the latter months of 1921 the interior of the church was completely redecorated, including the changing of the wood stain to a dark oak. After the Eaton Avenue church was constructed, this building housed other church groups. The church building and parish house were demolished in February 1961.

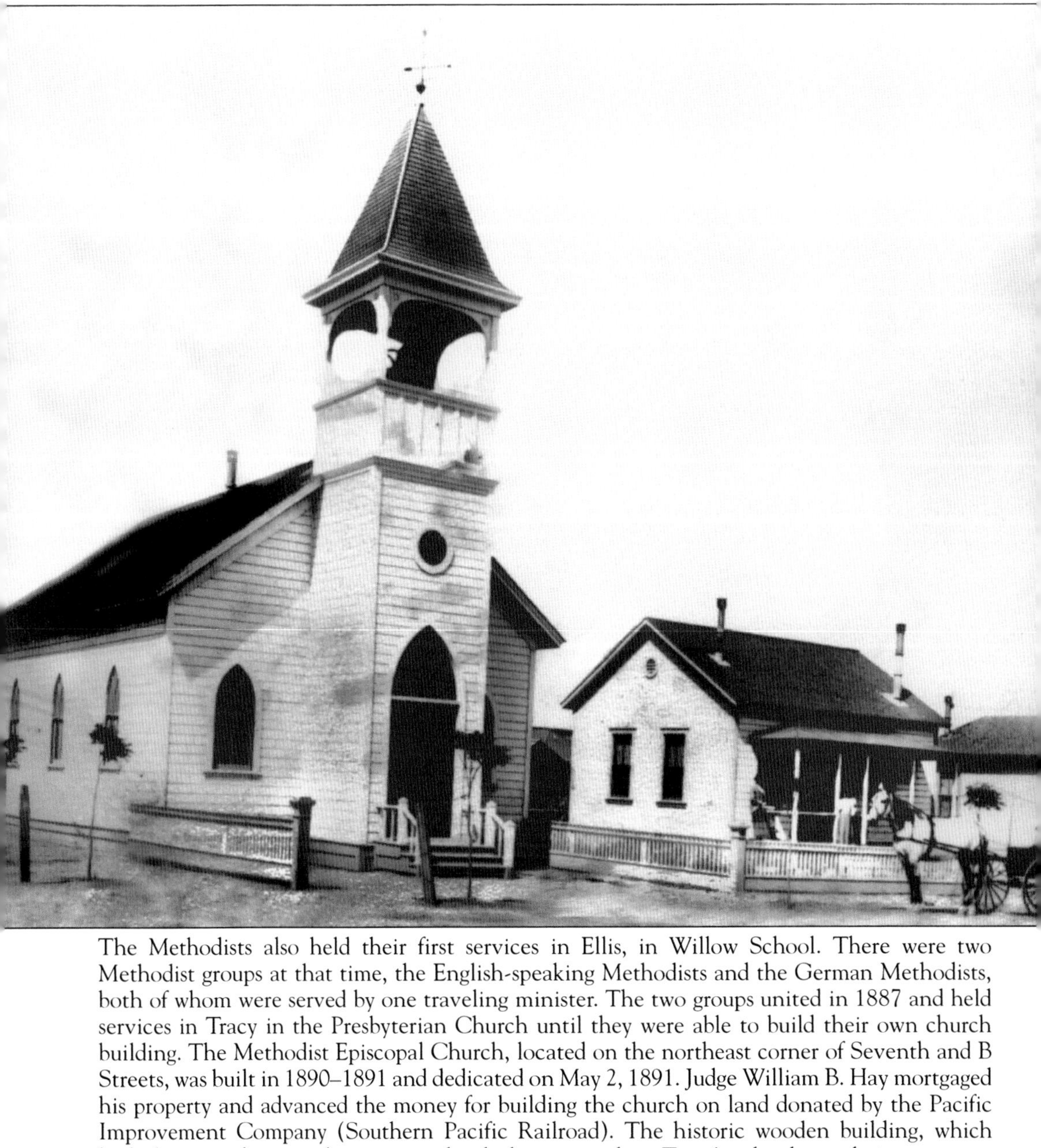

The Methodists also held their first services in Ellis, in Willow School. There were two Methodist groups at that time, the English-speaking Methodists and the German Methodists, both of whom were served by one traveling minister. The two groups united in 1887 and held services in Tracy in the Presbyterian Church until they were able to build their own church building. The Methodist Episcopal Church, located on the northeast corner of Seventh and B Streets, was built in 1890–1891 and dedicated on May 2, 1891. Judge William B. Hay mortgaged his property and advanced the money for building the church on land donated by the Pacific Improvement Company (Southern Pacific Railroad). The historic wooden building, which had also served as an elementary school classroom when Tracy's school population outgrew Willow School in the early 1900s and as an emergency ward during the 1918 flu epidemic, was destroyed by a fire on Sunday morning, November 3, 1929.

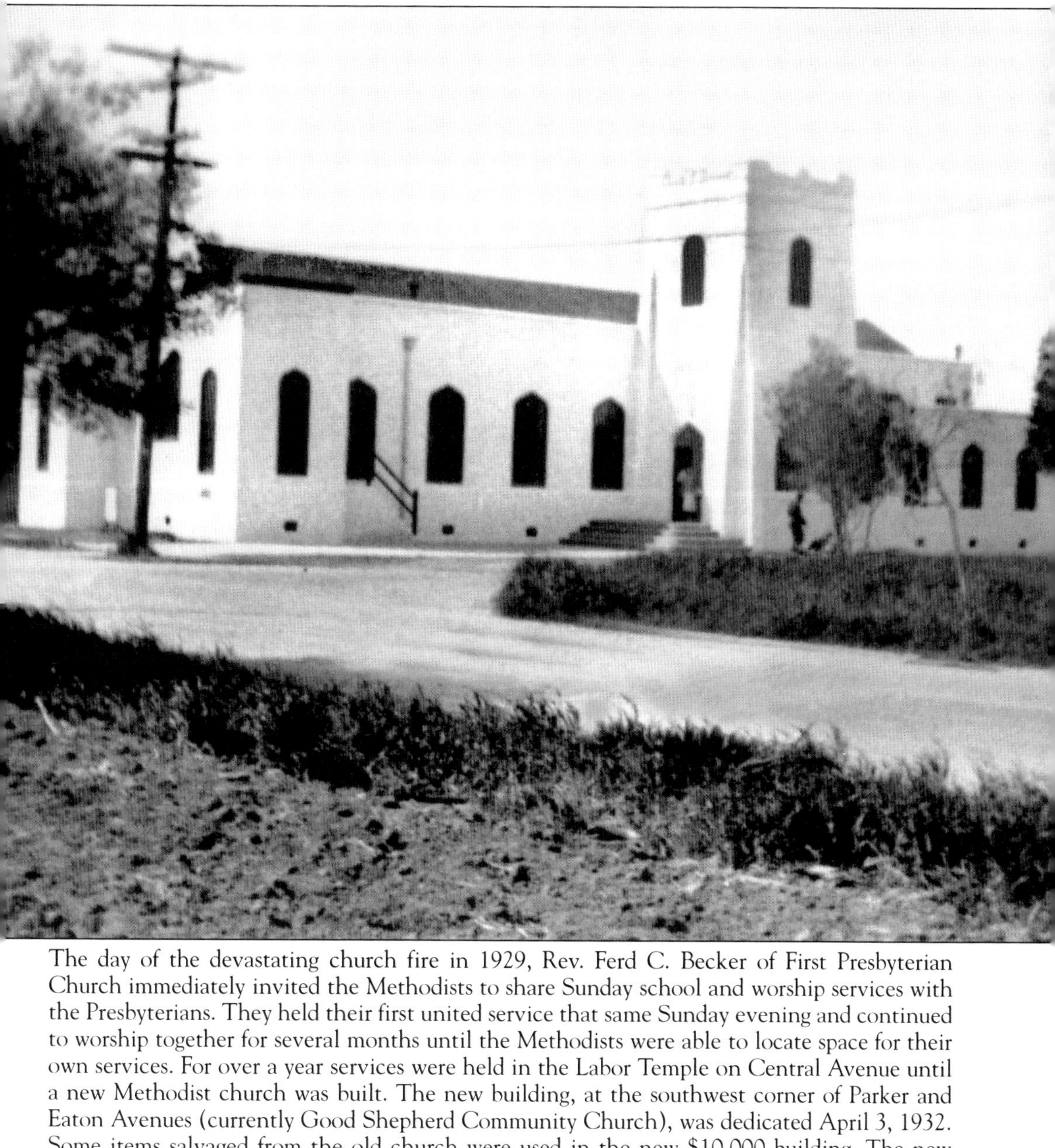

The day of the devastating church fire in 1929, Rev. Ferd C. Becker of First Presbyterian Church immediately invited the Methodists to share Sunday school and worship services with the Presbyterians. They held their first united service that same Sunday evening and continued to worship together for several months until the Methodists were able to locate space for their own services. For over a year services were held in the Labor Temple on Central Avenue until a new Methodist church was built. The new building, at the southwest corner of Parker and Eaton Avenues (currently Good Shepherd Community Church), was dedicated April 3, 1932. Some items salvaged from the old church were used in the new $10,000 building. The new church, with a seating capacity of 500, was home to the congregation until the current church was built in 1957 on the southeast corner of East and Acacia Streets.

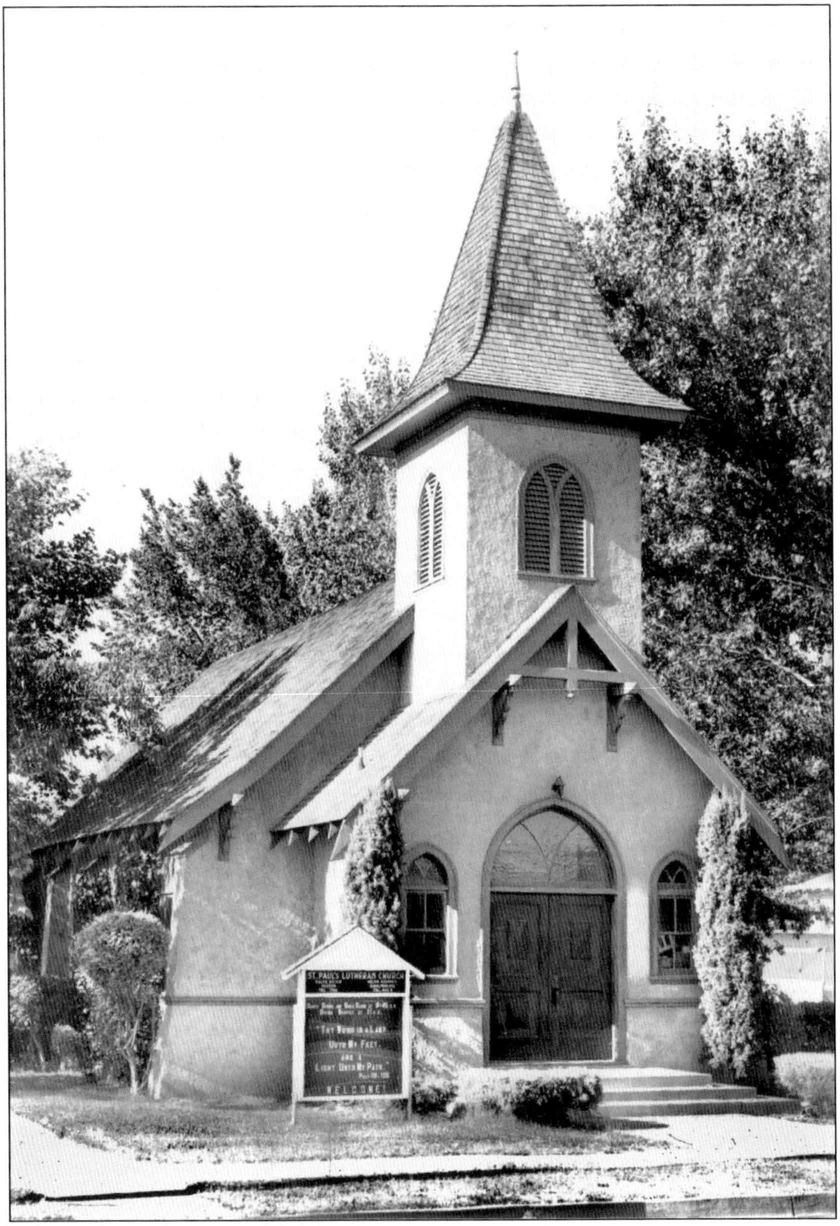

St. Paul's Lutheran Church, a stucco building designed in the Gothic style by William Cohrs, was built on the southwest corner of East Tenth and F Streets in 1920–1921 and dedicated on April 3, 1921. This building was later moved to the location of the present St. Paul's Lutheran Church on Chester Drive. The Lutherans, both in Ellis and the early years in Tracy, had been served by ministers who made periodic visits to the valley from San Francisco or Stockton to conduct services and perform sacraments. The local congregation organized in 1891–1892. On December 9, 1891, Rev. Otto Kitzmann opened a Saturday school of religion in the old Jefferson schoolhouse, then located near Carbona, and began church services in New Jerusalem and Tracy. The Lutherans had helped build the Presbyterian church in Tracy and shared that building for their own worship services until they were financially able to build a church of their own.

Four

ORGANIZATIONS

Among the fraternal, civic, and social organizations formed in the early years of Ellis and Tracy were such farm groups as the Grange, fraternal organizations, a debating club, a literary club, brass bands, orchestras, choirs, women's social and service groups, a gun and rifle club, baseball teams, and card clubs. Many of the organizations held annual picnics, banquets, dances, and costume balls and provided entertainment as well as fund-raising activities for the betterment of the community. Travel to meetings by those members who lived outside the town was done by horseback, buggy, or walking. These organizations provided a vital cultural and social dynamic to the community and were very important in the lives of individual members.

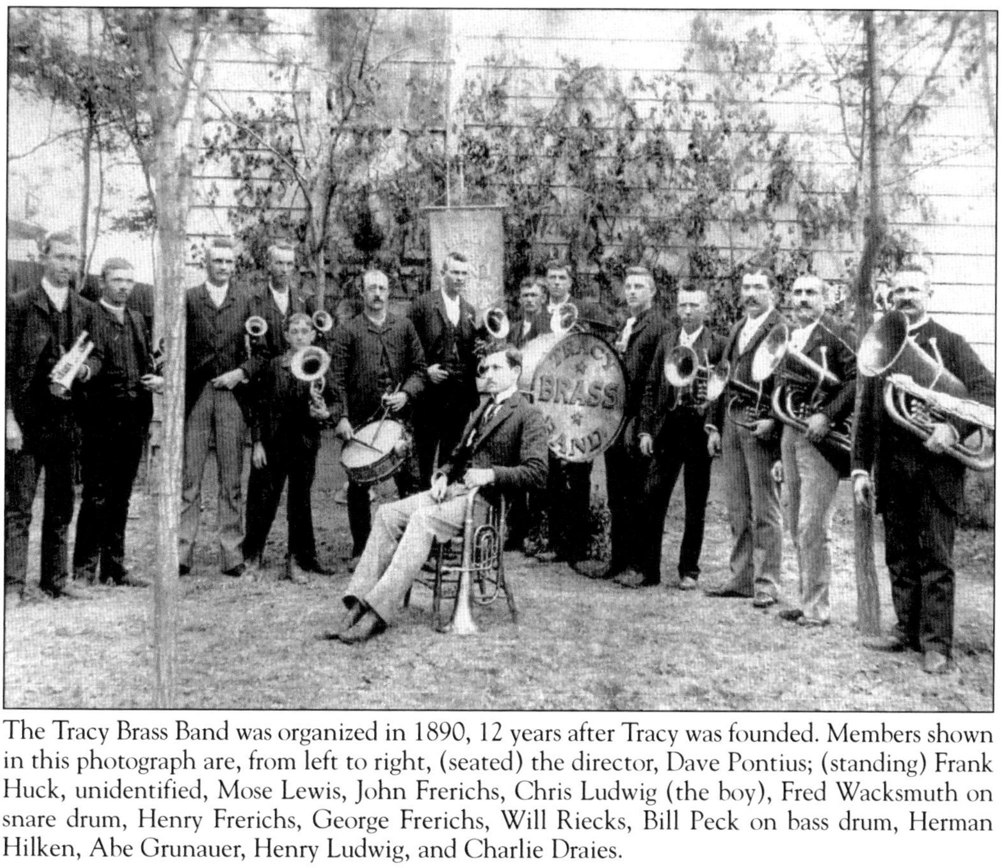

The Tracy Brass Band was organized in 1890, 12 years after Tracy was founded. Members shown in this photograph are, from left to right, (seated) the director, Dave Pontius; (standing) Frank Huck, unidentified, Mose Lewis, John Frerichs, Chris Ludwig (the boy), Fred Wacksmuth on snare drum, Henry Frerichs, George Frerichs, Will Riecks, Bill Peck on bass drum, Herman Hilken, Abe Grunauer, Henry Ludwig, and Charlie Draies.

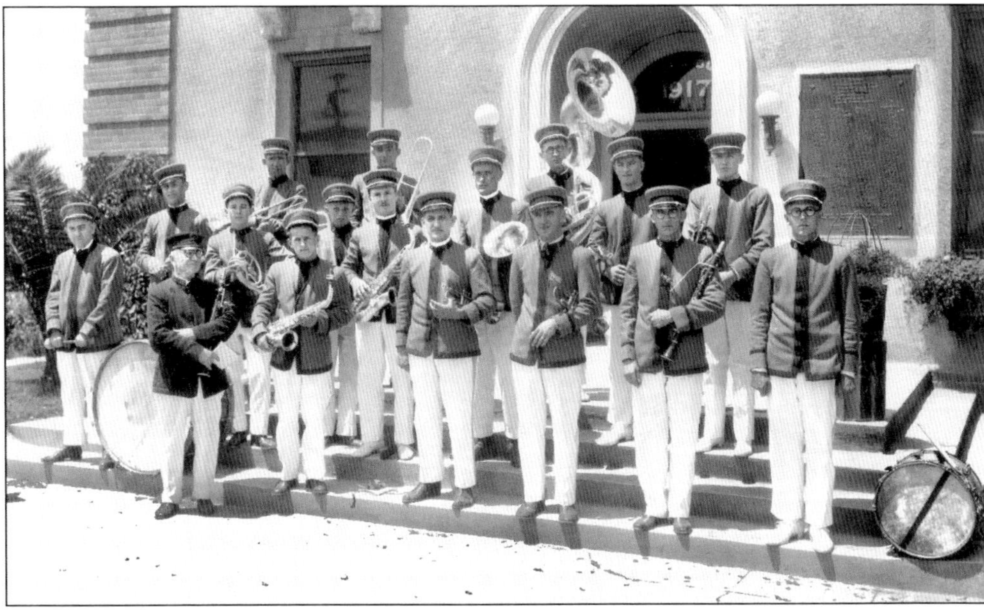

Arnold A. "Pop" Graham, standing in front of the bass drum, headed the music department at West Park School and was later at the high school for 22 years. Thomas E. Eagan, the saxophone player to the right of Pop in this photograph of Pop Graham's Band taken between 1919 and 1924, became a music professor at San Jose State. Jim Maxwell, another of Pop's students, played cornet in Johnny Carson's band.

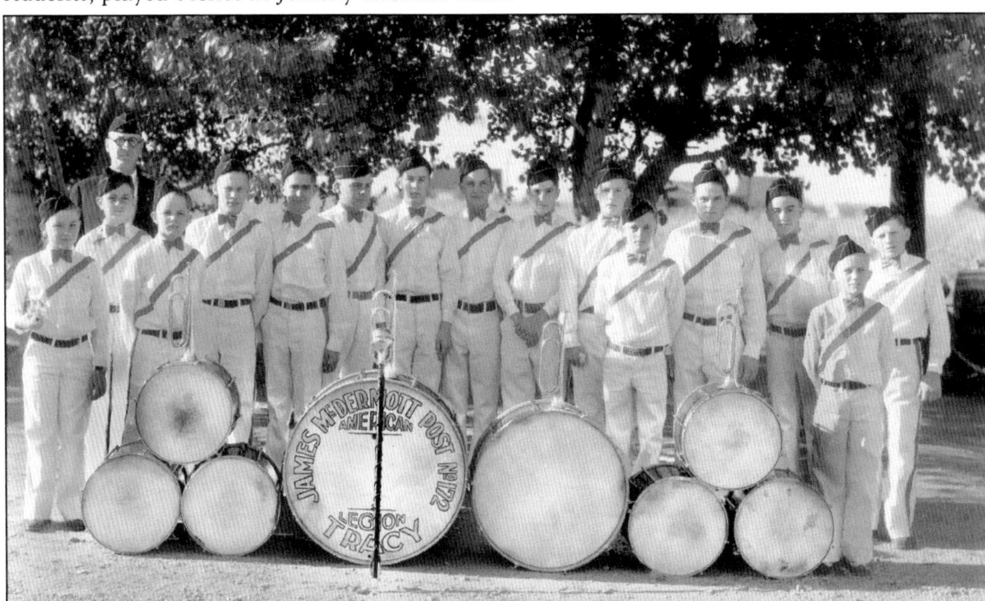

The American Legion Drum and Bugle Corps, pictured here in 1931, was part of James McDermott Post No. 172. Pictured, from left to right, are (front row) Allan Powers, Harris Drake, Raymond Wright, Sherman Westmeir, Clyde Mehring, Jim Isbell, Max Farnsworth, Waldo Coffman, Bob Sipe, Vernon Jeffries, Ralph Sipe, unidentified, Fred Garrison, Phillip Delgado, and Howard Costello; (back row) the director, Mr. Sharp.

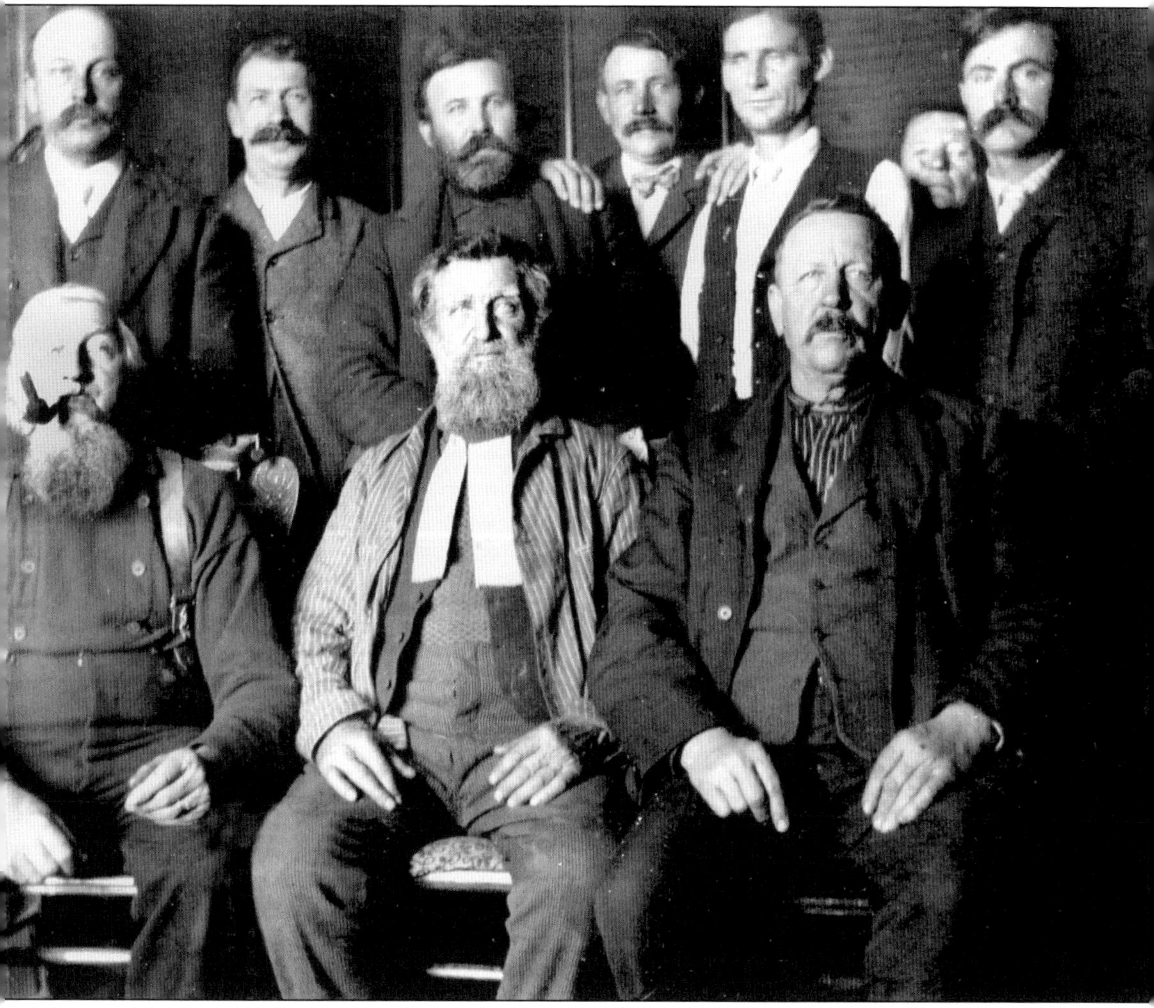

Pictured here in a 1903 picture, taken at the home of William and Anna Pruser, are members of the Solo Club. In the early years members met in each other's homes to play Solo, a card game similar to Euchre. Both husbands and wives attended these get-togethers. From left to right are (front row) William Pruser, Frank Pagel, and John Bruhns; (back row) Christoph Batterman, George Messer, Paul Harder, John Krohn, Fritz Hilken, Anna Pruser, and Amos McGee. In later years some of these men continued playing cards, usually penny ante (poker), at Shockley's pool hall on Central Avenue instead of in each other's homes.

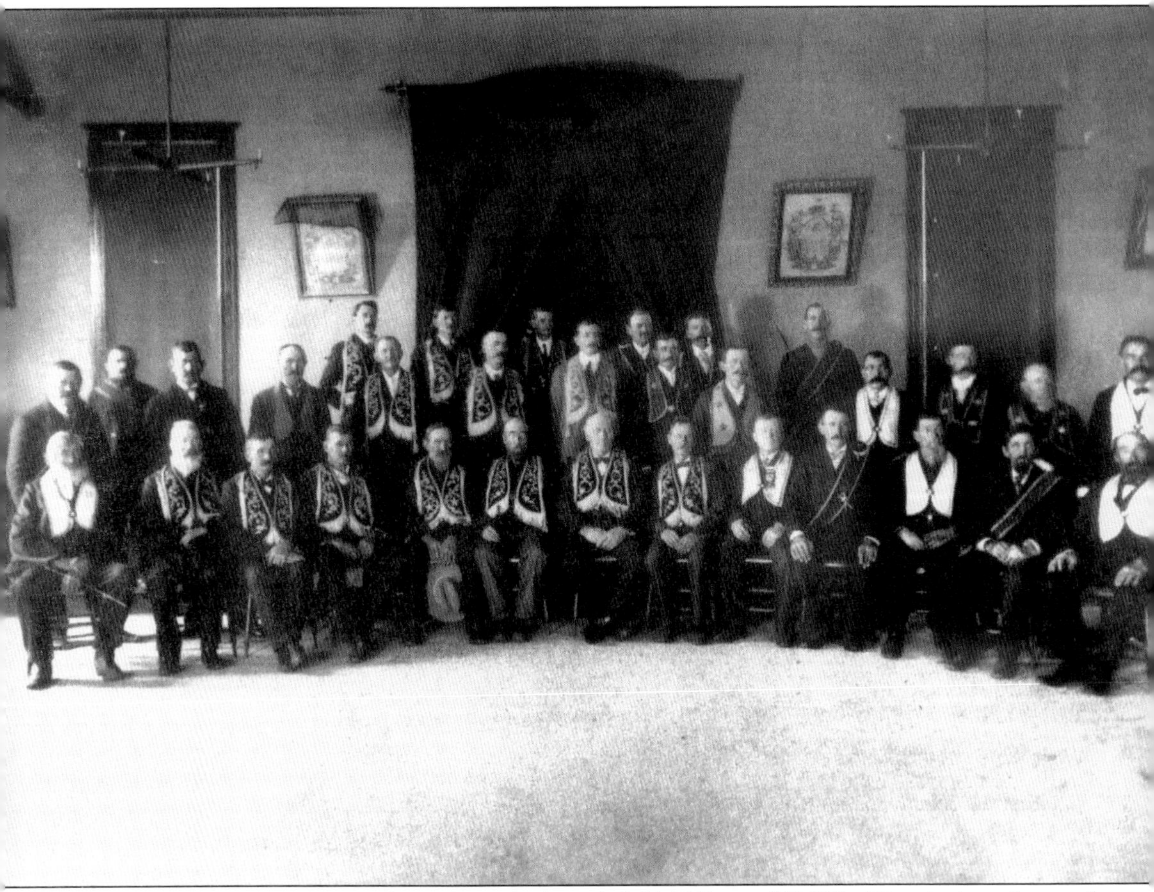

Sumner Lodge of the Independent Order of Odd Fellows (IOOF), Tracy's first fraternal organization, was instituted September 1, 1870, in Ellis. When the citizens of Ellis moved to Tracy, the IOOF lodge building was also moved. One dedicated, early member of the lodge was reported to have walked from his home located 13 miles from Tracy on more than one occasion to attend lodge meetings. Pictured sometime before 1908, from left to right, are many of the early members: (front row) Washington Haynes, William Moran, William Sehrt, Adolph Windeler, Henry Banta, Jim Allen, Martin Lammers, Henry Finck, Lewis Parker, John Krohn, John Gardner, ? Schmidt, and Carl Walter; (back row) Henry Ahrens, unidentified, William Schmidt, unidentified, Frank Housken, William Johnsen, George Frerichs, Neil Howard, Frank Brown, Ed Steinmetz, George Luhrsen, Peter Hansen, William Braasch, Gus Rosin, Thomas Garner, Dan Canale, Pete Schmidt, Henry Heinbockel, and John Hess.

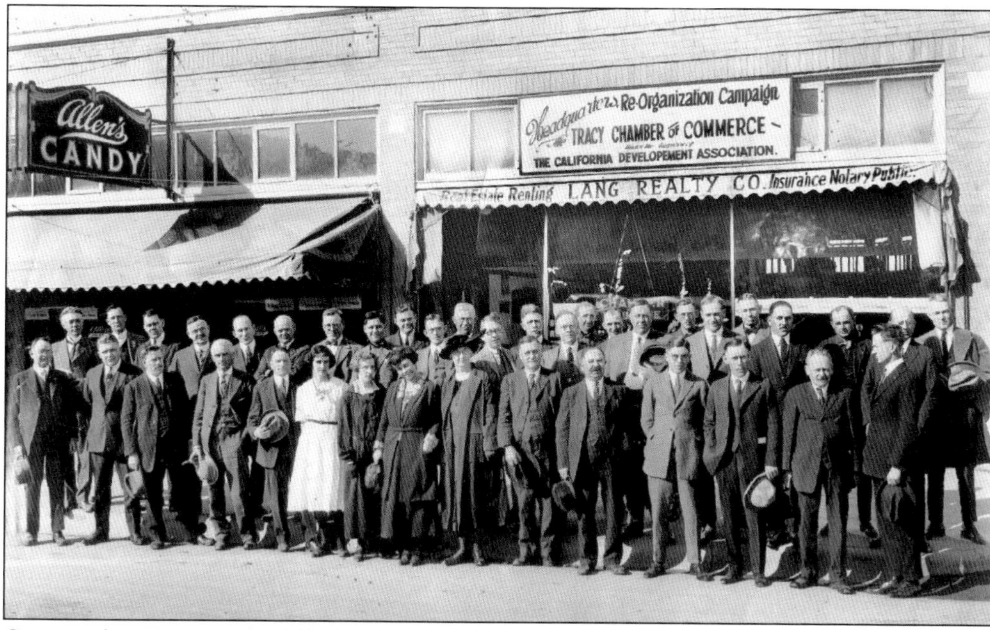

Organized in Tracy in the fall of 1909, the Tracy and West San Joaquin Board of Trade worked energetically for growth and civic improvement in Tracy. In 1919 the board reorganized, and the name was changed to the Tracy Chamber of Commerce. In this 1920 photo, members are shown in front of their headquarters, which opened for business in early March 1920 on Central Avenue.

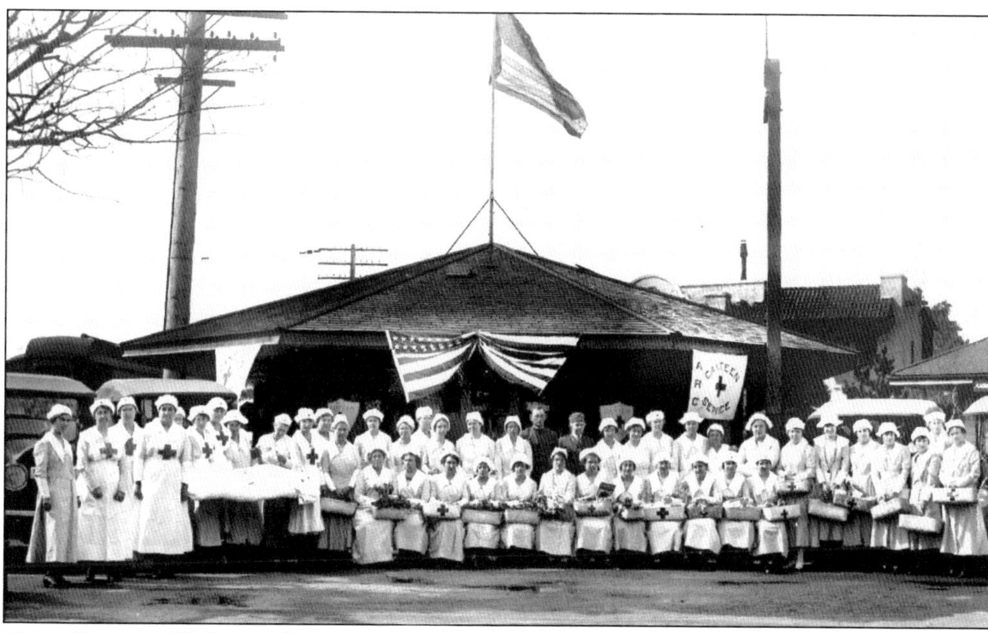

Tracy Canteen Club members posed in front of "The Hut" at the Southern Pacific station during World War I. Established in August 1918, the Canteen Club provided reading material, coffee, sandwiches, cigarettes, and so forth to servicemen passing through Tracy. Operated through the American Red Cross, the club had around 50 members during the height of its activity, making it the second largest Canteen Club in the state.

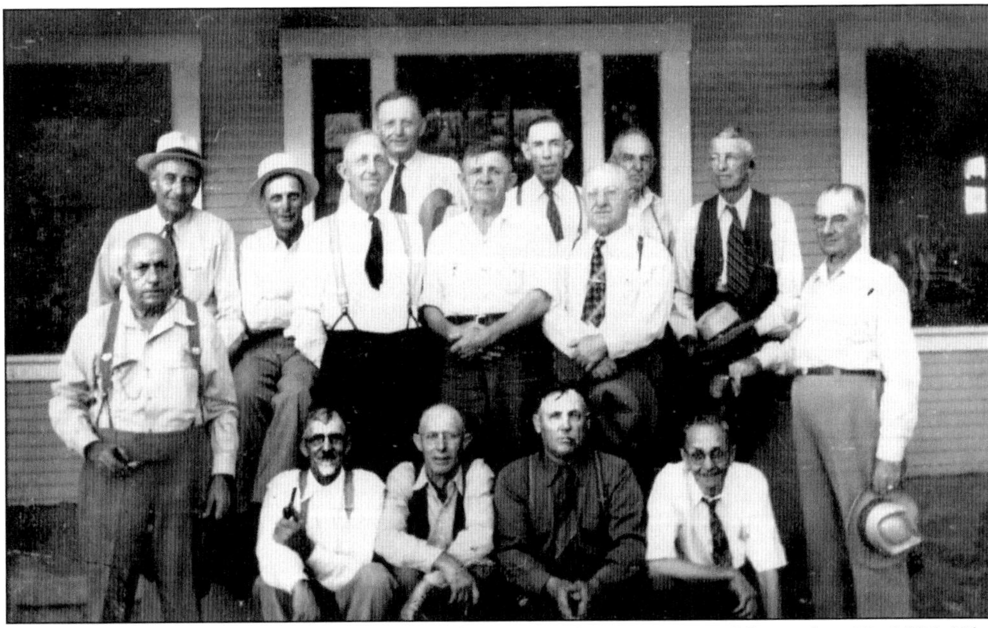

Atty. Frank Housken organized the West Side Pioneer Association on November 20, 1921. The organization, open to men over age 52 who had resided on the West Side for at least 30 years, sought to preserve Tracy area history. Seated in this 1941 picture are, from left to right, (front row) John Thoming, Walter Peterman, Ed Gerlach, and A. Anderson; (back row) Ben Canale, Fred von Sosten, Herman Walter, Frank Huck, Earl Paulson, John Kahlke, Fen Jackson, Fred Herzog, Ernest Schnabel, Henry Frerichs, and Victor Lee.

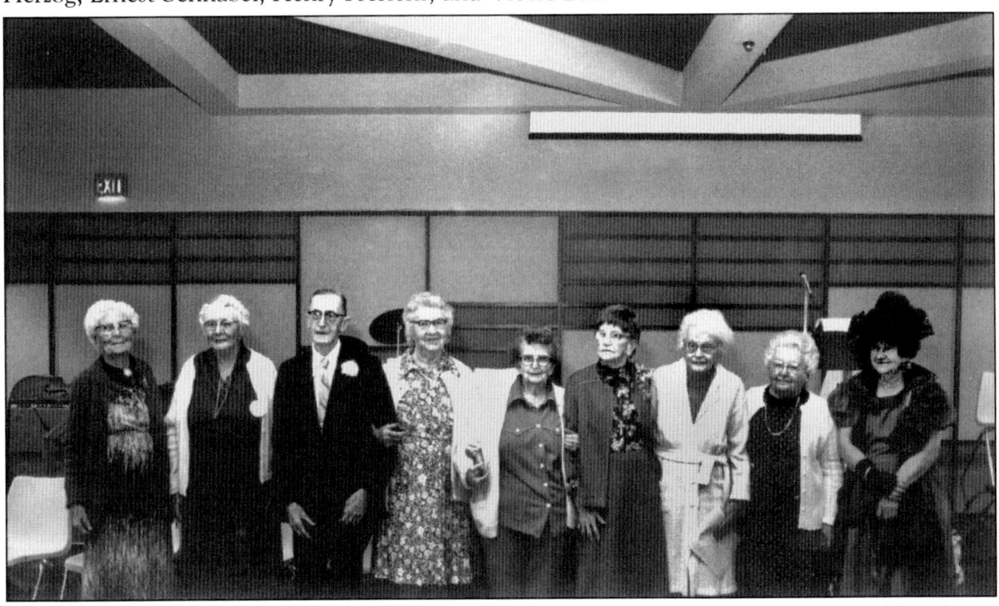

West Side Pioneer membership was opened to women around 1972, and age and residency requirements were eliminated. Pictured in 1982, from left to right, are early members Frieda Lehmann Strecker, age 98; Esther Luhrsen Poet, age 84; Jess Hansen, age 84; Meta Messer King, age 86; Katherine Taylor Hatfield, age 77; Toni Ohm Wessling, age 96; Annie Schroeder Walter, age 89; Bertha Hilken Rhodes, age 85; and Christine Bromell Asels, age 74.

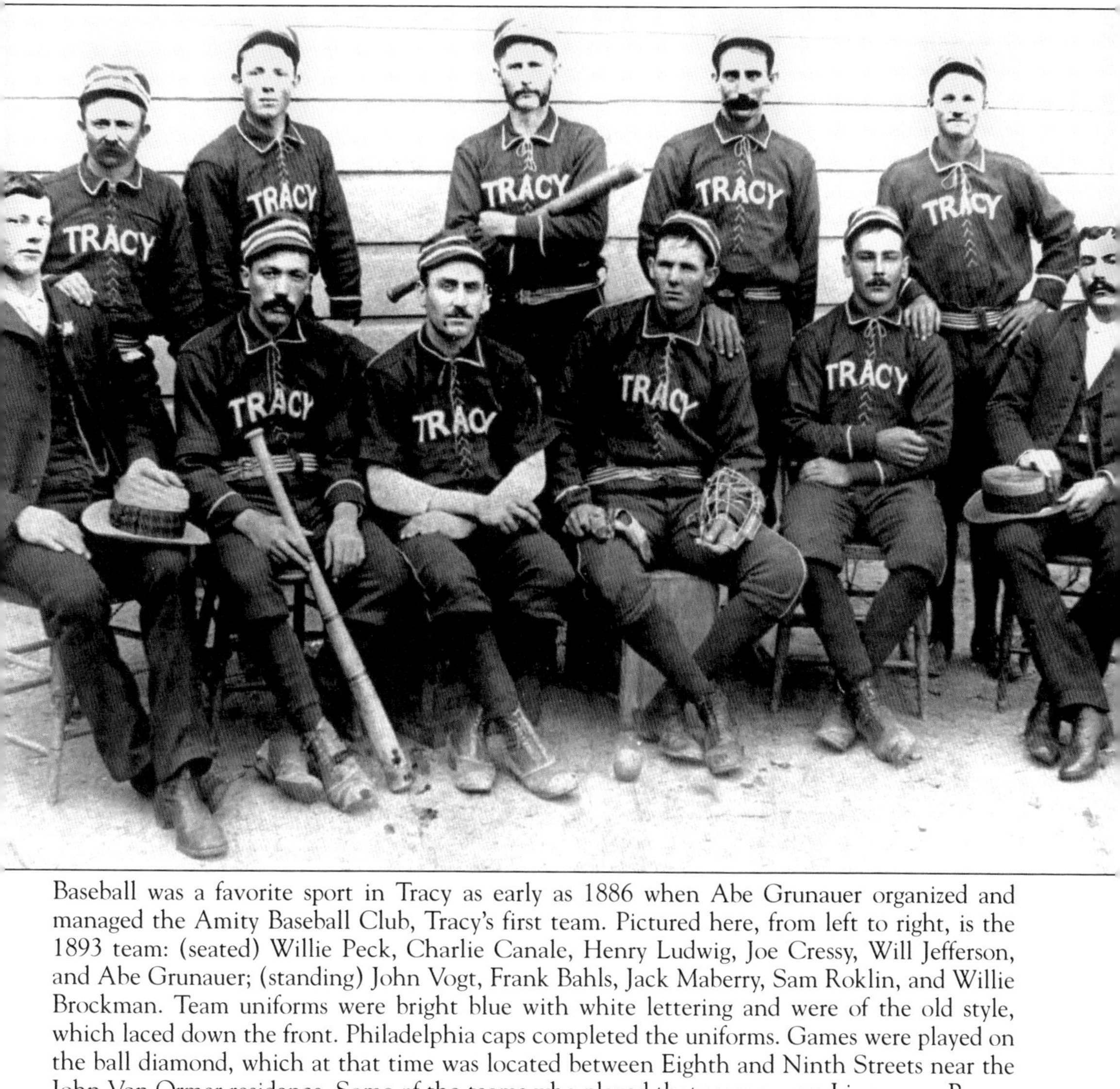

Baseball was a favorite sport in Tracy as early as 1886 when Abe Grunauer organized and managed the Amity Baseball Club, Tracy's first team. Pictured here, from left to right, is the 1893 team: (seated) Willie Peck, Charlie Canale, Henry Ludwig, Joe Cressy, Will Jefferson, and Abe Grunauer; (standing) John Vogt, Frank Bahls, Jack Maberry, Sam Roklin, and Willie Brockman. Team uniforms were bright blue with white lettering and were of the old style, which laced down the front. Philadelphia caps completed the uniforms. Games were played on the ball diamond, which at that time was located between Eighth and Ninth Streets near the John Van Ormer residence. Some of the teams who played that season were Livermore, Byron, and Tracy's arch-enemy, Lathrop.

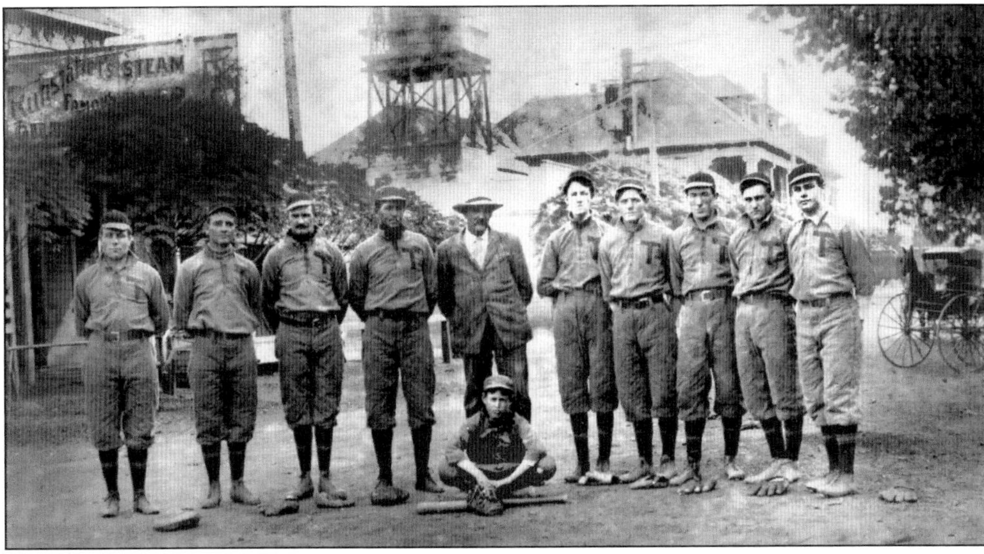

Baseball fever was at its height in the early 1900s in Tracy. Games were so popular that gate receipts were sufficient to defray all of the team's expenses. Members of the 1903 baseball team included, from left to right, Henry Gieseke, Bill Banta, Esau "Lefty" Lewis, ? Milsap, manager Adolph Windeler Sr., Earl Lindsay, Alfred "Allie" Gieseke, Adolph Windeler Jr., Ward Britton, and Honus Frerichs, the mascot.

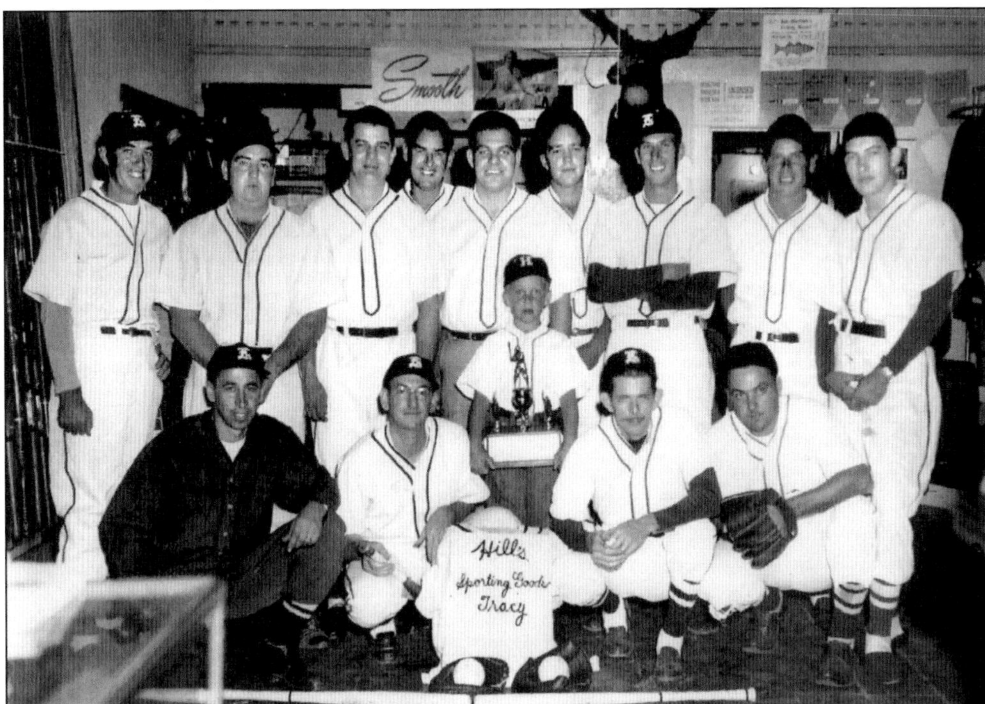

The Hill's Sporting Goods baseball team won the city championship in 1949. Displaying the championship trophy are, from left to right, (front row) Sam Hill, John Espinal, batboy Jere Hill, Don Duncan, and Jack Fisher; (back row) Tom Deadrick, Bruce Bailor, Ed Christian, Toby Grove, Bill Burdette, Jim Blaney, Jake Longmire, Ted Baskette, and Bob Stocking.

Five

SCHOOLS

As soon as families began settling on the West Side of San Joaquin County, there was an interest in establishing schools to educate the children. In 1866 local farmer Rufus Saddlemire circulated a petition to form a school district for the children around Ellis. Willow School District was formed, and Louisa Lynn donated land near the intersection of Byron Highway and Corral Hollow Road for the schoolhouse. When the town of Tracy was founded, the schoolhouse was moved from its location in the country to town. As the school population grew, the building became too small, and one of the classes was held in the annex of the Methodist church until a larger grammar school was opened in 1912. Rufus Saddlemire, who continued to be an ardent supporter of education in Tracy, received a rousing ovation when he was overcome with emotion and unable to speak at the dedication ceremony. As Tracy grew, additional schools and additions to the school campuses were built as residents continued to place a high value on quality educational opportunities for their children.

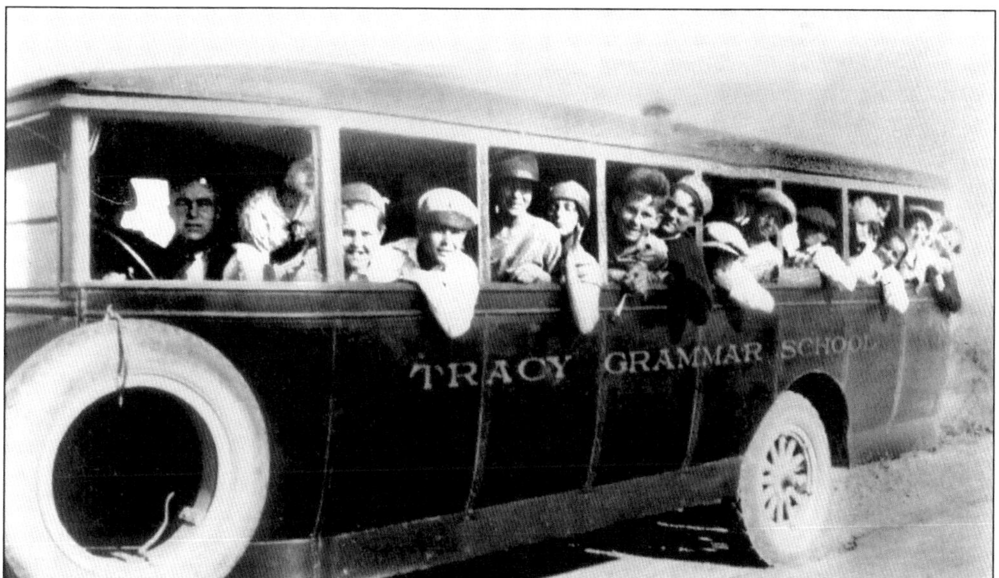

This Tracy Grammar School bus, loaded with pupils in 1925, was the first school bus used in Tracy. There were three grammar school buildings within the Tracy city limits in 1925: Central School (grades K–4), South Side School (grades 1–4), and West Park School (grades 5–8).

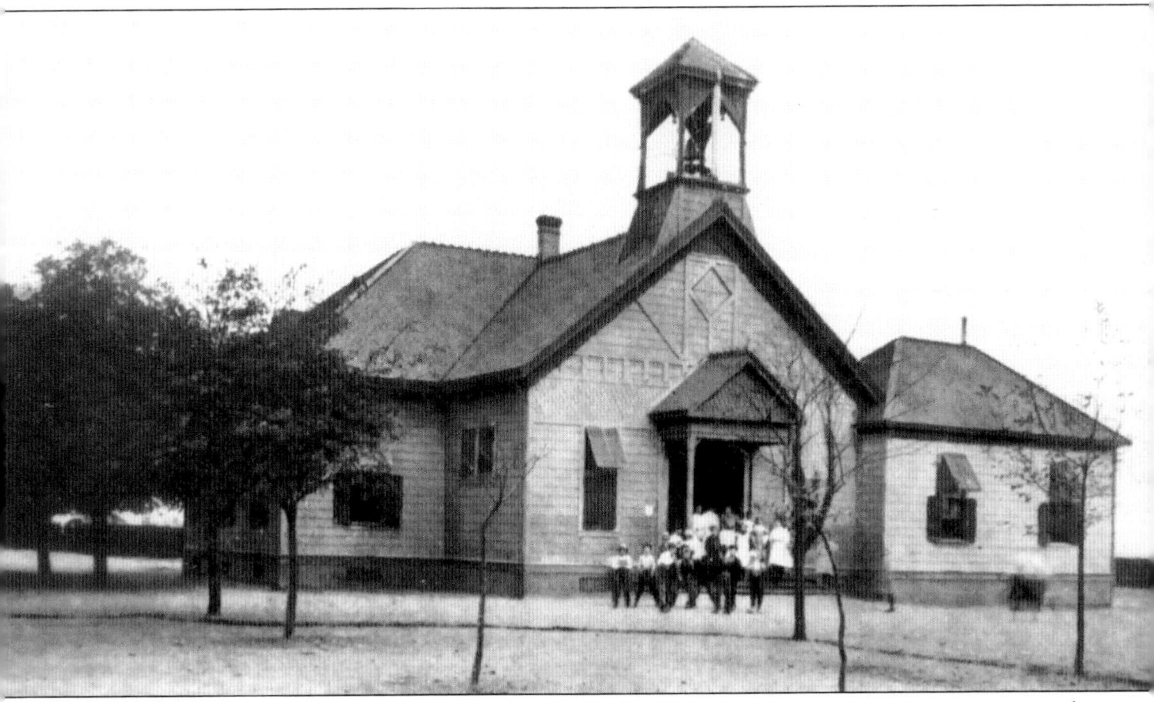

Willow schoolhouse, Tracy's first school, opened in the Ellis District in 1867 near the intersection of what is now Byron Highway and Corral Hollow Road. The interior of the one-room, country school was about 16 by 24 feet and had a center row of double desks with a row of single desks on either side. Early in 1879, after Tracy was established, the little yellow schoolhouse was moved to a lot in Tracy donated by the railroad and located on the triangular-shaped block at the intersection of Eighth and Ninth Streets (later known as the Van Ormer property). Nine years later the school moved to a much larger location on land also donated by the railroad at the southwest corner of Central Avenue and Eleventh Street (currently the Tracy Inn location). After a larger building was completed in 1912, the historic Willow School was reportedly sold to the highest bidder and moved near Canale's grocery store on East Sixth Street, where it became a "soft" drink establishment.

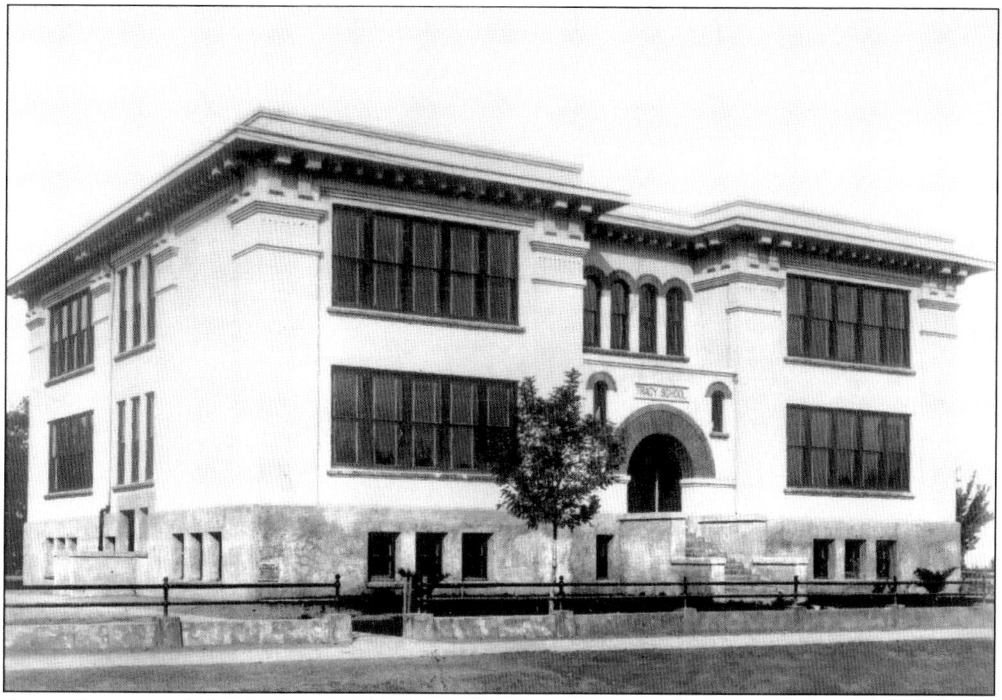

Tracy Grammar School, designed by Deule & Wright of Stockton, was dedicated March 1, 1912. Built on Central, in the same location as Willow School, the building contained eight classrooms, an assembly hall that could seat 250 people, and a full basement. After 1938, the building served different purposes, including use as the Service Men's Club and later as City Hall. It was torn down in 1961.

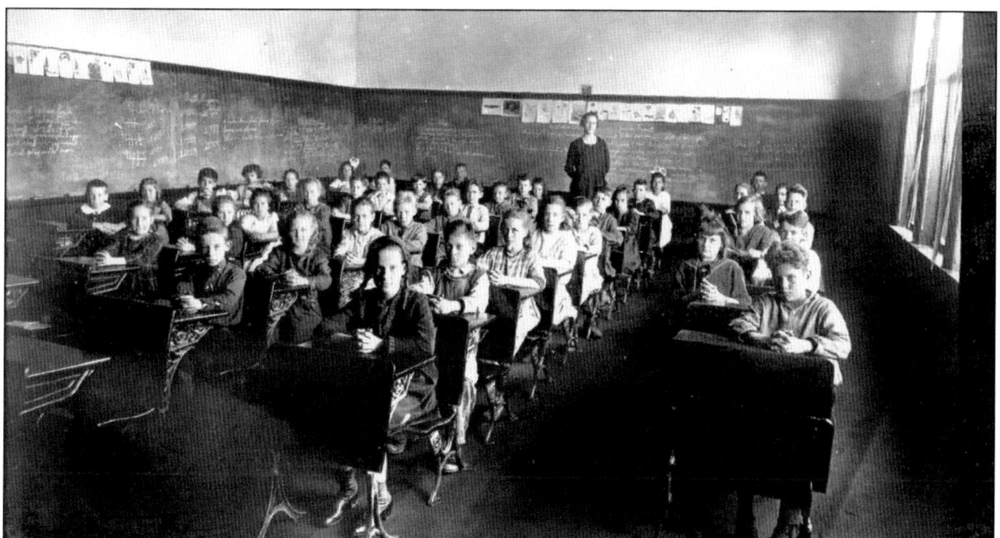

Miss Sehrt's class at Tracy Grammar School (later Central School) was photographed in 1919. Viola Sehrt, a former student at the school and a member of the first graduating high school class in 1915, began her 40-year teaching career in Tracy schools when she was hired to teach eighth grade at Tracy Grammar School in 1917. She later taught at West Park and Senior Elementary.

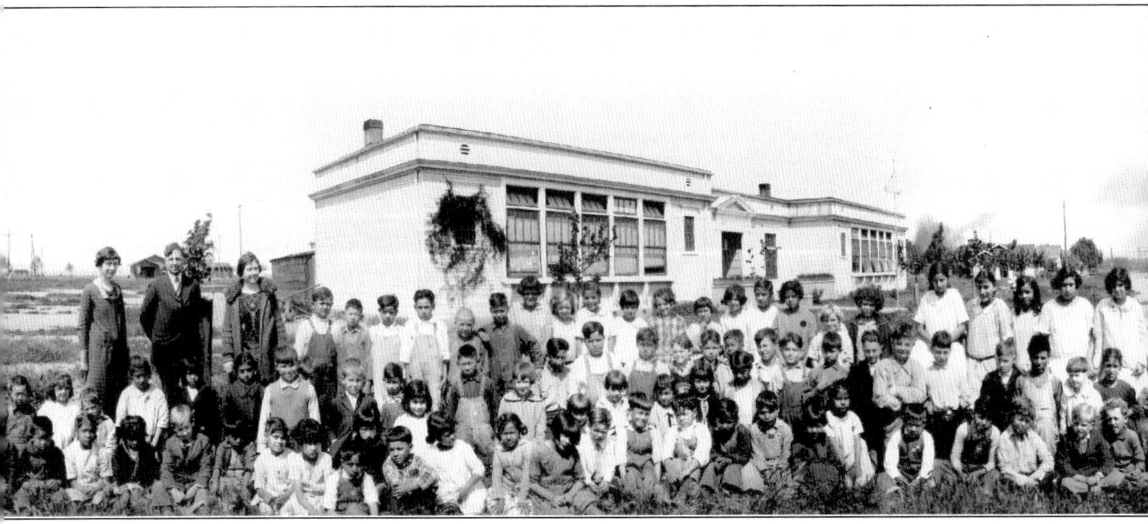

Two new grammar schools, West Park School and South Side School, were opened in September 1920 to meet the increasing need for more classrooms in Tracy. South Side School, with one teacher the first year, was a one-room, wooden frame building on Central Avenue and First Street (currently the site of McDonald Park). For several years in the 1920s the school had two teachers; Miss Mamie Sullivan was principal and taught the intermediate grades, and Miss Ethel Carlton taught the lower grades. An additional 25-by-38-foot regulation-size classroom, identical to the original, was added in the summer of 1925. The students and faculty were photographed at the dedication in 1925. Standing on the left in the back row is Miss Carlton, and third from the left is Miss Sullivan. South Side School (later called South School) expanded to a K–6 elementary school before it closed in 1951 when the new South School was opened on Mt. Diablo Avenue.

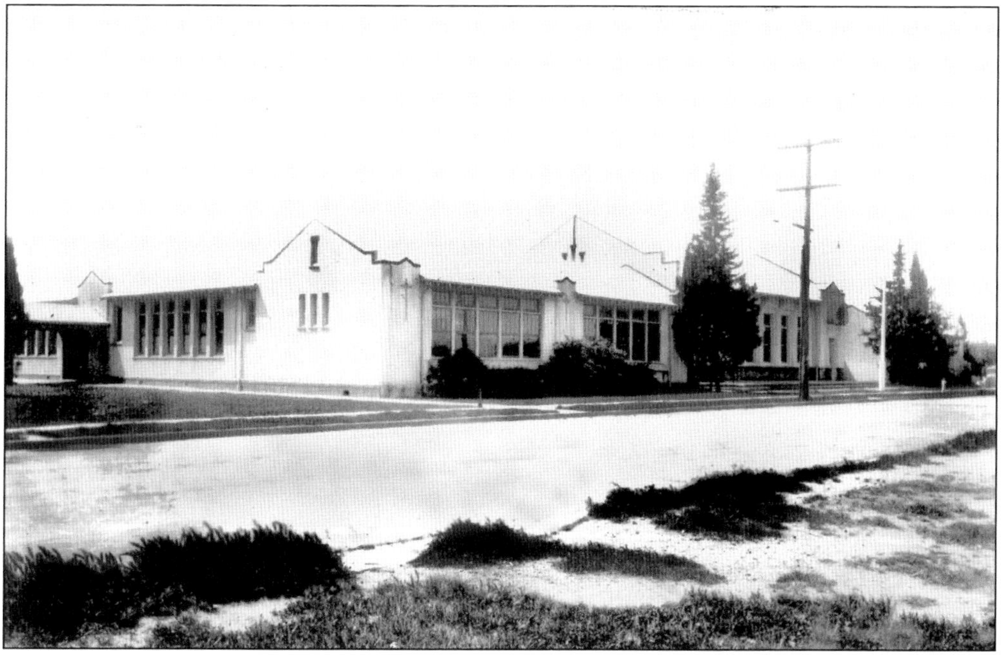

West Park School, a small brick structure built in 1920 on West Tenth Street (currently the site of the Discovery School), had two classrooms. Students in grades 5–8 attended this school, while those in K–4 attended Central. Pictured is the school after two more rooms and an auditorium were added in the summer of 1922 and dedicated in April 1923. For safety reasons, the school was replaced in the 1950s.

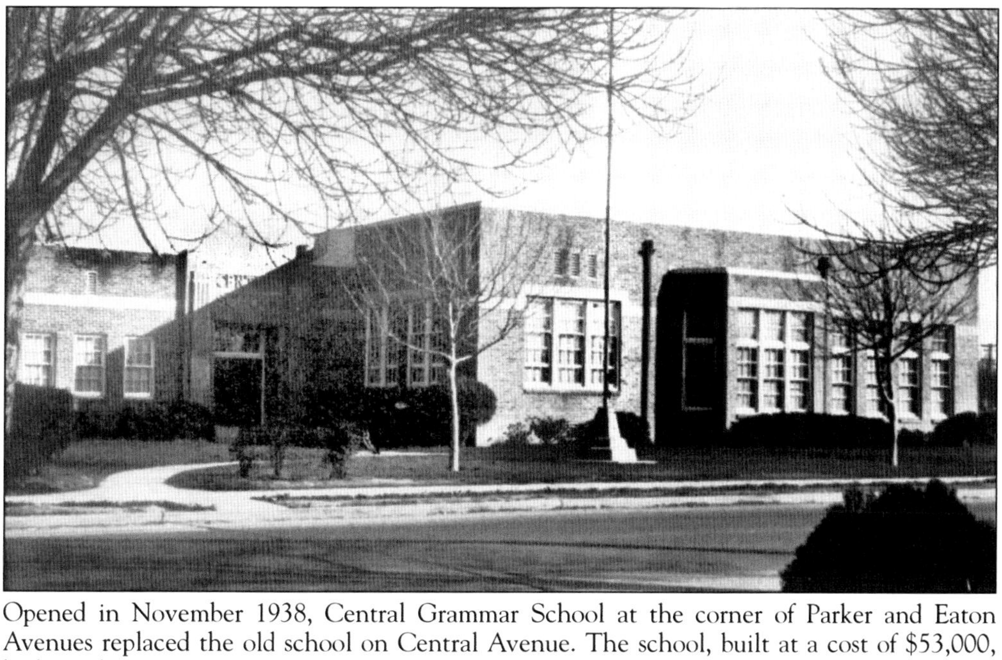

Opened in November 1938, Central Grammar School at the corner of Parker and Eaton Avenues replaced the old school on Central Avenue. The school, built at a cost of $53,000, had six classrooms, an office, an auditorium, a kitchen/cafeteria, and a teacher's/nurse's room. Miss Elsie Salcido, who had been a teacher and principal in Tracy schools for 25 years, was the principal.

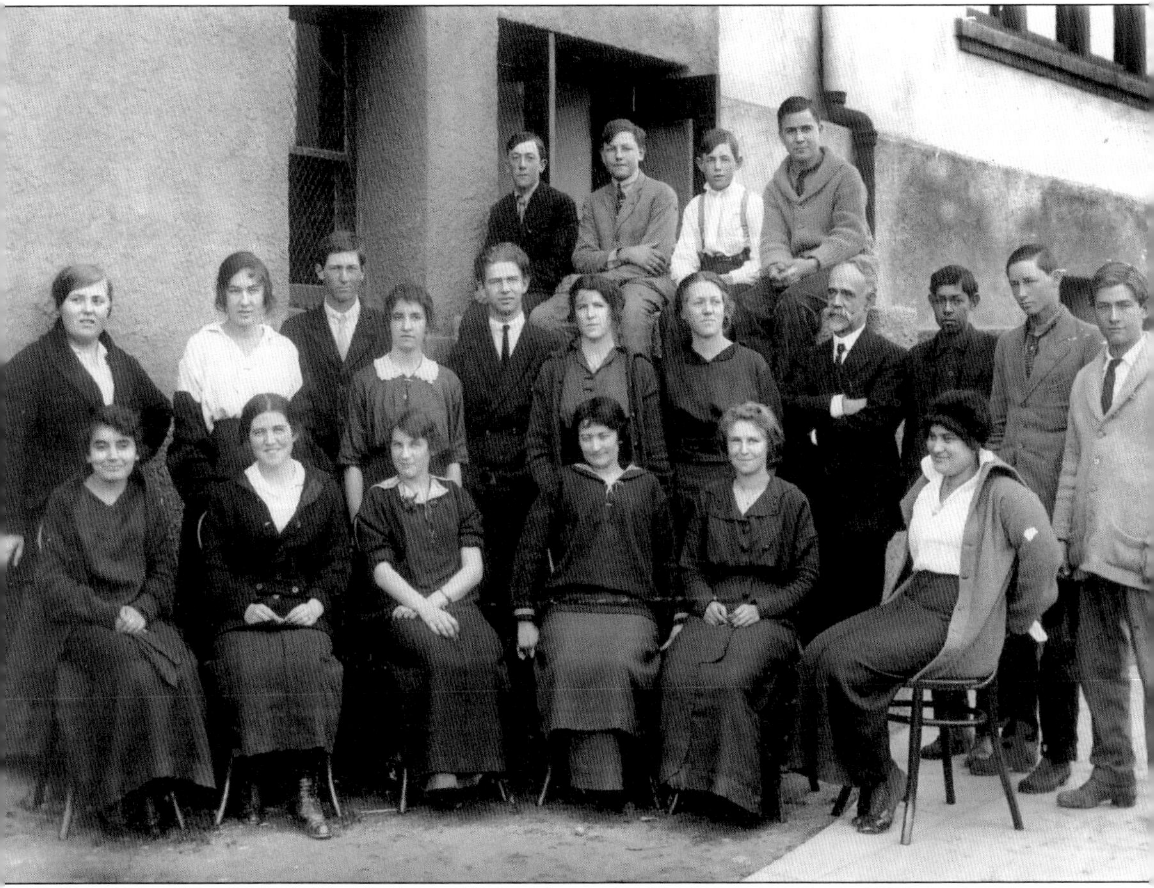

The first classes of West Side Union High School were held in two upstairs classrooms at the Tracy Grammar School. Principal A.D. Tenney and Assistant Mary Acheson were hired to teach three courses of study: the literary, the scientific, and the commercial. The literary curriculum included English, math, science, history, and language courses. The scientific curriculum emphasized science, math, and technical drawing courses. The commercial curriculum included business courses and could be completed in two years. Pictured in 1913 with the principal are the first students. From left to right are (front row) Vera Salcido, Dorothy O'Neil, Bertha Grunauer, Hazel Parker, Eva Schmidt, and Vesta Ludwig; (middle row) Margaret Garner, Elizabeth Dwelly, Earle Williams, Mildred Westlake, Paul Tenney, Elizabeth O'Neil, Viola Sehrt, Professor A.D. Tenney, Arcadio Alviso, Harris Williams, and Herbert Buschke; (back row) Jess Hansen, Henry Schmidt, Francis McKeany, and Warner Culver. The first students to graduate from the local high school were Viola Sehrt and Elizabeth O'Neil in 1915.

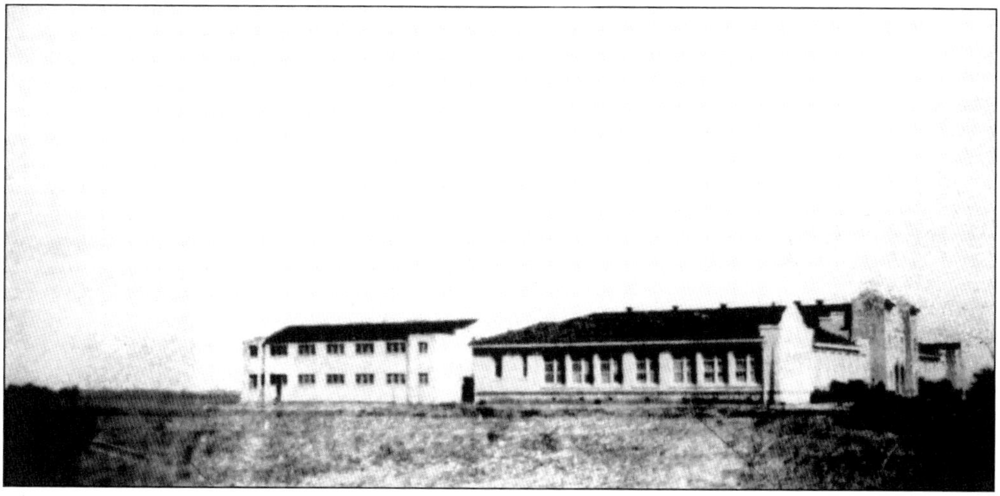

The West Side Union High School, renamed Tracy Union High School in 1928, was located on Tracy's eastern edge on 12 acres of land on Eleventh Street. Prior to its opening in 1917, high school students attended classes in second-floor classrooms at Tracy School on Central. Before 1912 students desiring a high school education had to attend school in Stockton or elsewhere.

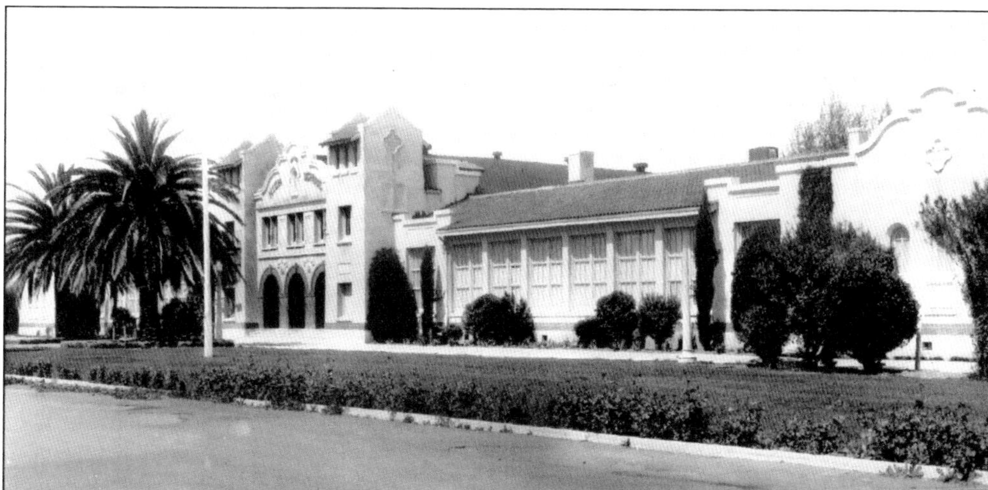

The high school, designed by W.H. Weeks in the Mission style, was built on the unit system so additions could be made without changing the building's style. Costing about $65,000, the school was originally built with 14 classrooms and an auditorium with seating for about 1,000 people. This photo shows the landscaped exterior of the building, currently known as the West Building, on the Tracy High School campus.

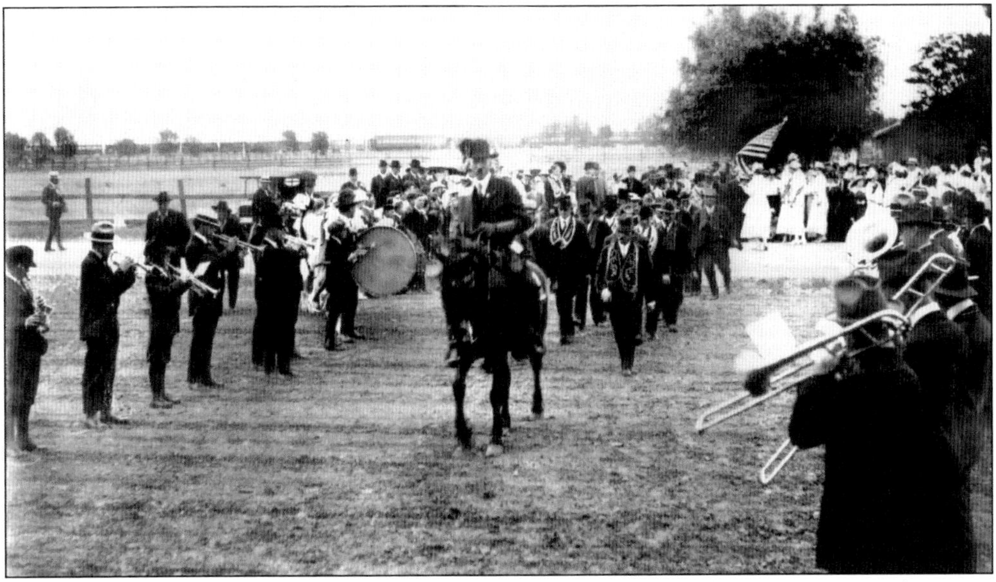

Photographed leading the parade procession at the dedication ceremonies for West Side Union High School on May 1, 1917, is the grand marshall, Judge Samuel S. McLain, on horseback. Parade participants included Grand Officers of the IOOF, delegates from the Stockton Chamber of Commerce, Tracy school students, Boy Scouts, fraternal organizations, city and school trustees, citizens, and visitors. The Tracy Band provided music for the occasion.

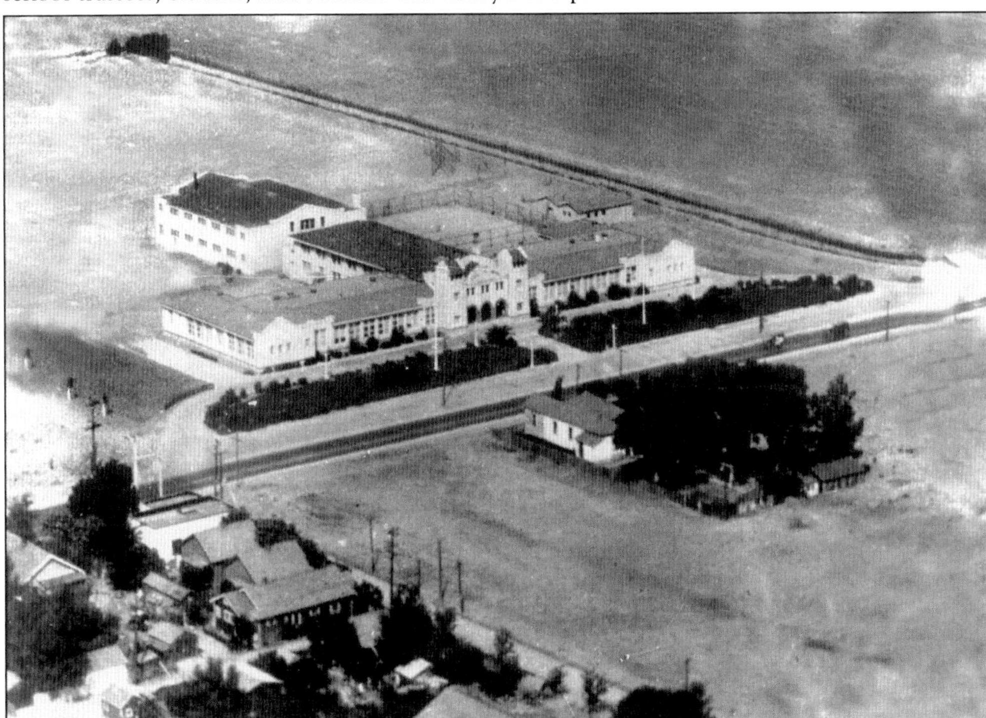

This aerial view of Tracy West Side Union High School, which appeared in the 1925 yearbook, the *Orange and Green*, shows the campus with the addition of the gymnasium. The gymnasium was added in 1922 so the school would meet California accreditation requirements.

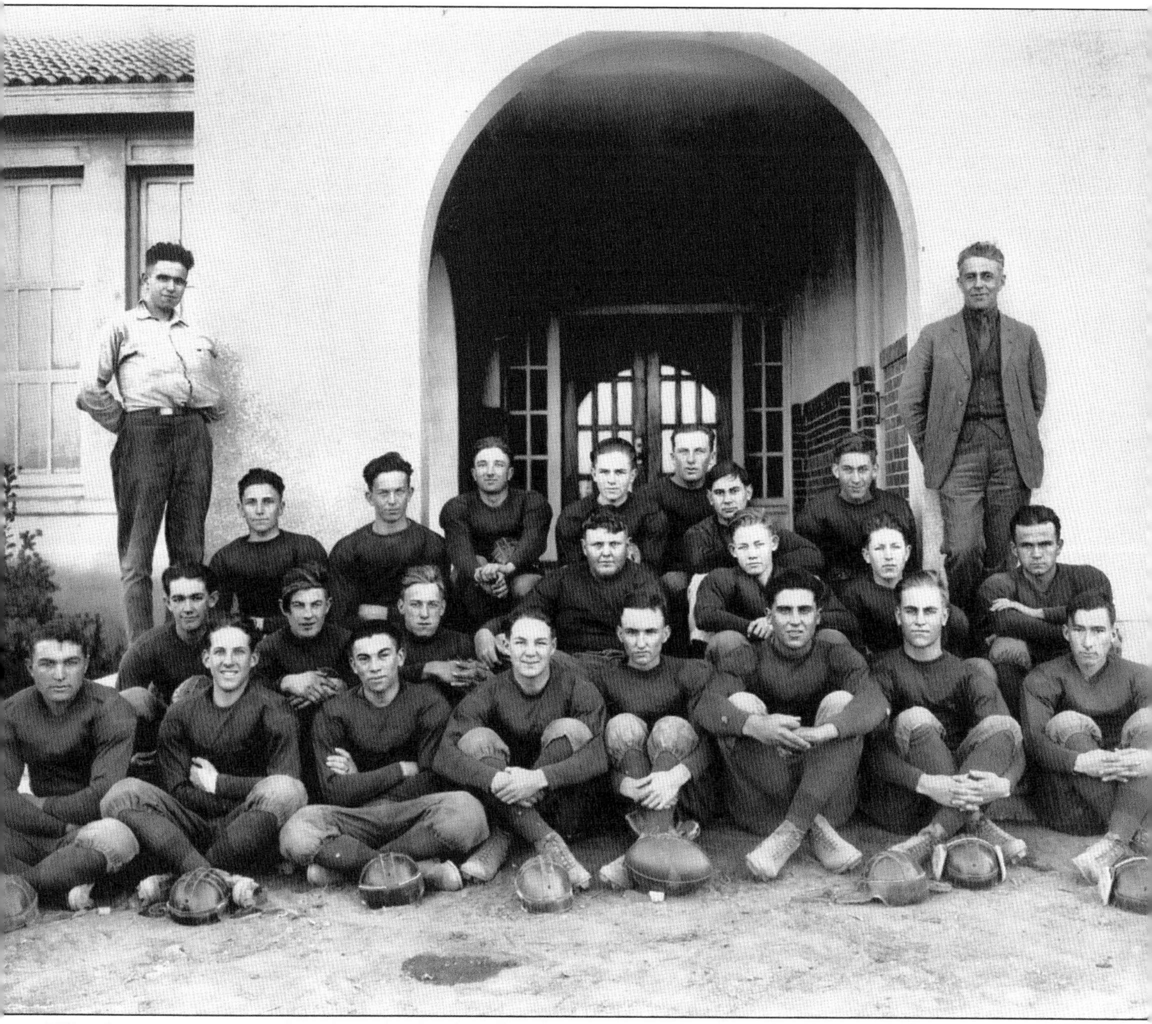

The first two sports played at the high school were baseball and football. Coached by G.M. "Bull" Hunter (standing on the right) and Asst. Coach Pat Bone (not pictured), Tracy's West Side Union High School football team lost all eight games in 1921 in their first season. The "varsity" and "scrubs" team members pictured that year, from left to right, are (front row) unidentified, Louis Strahorn, Sammy Gallego, Dale Strahorn, quarterback and varsity captain Leonard Gibson, Leonard "Dink" King, John von Sosten, and Herman Moller; (middle row) Malcolm Tisher, two unidentified members, Henry "Tiny" Batterman, Maxwell Conklin, John McCusker, and ? McGlothlan or McLaughlin; (back row) Ralph Fitzsimmons (standing), Norman Gonzales, Leland Tschierschsky, Art Affonso, Charlie Payne, Walter Ekenberg, and two unidentified people. The names of the unidentified players are Nelson Dwelly, Carl Quadros, John Arthur, Joe Hart, and Robert Carlton. Notice the style of the uniforms, especially the helmets.

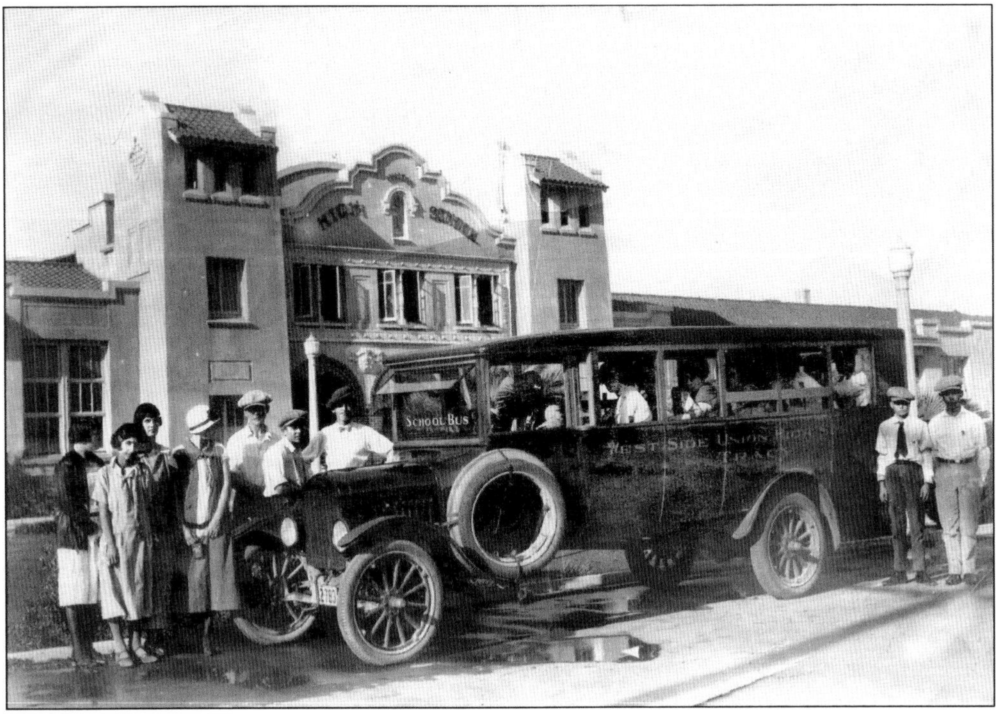

This West Side Union High School bus, pictured in the 1920s, was Virgil Poet's bus. Virgil, the first school bus driver in Tracy, bought a bus and began busing grade school students in 1923. About five years later he added the high school students to his routes. Beginning in 1927, Esther Luhrsen Poet, Virgil's wife, also drove a bus for the schools.

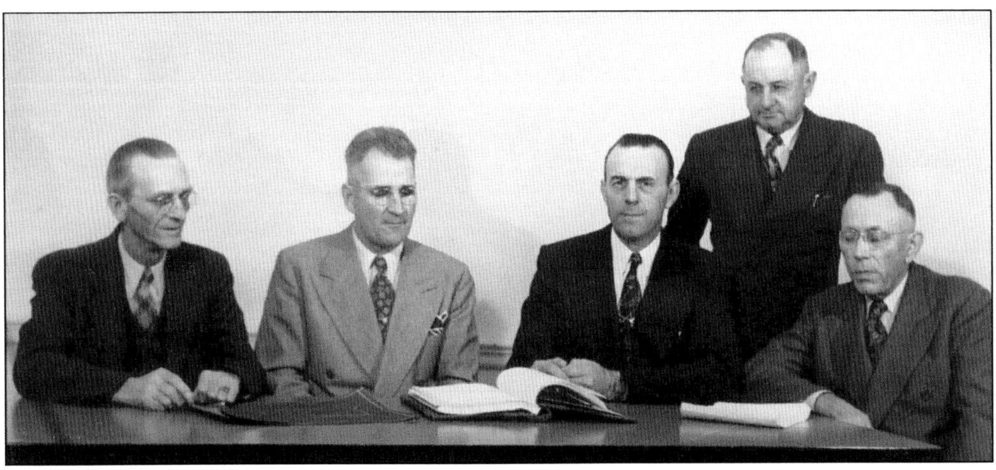

Photographed in 1933 around a conference table are the Tracy Union High School trustees. Pictured, from left to right, are Bill Costello, William Koster, Irvin Petz, Bert Banta, and James Mullaly. William Koster served as a trustee for 21 years before retiring. (Courtesy of Clifford W. Koster.)

Six

BUILDINGS AND BUSINESSES

Tracy's first businesses and buildings were those moved from Ellis to the new town of Tracy. Among those businesses, which were located on the north side of the tracks along Front Street (Sixth Street) and along Seventh Street in the first blocks on either side of Central Avenue, were G.A.D. Buschke's harness shop, Thomas Castle's hotel and saloon, Philip Fabian's general merchandise store, John Hay's blacksmith shop, Charles Landgraf's blacksmith shop, Christian Ludwig's hotel, Joseph Matevia's saloon and livery stable, Sebastian Questa's general store, Peter Sohn's boot and shoe making business, and Edward Wacksmuth's hotel. A few early businesses also developed on Fourth Street south of the railroad tracks. As the population grew, new buildings were constructed and new businesses opened to meet the needs of the community. As a result of fires that destroyed some of the early buildings, especially the large fire of 1898, the wooden buildings were gradually replaced with ones made of brick.

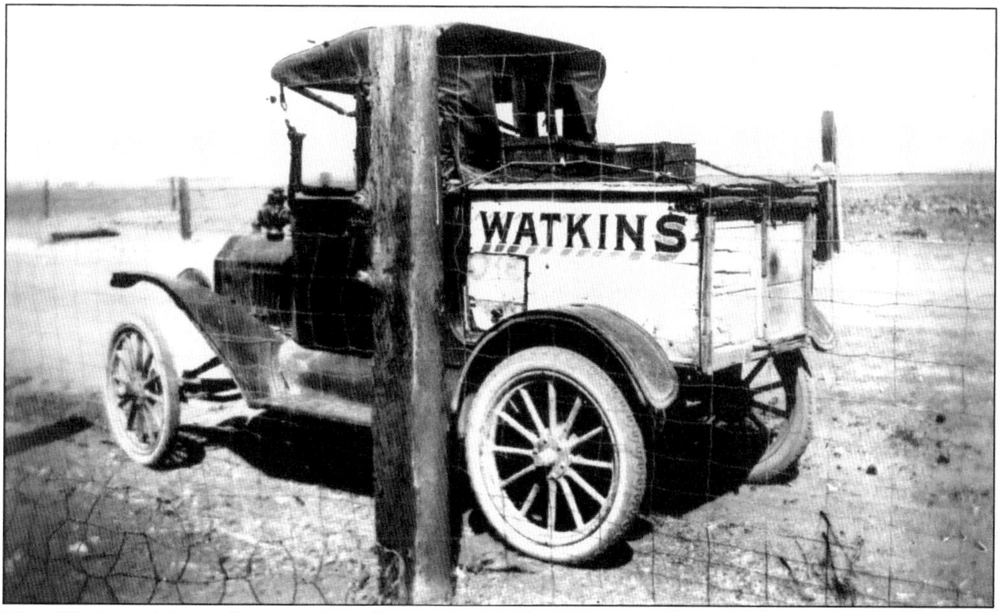

The Watkins Man, photographed here in a Ford pickup in 1922 on the Cordes ranch, sold household gadgets, liniments, tonics, salves, kitchen spices, and other household items to rural families. The arrival of the Watkins Man, with his colorful displays, was almost as exciting to farm and ranch children as the arrival of the Sears Roebuck Catalog. (Courtesy of Paul Andersen.)

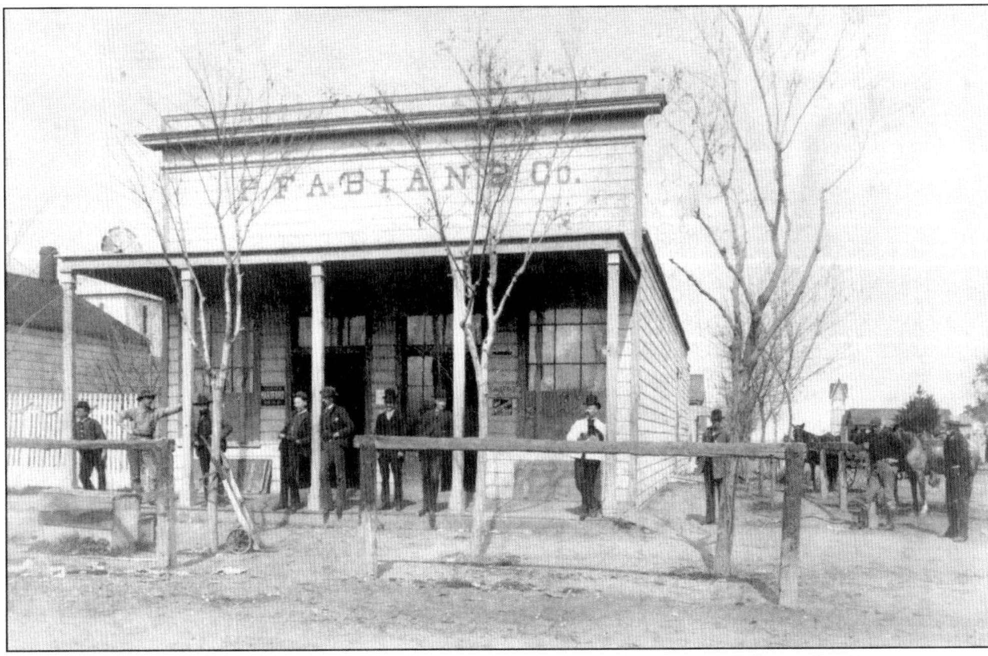

One of the first businesses moved from Ellis to Tracy in 1878. P. Fabian & Co., a general merchandise store operated by Philip Fabian and Louis Levinsky, was located on West Sixth Street at the corner of Sixth and Central Avenue (currently a vacant lot). Tracy's first post office was located in this building, and Philip Fabian was the first postmaster. The building was destroyed in the 1898 fire.

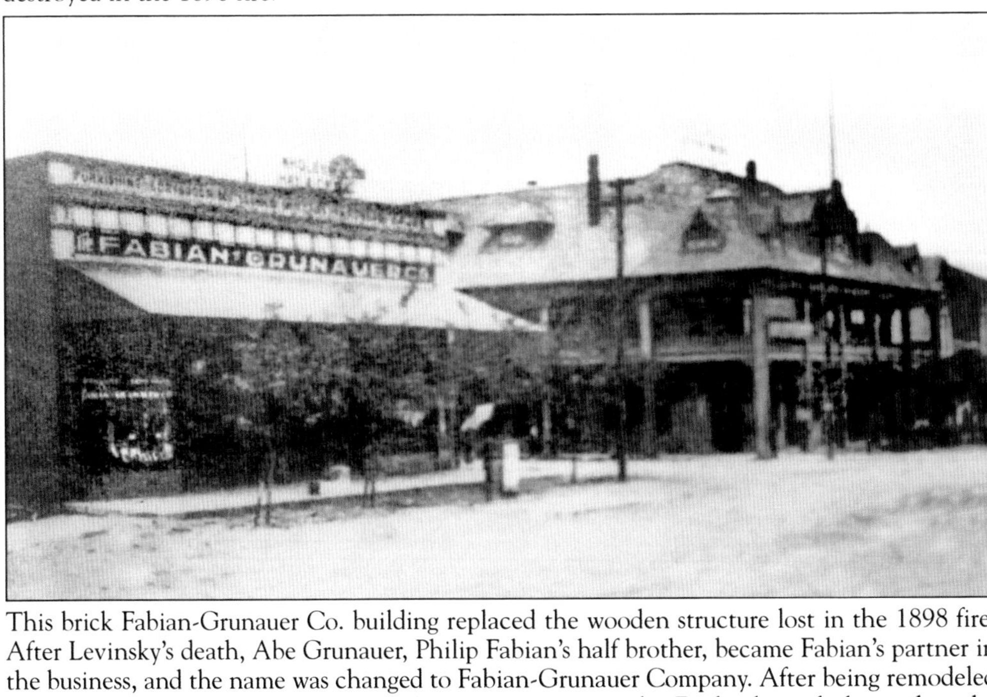

This brick Fabian-Grunauer Co. building replaced the wooden structure lost in the 1898 fire. After Levinsky's death, Abe Grunauer, Philip Fabian's half brother, became Fabian's partner in the business, and the name was changed to Fabian-Grunauer Company. After being remodeled in the early 1900s, it was known as The Big Store. Note the Fairbanks scale located in the street. (See the Fabian-Grunauer warehouse caption in the agriculture chapter.)

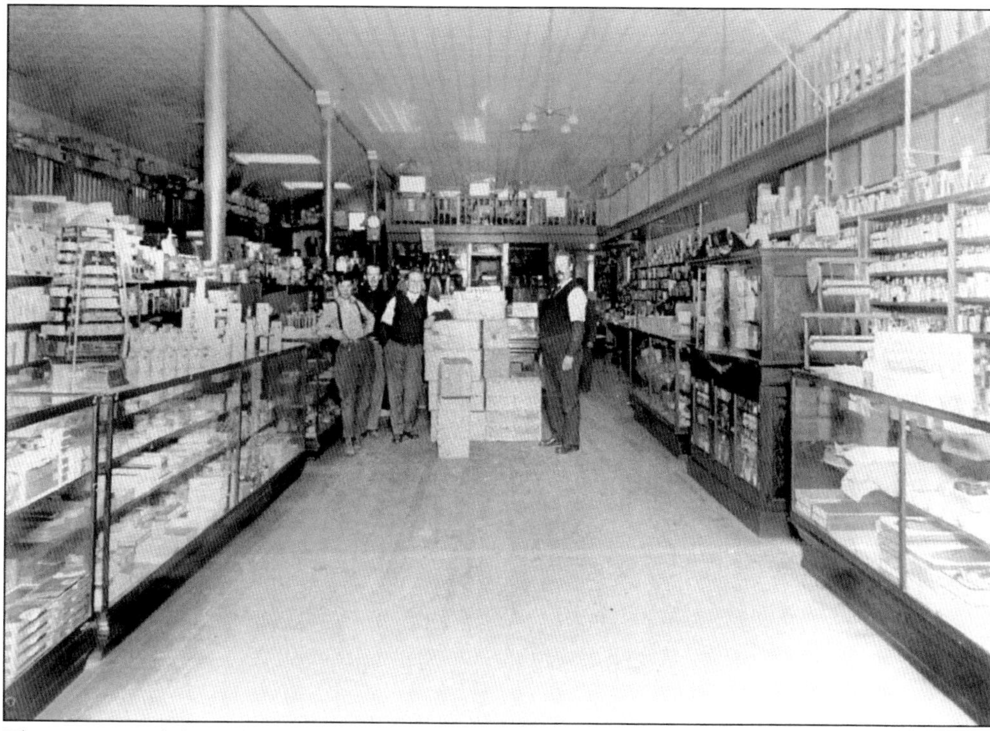

The interior of the Fabian-Grunauer store shows a portion of the wide variety of items sold in Tracy's largest store. Items sold included all sorts of general merchandise, from groceries, household items, hardware, medicine, and shoes to farm equipment and automobiles. After the store closed in 1926, the building housed other businesses for many years. It was torn down in 1985.

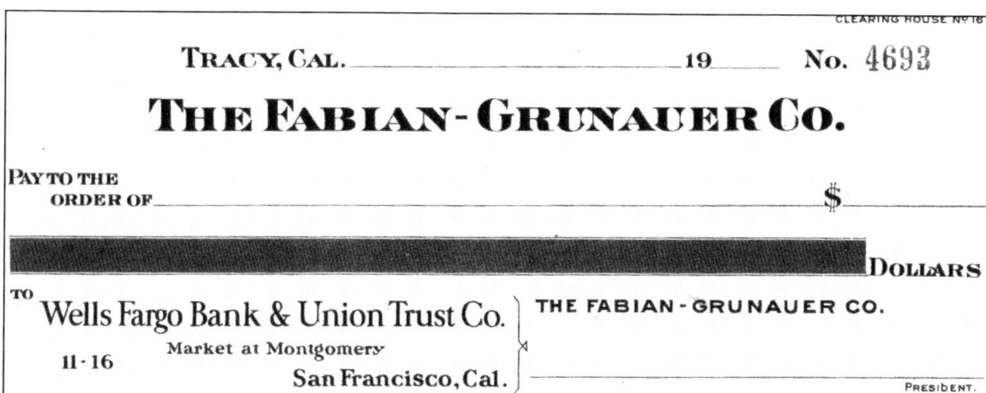

CLEARING HOUSE No 16

TRACY, CAL. ______ 19___ No. 4693

THE FABIAN-GRUNAUER CO.

PAY TO THE ORDER OF ______ $______

______ DOLLARS

TO Wells Fargo Bank & Union Trust Co.
Market at Montgomery
San Francisco, Cal.
11-16

THE FABIAN-GRUNAUER CO.

______ PRESIDENT. SECRETARY.

Pictured is a blank check from the Fabian-Grunauer Co. There were no banks in Tracy until 1909 so the Fabian-Grunauer Co. fulfilled some of the functions of a banking institution for local citizens in the early years. They granted credit, especially to railroad employees and farmers. They also loaned money to merchants and farmers, with land or crops often used as collateral until the crops were harvested.

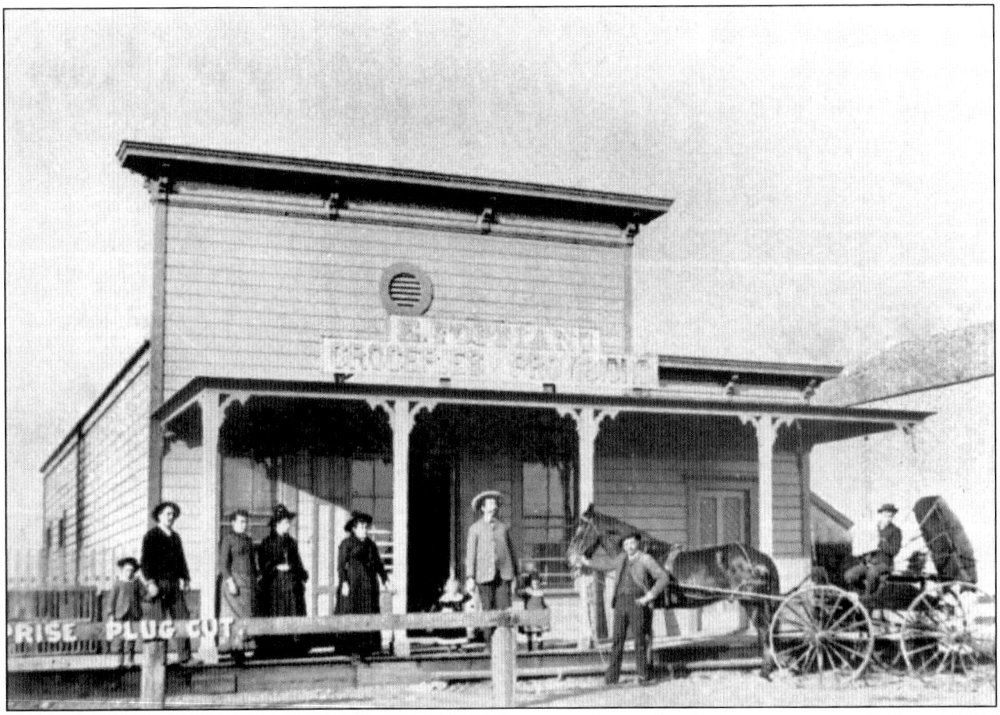

Emanuel Foppiano Groceries and Provisions was on East Sixth Street, east of the IOOF building. Foppiano later went into partnership with his brothers-in-law Dan and Charles Canale, who bought him out in 1887, after which the business was known as Canale Brothers. This building burned in the 1898 fire and was replaced by a new building on the same site. The store closed in 1943.

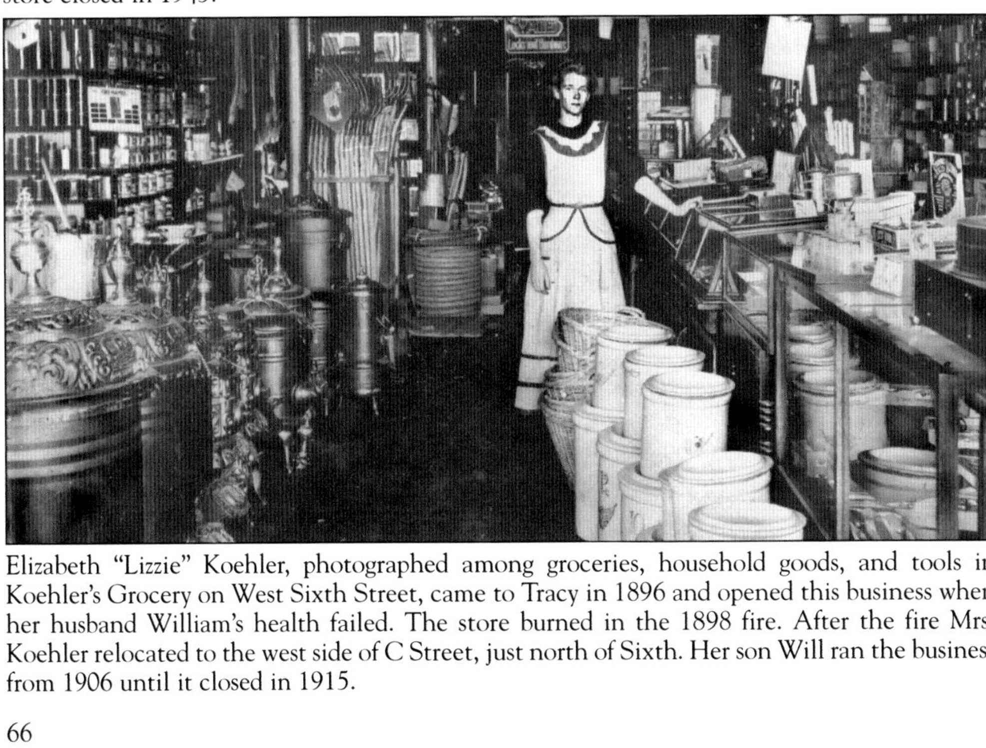

Elizabeth "Lizzie" Koehler, photographed among groceries, household goods, and tools in Koehler's Grocery on West Sixth Street, came to Tracy in 1896 and opened this business when her husband William's health failed. The store burned in the 1898 fire. After the fire Mrs. Koehler relocated to the west side of C Street, just north of Sixth. Her son Will ran the business from 1906 until it closed in 1915.

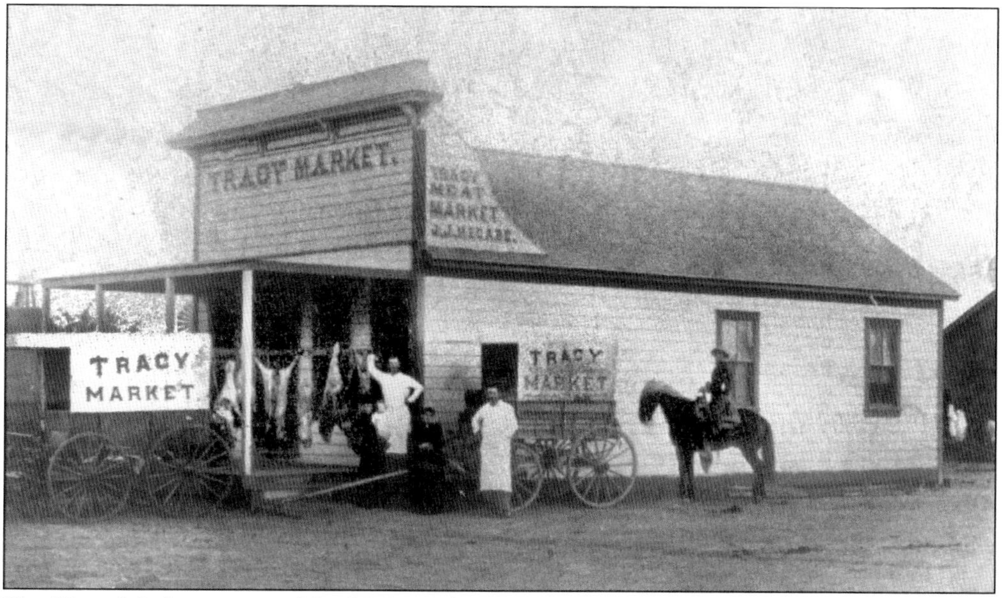

The Tracy Market, operated by J.J. McCabe *c.* 1894, was an early day meat market on West Eighth Street in Tracy. The meat carcasses hanging in front of the market were waiting to be cut up and sold. Meat was delivered to customers in the two delivery wagons parked by the store.

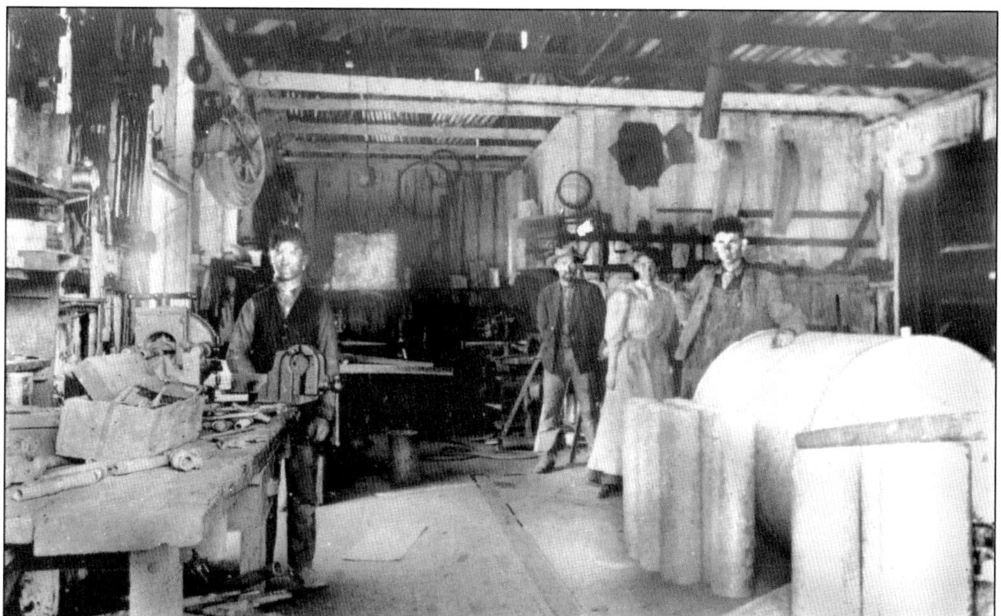

In 1895 Benjamin Bramman established Bramman Plumbing Co., a hardware and plumbing business, on the east side of Central Avenue near the alley between Eighth and Ninth Streets. Later he went into partnership with his wife's brother Frank Brown, and the business became Bramman and Brown Plumbing Co. Following her husband's death in 1904, Maria Bramman and her brother operated the business and later moved it to East Ninth Street.

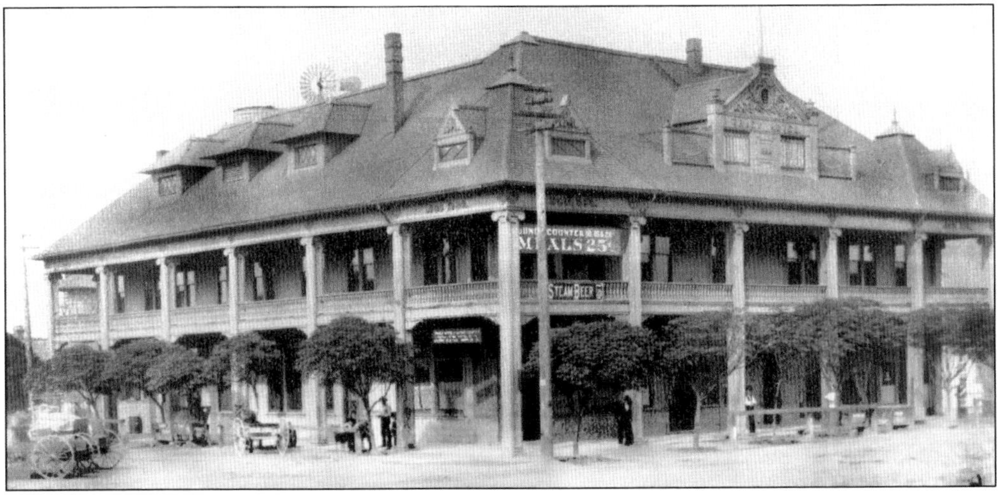

Owner Edward Wacksmuth had the Tracy Hotel, formerly the Ellis Hotel, moved from Ellis to the northeast corner of East Sixth Street at Central Avenue. In 1891, Wacksmuth's son-in-law Charles Slack took over the business. Pictured here is the new Tracy Hotel built after the 1898 fire destroyed the original, smaller structure. In 1911 this second building was also destroyed by fire and was replaced with a brick building.

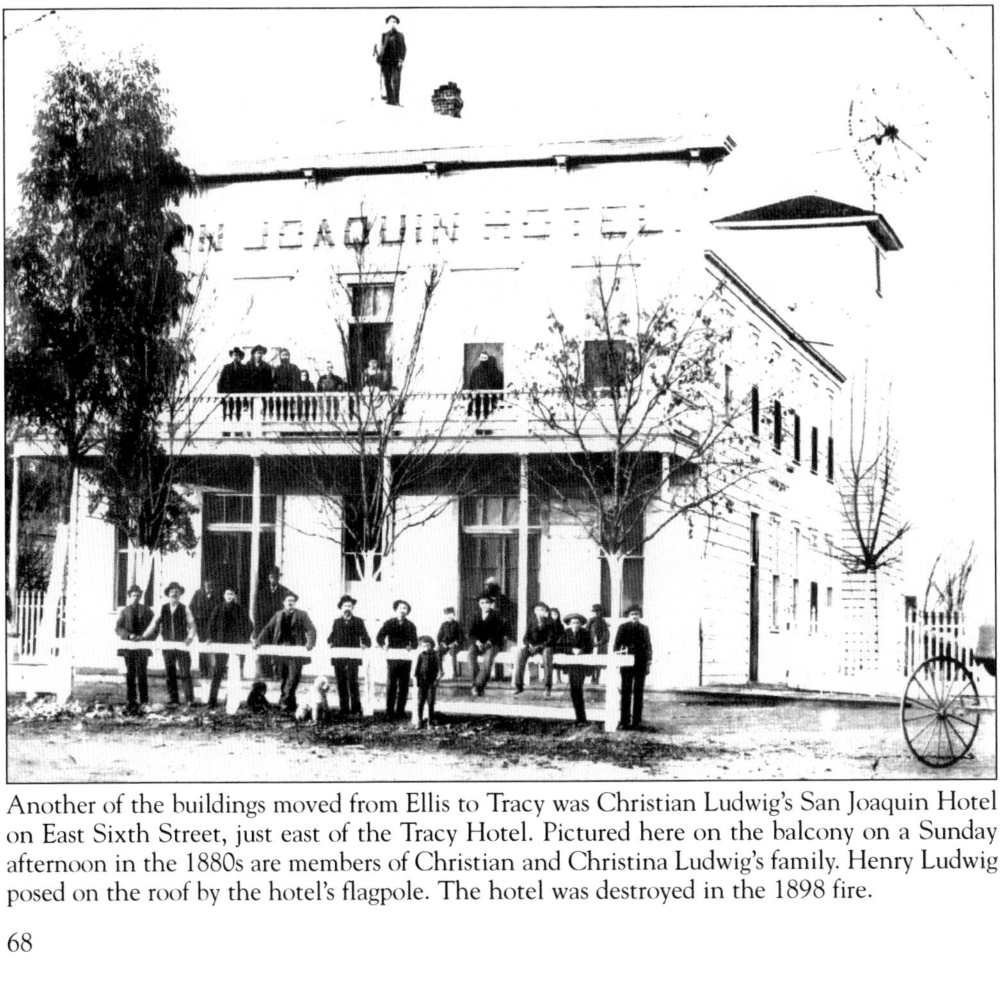

Another of the buildings moved from Ellis to Tracy was Christian Ludwig's San Joaquin Hotel on East Sixth Street, just east of the Tracy Hotel. Pictured here on the balcony on a Sunday afternoon in the 1880s are members of Christian and Christina Ludwig's family. Henry Ludwig posed on the roof by the hotel's flagpole. The hotel was destroyed in the 1898 fire.

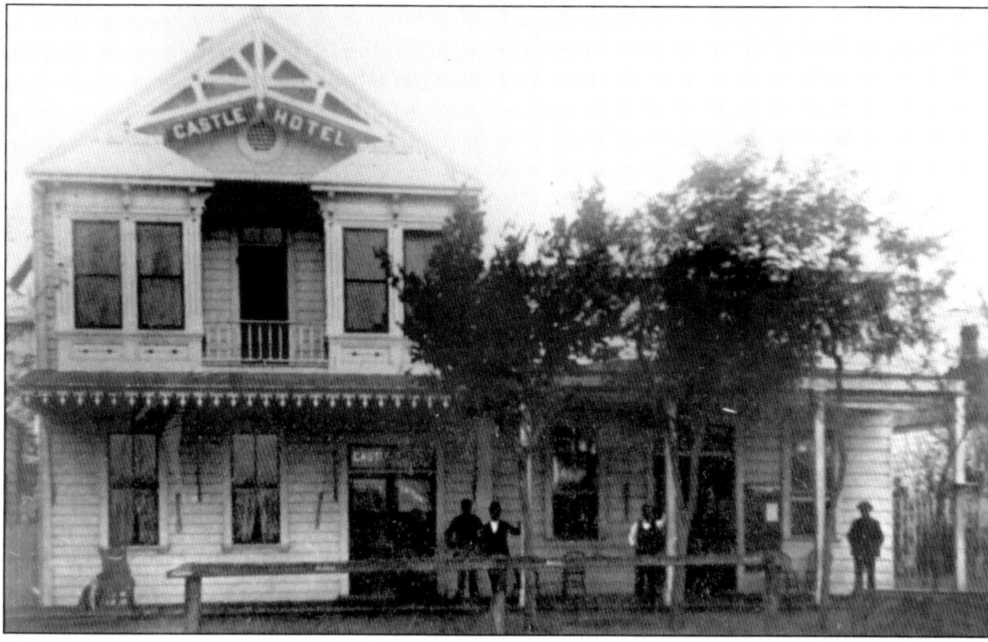

Thomas Castle moved the Castle Hotel from Ellis to Tracy in 1878 onto lots next to P. Fabian & Co. on West Sixth Street. After the hotel burned in an 1879 fire in Tracy, Castle built a saloon on the property. In 1889 he built a new Castle Hotel, which is pictured here.

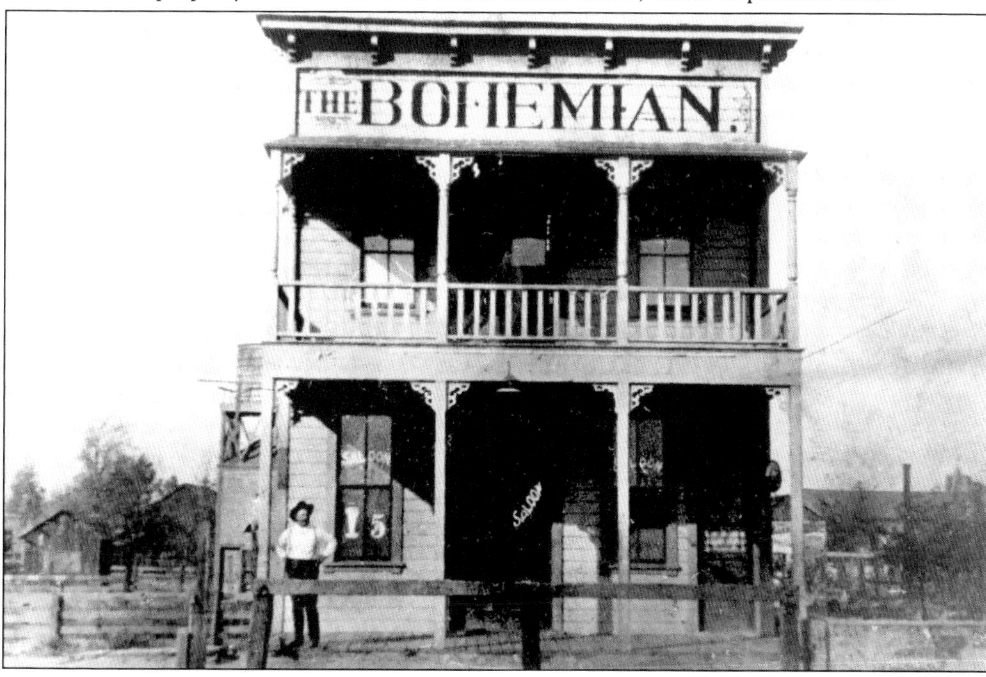

Charlie Guerra operated the Bohemian Hotel and Saloon on West Sixth Street, which was built after the 1898 fire. The upper level was a small hotel, and the lower level was a saloon with a special entrance to a private drinking room for the ladies at the lower right. The Bohemian was destroyed in a 1913 fire that consumed many of the businesses on West Sixth Street.

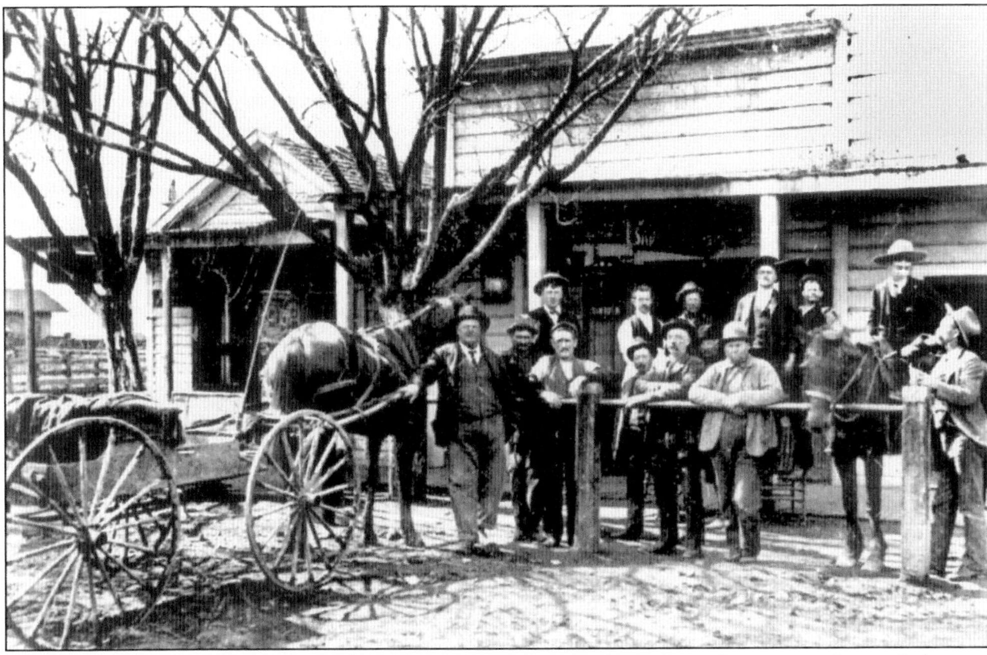

In contrast to the hotels on Sixth Street, this saloon and rooming house on Central Avenue offered "simple rooms." Because German was spoken in the saloon, it especially appealed to men of German heritage and became a favorite gathering place. Here they heard news from "home" and discussed farming, weather conditions, and local happenings.

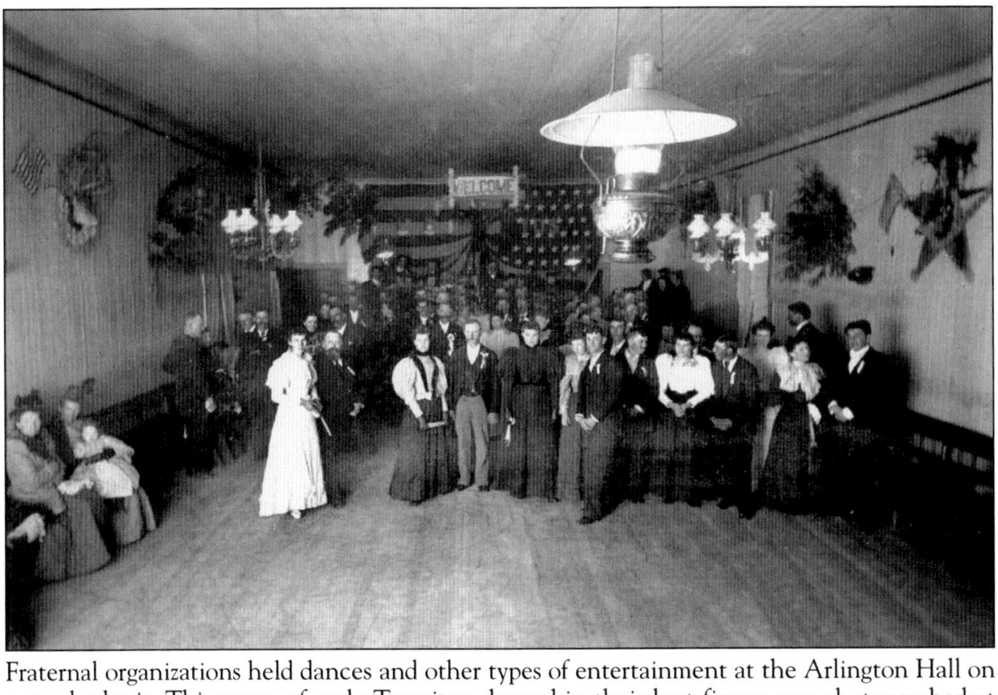

Fraternal organizations held dances and other types of entertainment at the Arlington Hall on a regular basis. This group of early Tracyites, dressed in their best finery, was photographed at a dance in the Arlington on February 29, 1896. Note the light fixtures, which were filled with kerosene, as there was no electricity. The hall burned in the 1898 fire.

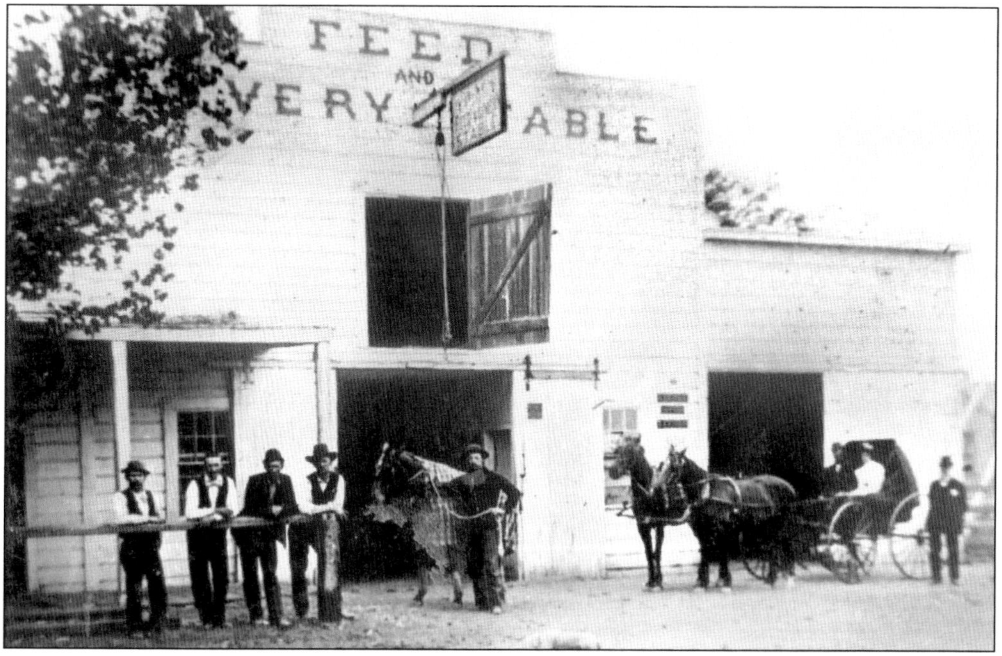

One of downtown Tracy's thriving businesses in 1909 was Schluter Brothers Feed and Livery Stable, located on the west side of Central Avenue between Seventh and Eighth Streets (currently the site of the Grand Theater). Along with several other buildings on Central and Eighth, this building was destroyed by fire in August 1909.

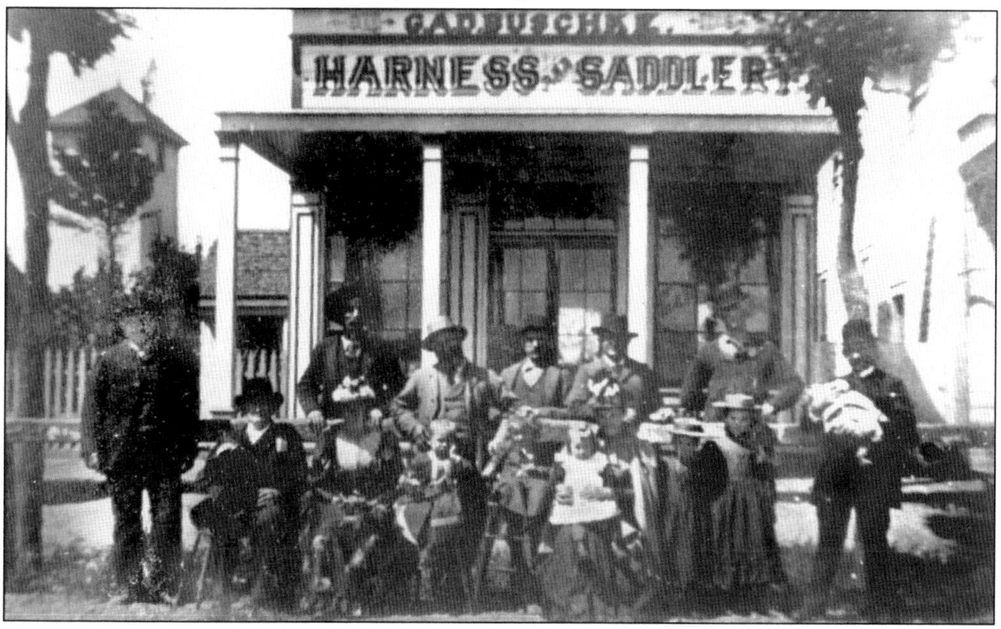

The original G.A.D. Buschke Harness & Saddlery shop, pictured here, was located on West Sixth Street on the west side of the Castle Hotel and Saloon (later the Arlington). Buschke had operated the Ellis Harness Shop for one year before moving his business to Tracy. He later rented this building out and moved his business to West Eighth Street. This building burned in the 1898 fire.

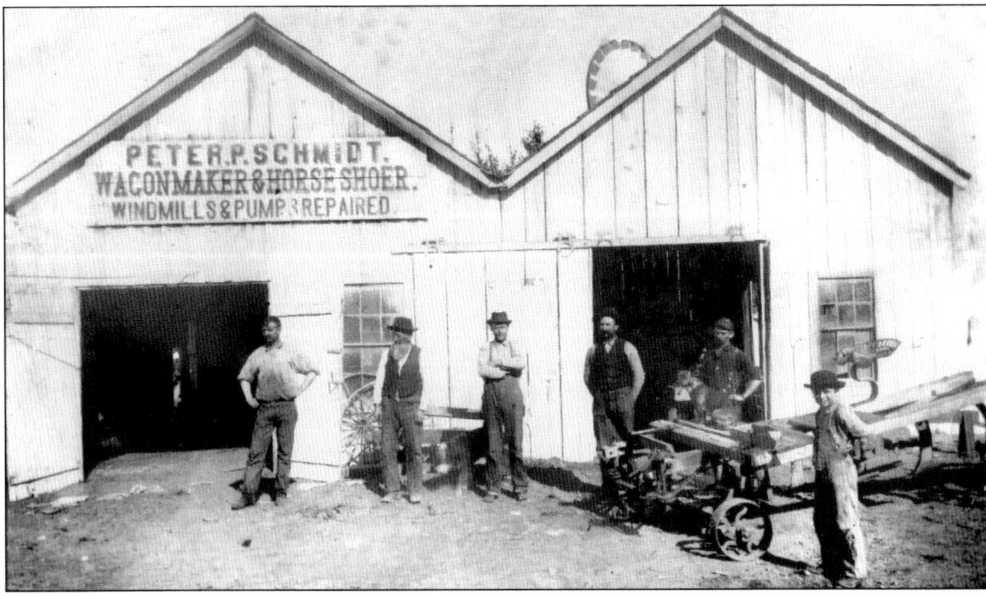

Peter P. Schmidt's blacksmith shop was located on the northeast corner of Central Avenue and Seventh Street. Originally Charles Landgraf's blacksmith shop, it had been moved to Tracy from Ellis. Schmidt worked as a blacksmith for Landgraf from 1881 until purchasing the business in 1887. Pictured, from left to right, in this 1902 photograph are Walter McArdle, Pete Knollenburg, Pete McCaskel, unidentified, Pete Schmidt, and Jess Schmidt (boy).

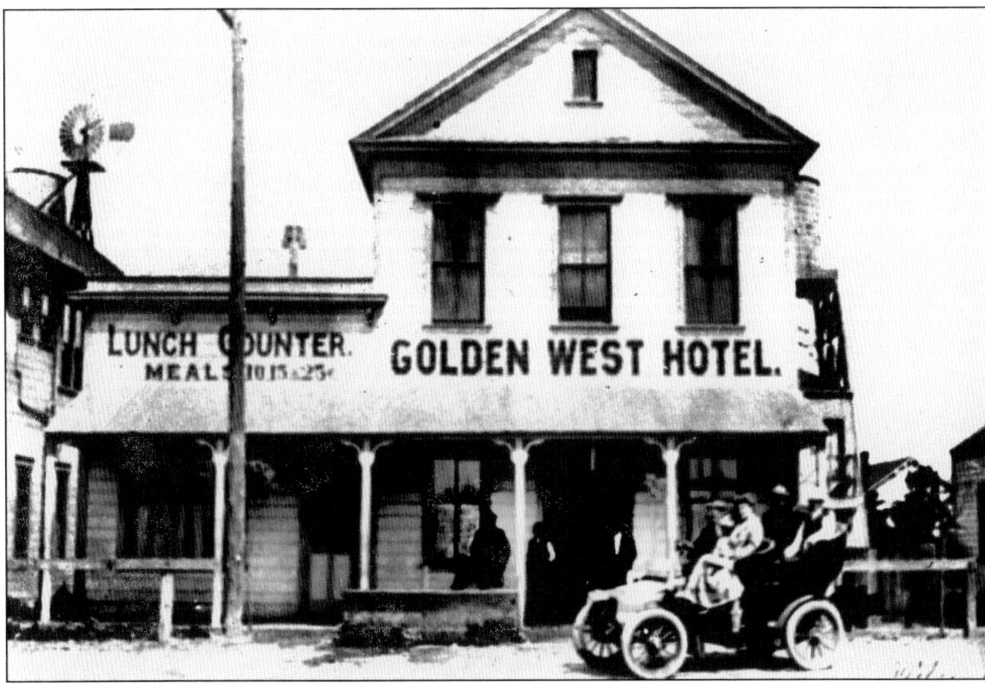

In 1908 a building was moved from the corner of Seventh and D Streets to Sixth Street to the site of the former San Joaquin Hotel, which had been destroyed in the 1898 fire. This building became the Golden West Hotel & Lunch Counter. While most of the hotels advertised their saloons, this hotel's sign advertised its lunch counter rather than its bar.

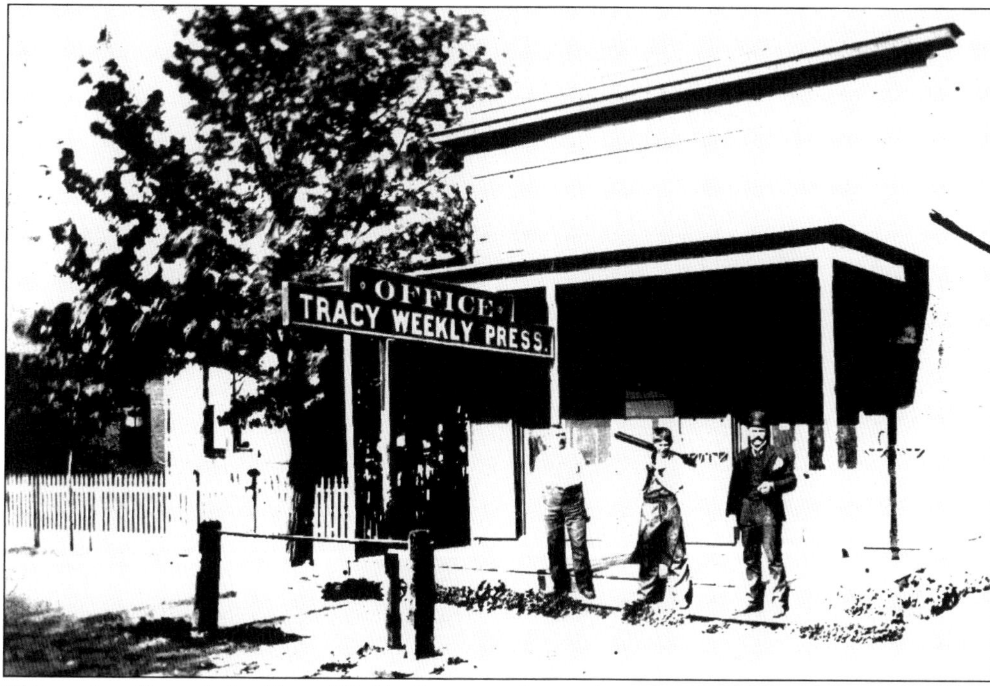

This early office of the *Tracy Weekly Press* was located on the east side of Central Avenue between Seventh and Eighth Streets. Pictured in front of the building, from left to right, are a printer, a printer's "devil" with a press roller on his shoulder, and Dennis J. Looney, the owner and publisher of the newspaper in the early 1900s.

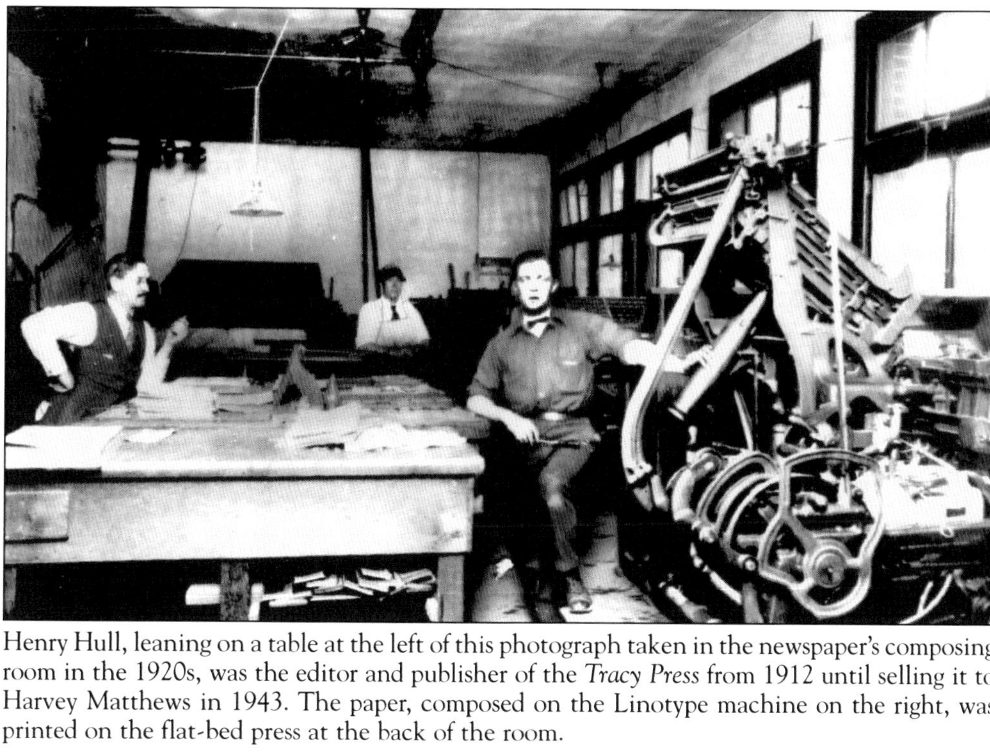

Henry Hull, leaning on a table at the left of this photograph taken in the newspaper's composing room in the 1920s, was the editor and publisher of the *Tracy Press* from 1912 until selling it to Harvey Matthews in 1943. The paper, composed on the Linotype machine on the right, was printed on the flat-bed press at the back of the room.

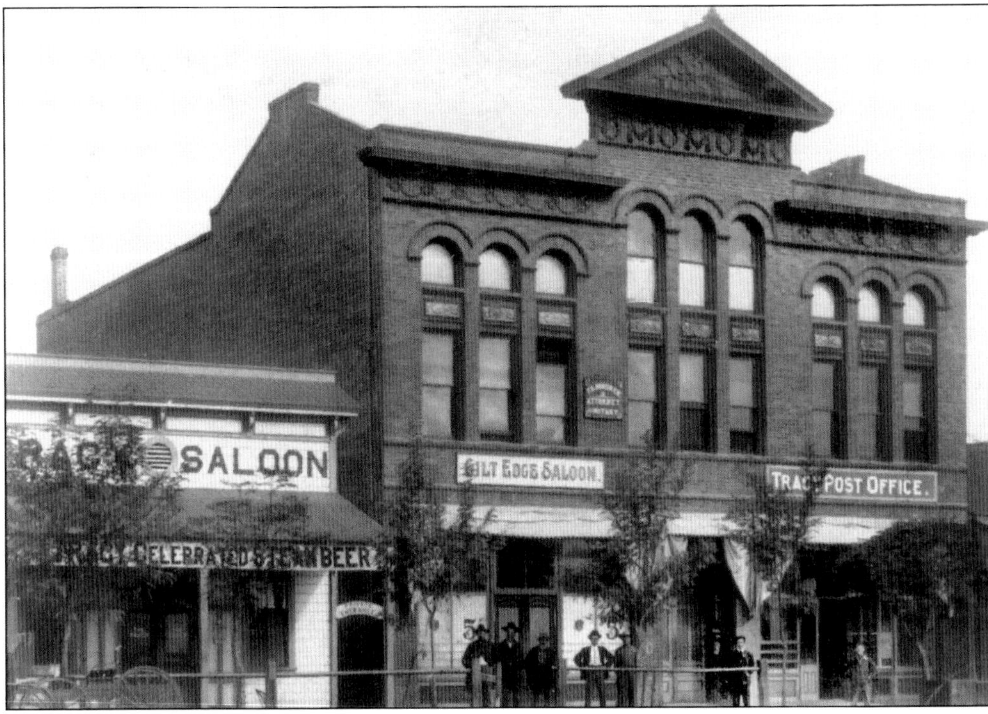

Two buildings on East Sixth Street in 1900 were the IOOF Hall and the Tracy Saloon. The IOOF Hall was built on the same site as the one lost in the 1898 fire. One of the oldest buildings in Tracy, it is still in use as the Tracy Moose Lodge. The Tracy Saloon, operated by the Ludwig brothers, had a billiard room as well as a cigar store and bar.

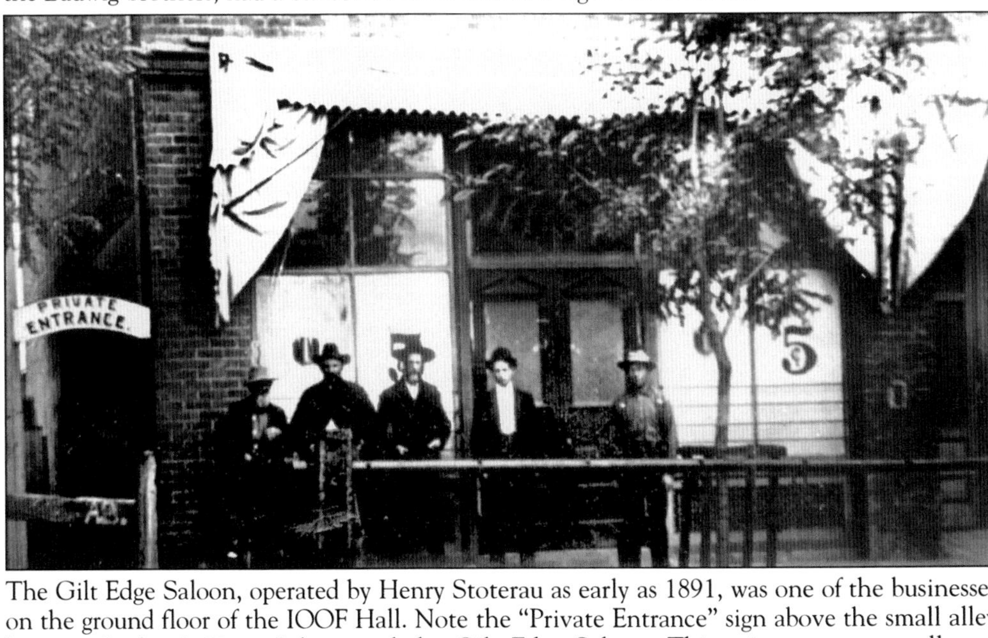

The Gilt Edge Saloon, operated by Henry Stoterau as early as 1891, was one of the businesses on the ground floor of the IOOF Hall. Note the "Private Entrance" sign above the small alley between Ludwig's Tracy Saloon and the Gilt Edge Saloon. This private entrance allowed women to enter without being seen from the street. Stoterau sold the saloon to William Lampkey in February 1913.

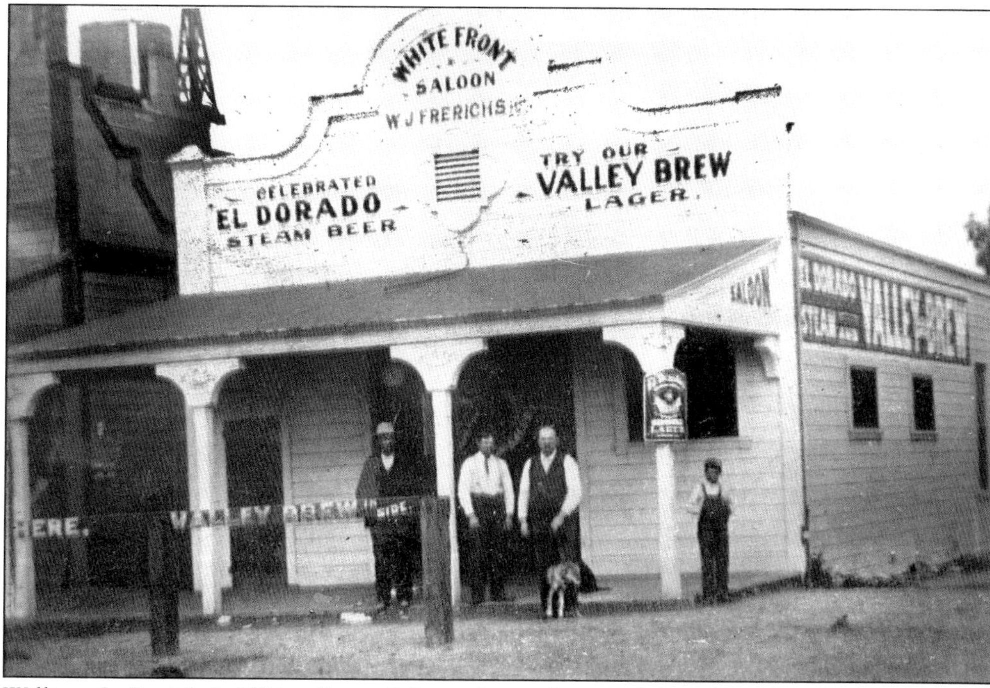

William J. Frerichs's White Front Saloon, located east of Canale Brothers on East Sixth Street, was one of several Tracy businesses operated by Frerichs. He added onto this building and turned the addition into the Opera House, with opera chairs for 200 people. Plays, silent movies, dances, and other entertainments were held there. Later he added the Opera Lunch Room onto the front of the building.

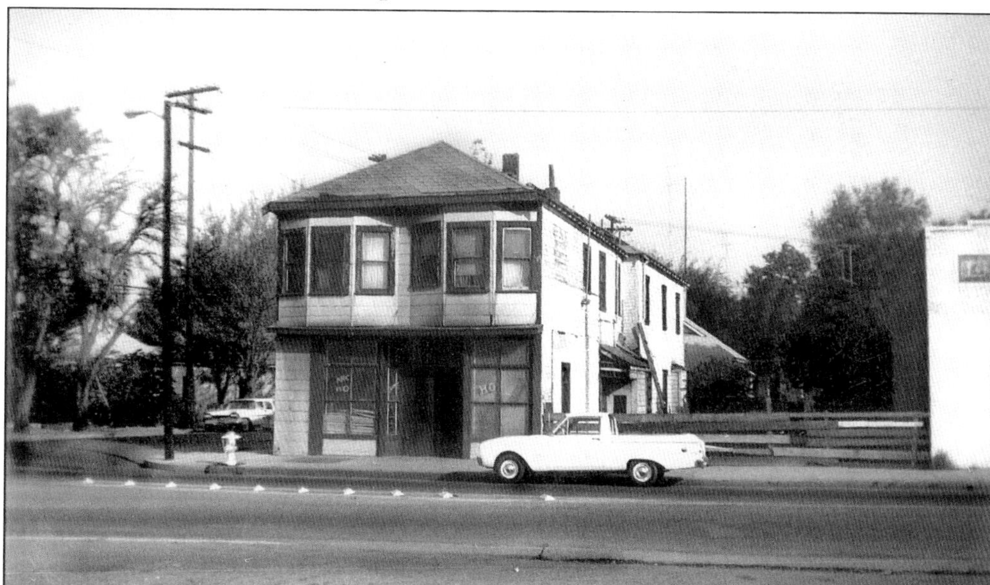

Prior to the 1898 fire, Lydia J. (Higgins) Cross established a ladies dry goods and millinery store in Tracy. After the fire she moved her business to the northeast corner of Sixth and C Streets to the lower floor of the Acacia Hotel building, pictured here just before being demolished in the mid-1960s. She closed her shop in 1920 and became manager of the Acacia.

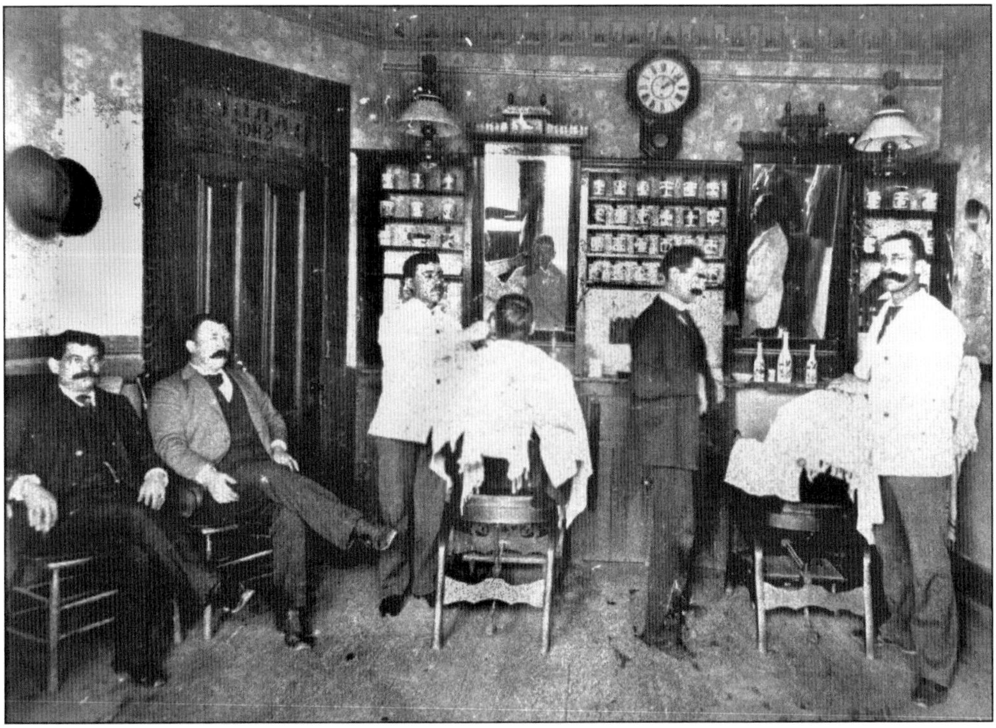

Photographed in 1907, the Tracy Hotel Barber Shop, located in the Tracy Hotel on East Sixth Street, was one of several barbershops in Tracy. Sam McLain, the proprietor (standing on the right in the photo), became Tracy's justice of the peace in 1914 and was known as Judge McLain thereafter. On the back wall are shaving mugs for regular customers.

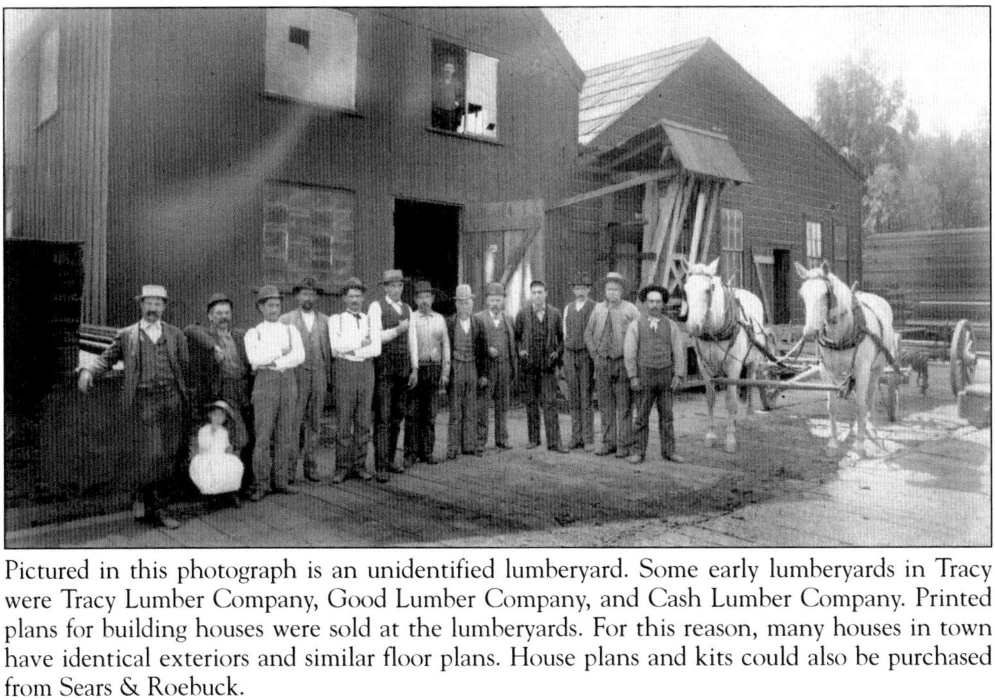

Pictured in this photograph is an unidentified lumberyard. Some early lumberyards in Tracy were Tracy Lumber Company, Good Lumber Company, and Cash Lumber Company. Printed plans for building houses were sold at the lumberyards. For this reason, many houses in town have identical exteriors and similar floor plans. House plans and kits could also be purchased from Sears & Roebuck.

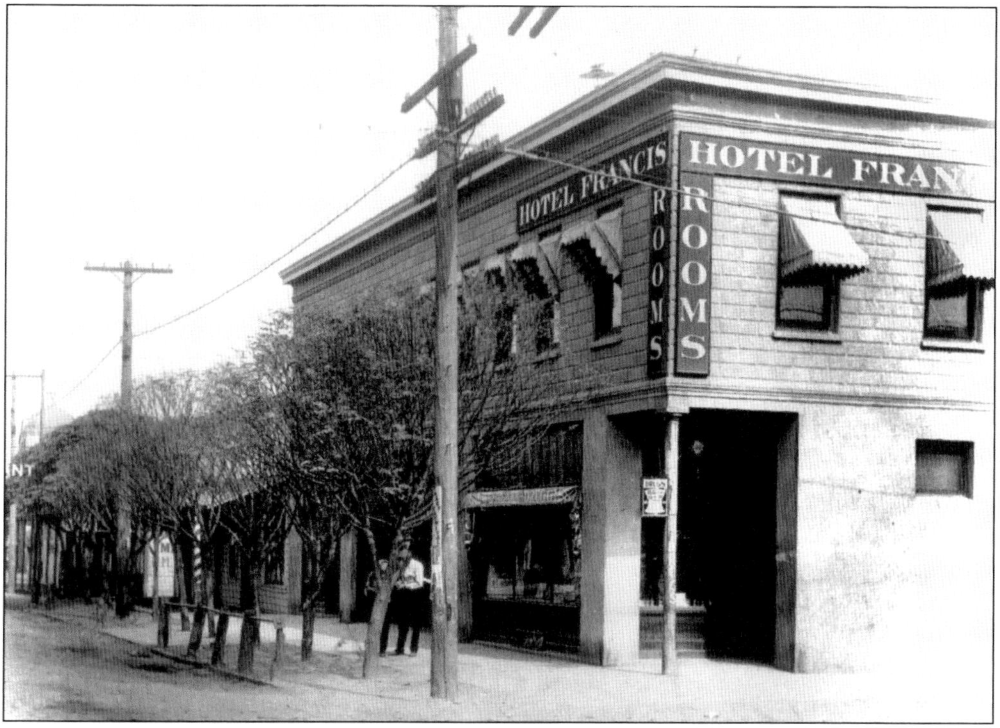

The Hotel Francis opened in September 1910 in the new fireproof Schmidt Building on the northeast corner of Central Avenue and Seventh Street. This corner was the former location of Peter P. Schmidt's blacksmith shop. The hotel, with its main entrance on Seventh, was located on the top floor. Mr. and Mrs. W.D. Cook managed this hotel along with another hotel, built earlier.

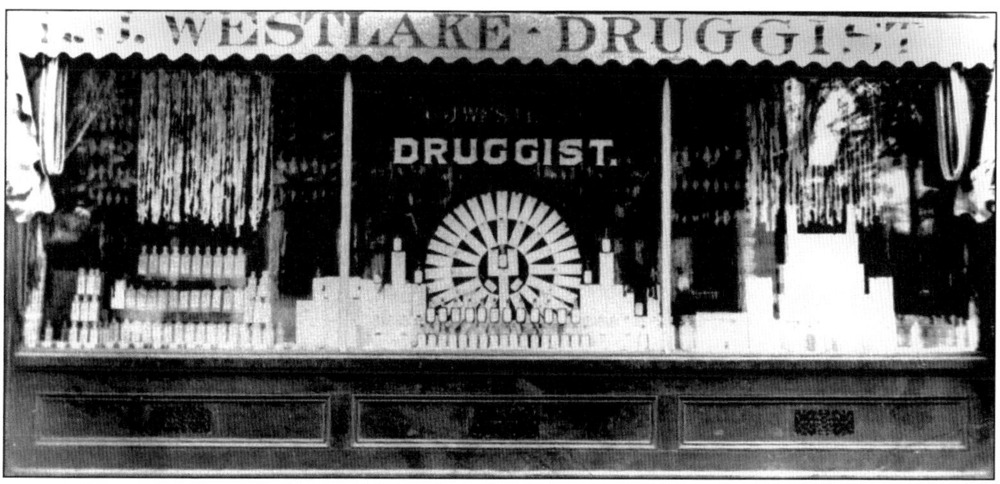

The Schmidt Building also housed L.J. Westlake Druggist, operated by Leonard J. Westlake, on the first floor of the building. Westlake Drug was a traditional drug store that mainly carried medicines and offered a prescription drug service. After it had been vacant for a number of years, this building was removed.

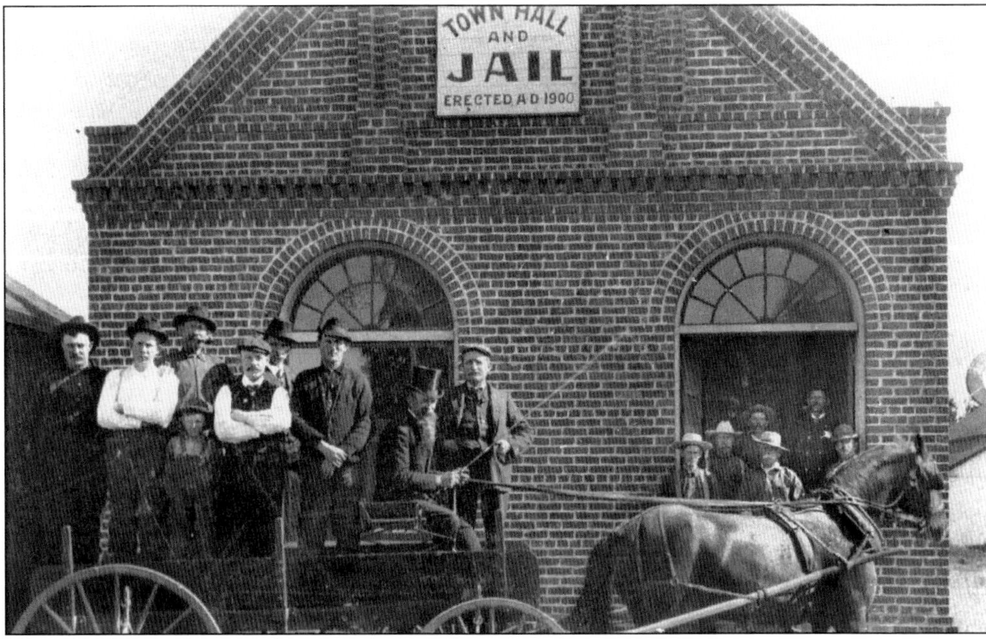

Listed on the National Register of Historic Places, the old Tracy Town Hall and Jail on West Seventh Street, was built c. 1900 and still stands today. Pictured in front is the horse-drawn patrol wagon driven by Pete Knollenburg. Even after a new city hall was built in 1917, this building continued to be used as a jail and courtroom until 1940.

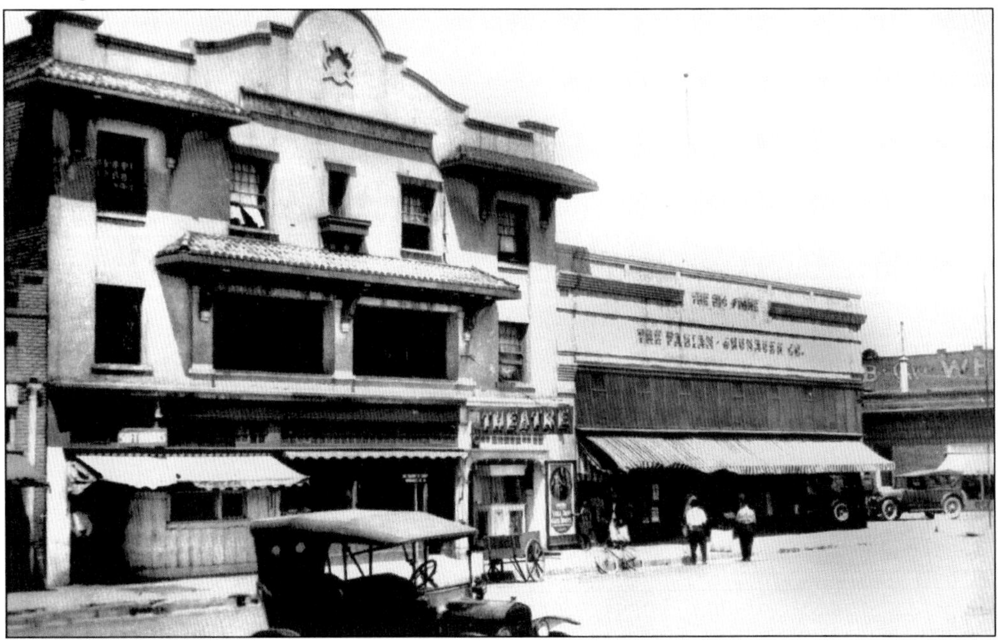

Pictured here in 1917, the Arlington Opera House was built in 1910 on West Sixth Street. The ground floor had space for two businesses, with a modern opera house behind a wide hall and stairway. Besides a magnificent stage, the opera house also boasted a moving picture machine. The upper floors housed a mezzanine and balcony area as well as 30 hotel rooms. The building burned in 1966.

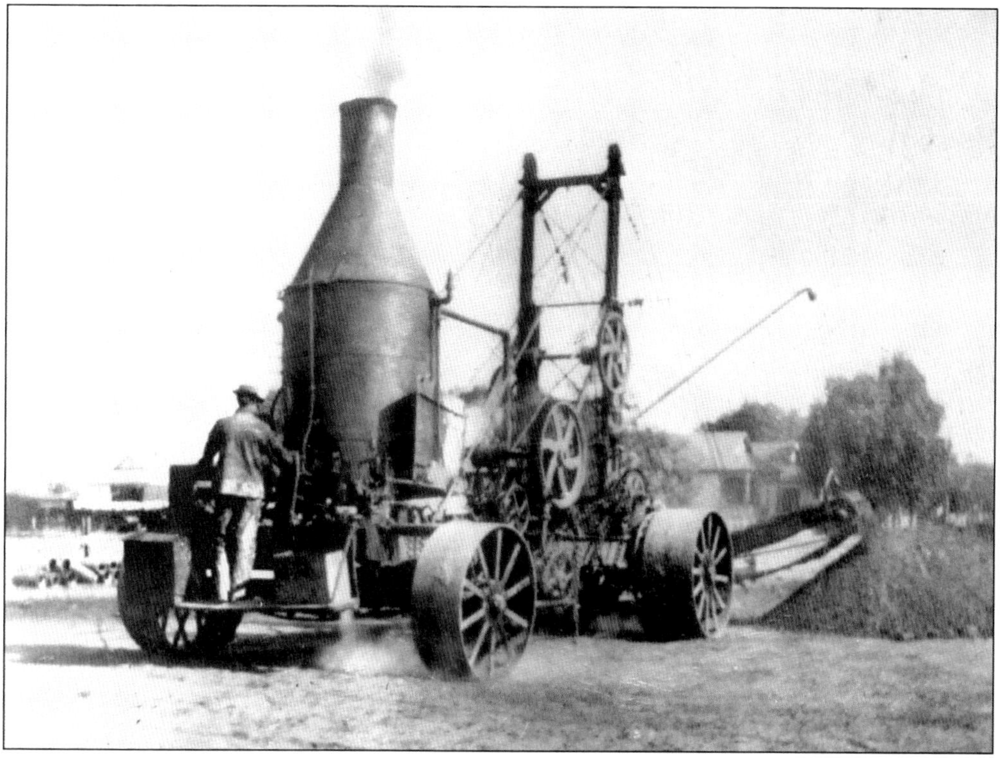

In 1911 a steam-powered digger was used to dig the first trenches for Tracy's municipal water and sewer system. The digger cut trenches and removed excavated dirt along a conveyor belt to horse-drawn wagons. Some residents refused to hook up to the new system, because they had previously spent considerable money to have independent septic systems put in on their lots.

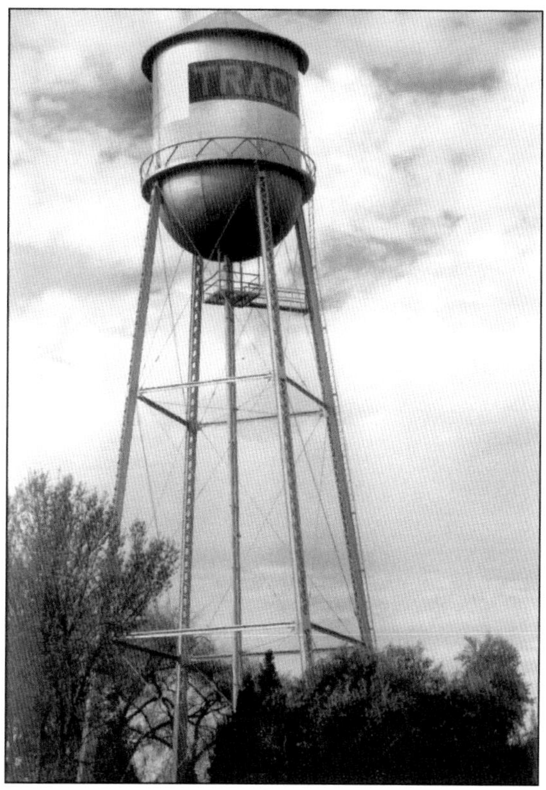

In order to provide the water pressure needed to operate Tracy's new sewer and water system as well as fire hydrants, an elevated water tank was required. A water tower with a capacity of 100,000 gallons was constructed 200 feet in the air at the city pumping plant on West Sixth Street. An additional water tower was added in 1928 on Tenth Street.

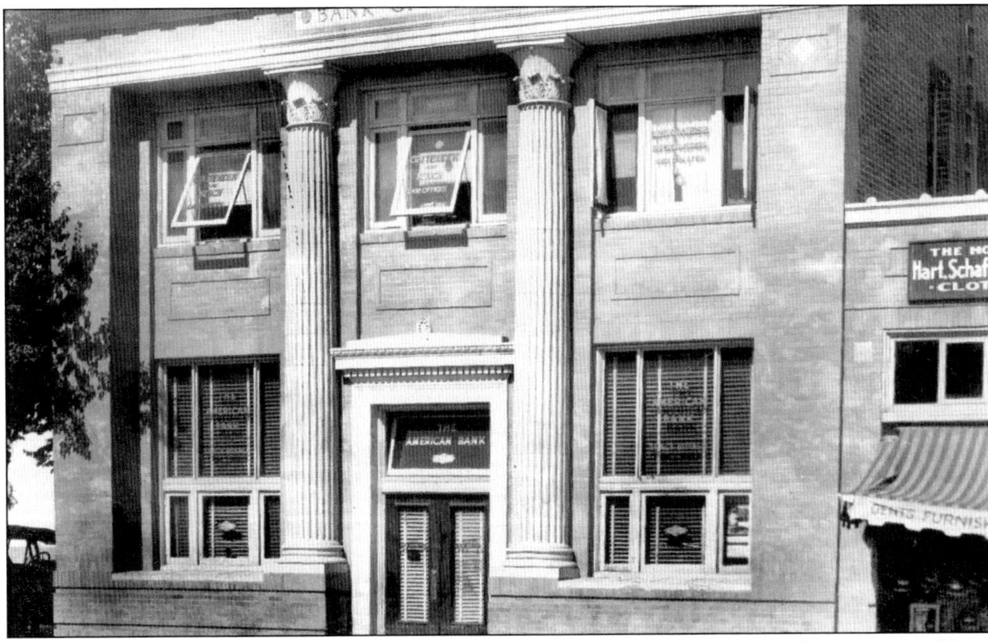

The first bank established in Tracy was the Bank of Tracy, which was organized by a group of local investors headed by John C. Droge. It opened for business on June 21, 1909, on the west side of Central Avenue between Seventh and Eighth Streets. In 1920 a new, larger bank building, pictured here, was built on the northwest corner of Central Avenue and Eighth Street.

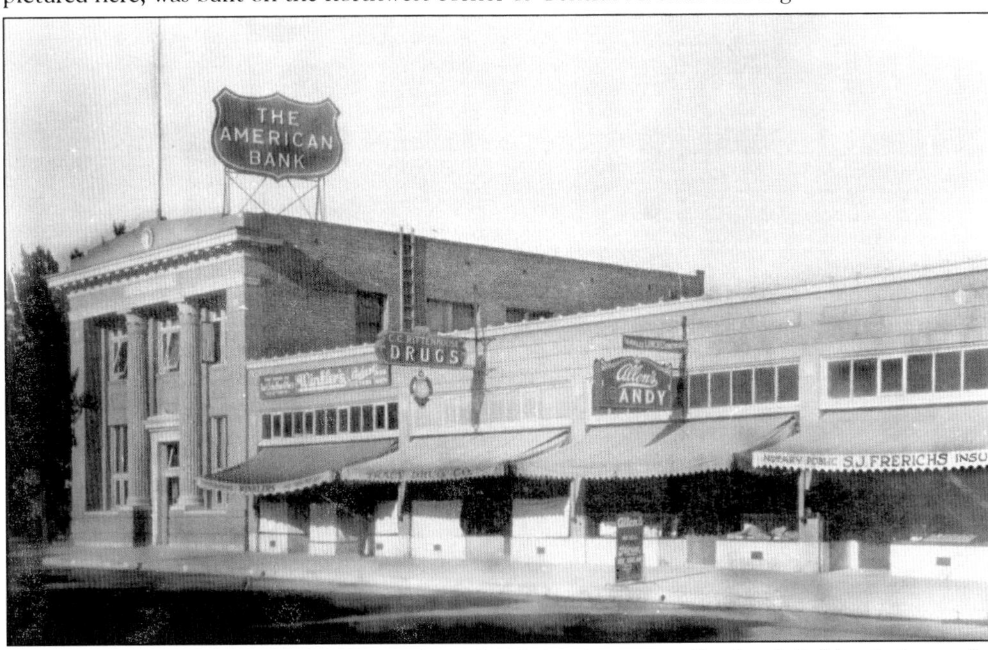

In 1923 the Bank of Tracy became a branch of the American Bank of Oakland. Later the name became the American Trust Co. William Larsen was bank manager for many years. The bank moved from this building to 1023 Central Avenue in 1947 and eventually became Wells Fargo Bank. Listed on the National Register of Historic Places, this building still exists and is currently the Burke Chiropractic Clinic.

Organized by Abraham Grunauer, the West Side Bank was the second bank established in Tracy and opened for business in 1910 on West Sixth Street. Pictured in the early years, from left to right, are cashier A.R. Arnold, stenographer Myrtle Frerichs Fisk, and bookkeeper Walter Johnson. The building is listed on the National Register of Historic Places and is currently home to the Design Center.

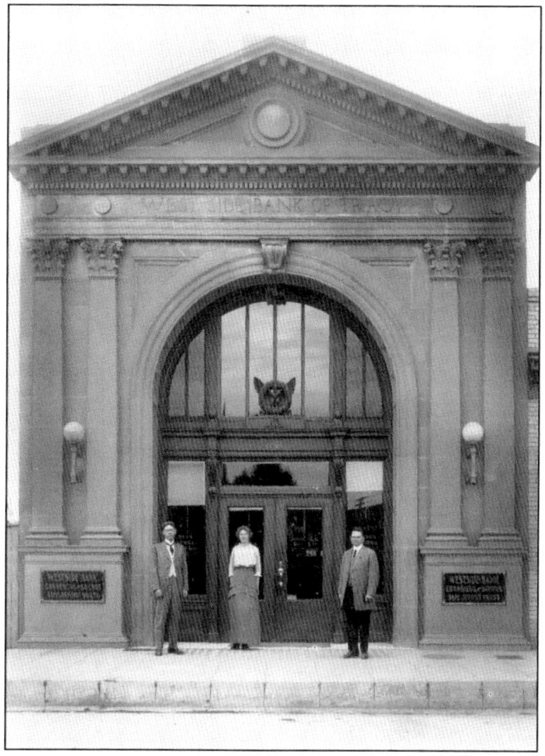

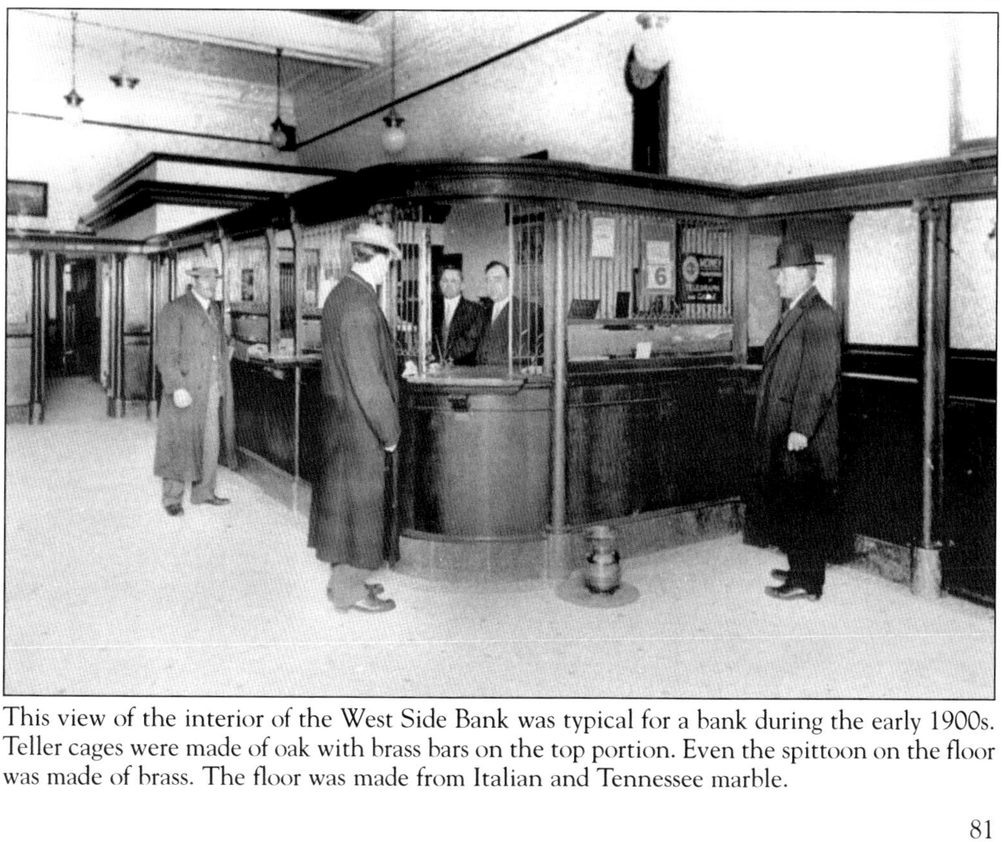

This view of the interior of the West Side Bank was typical for a bank during the early 1900s. Teller cages were made of oak with brass bars on the top portion. Even the spittoon on the floor was made of brass. The floor was made from Italian and Tennessee marble.

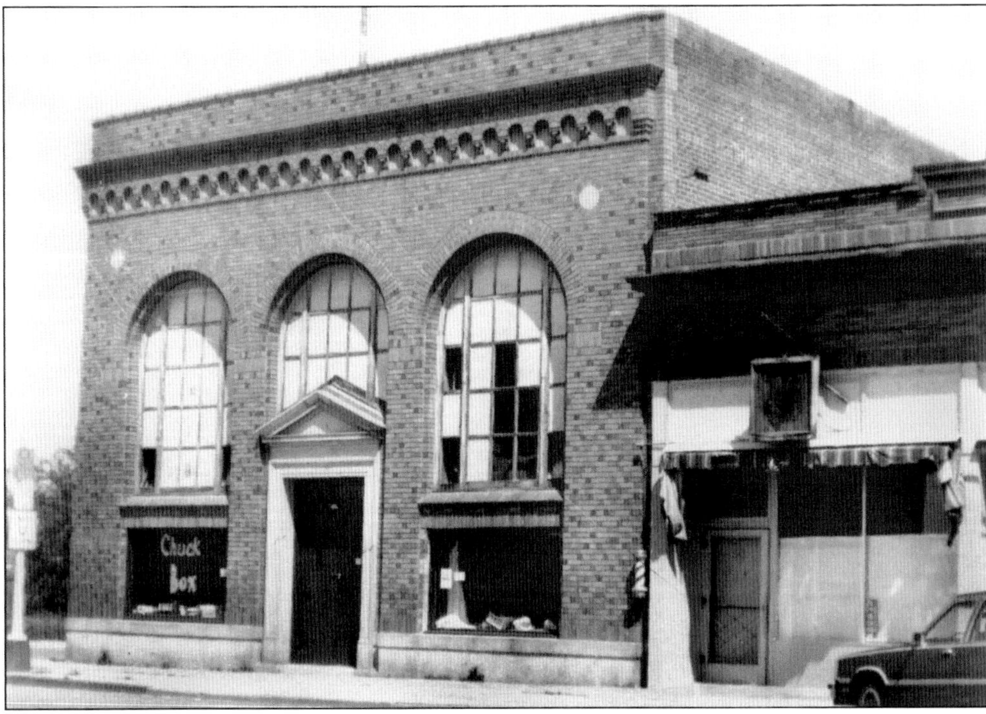

In July 1919 the West Side Bank moved to the southeast corner of Central Avenue and Seventh Street. The name was changed to American Bank and then sold to the Bank of Italy in 1921. It later became Bank of America. After Bank of America moved to a new location, this building housed various businesses, such as the Chuck Box, which is shown here.

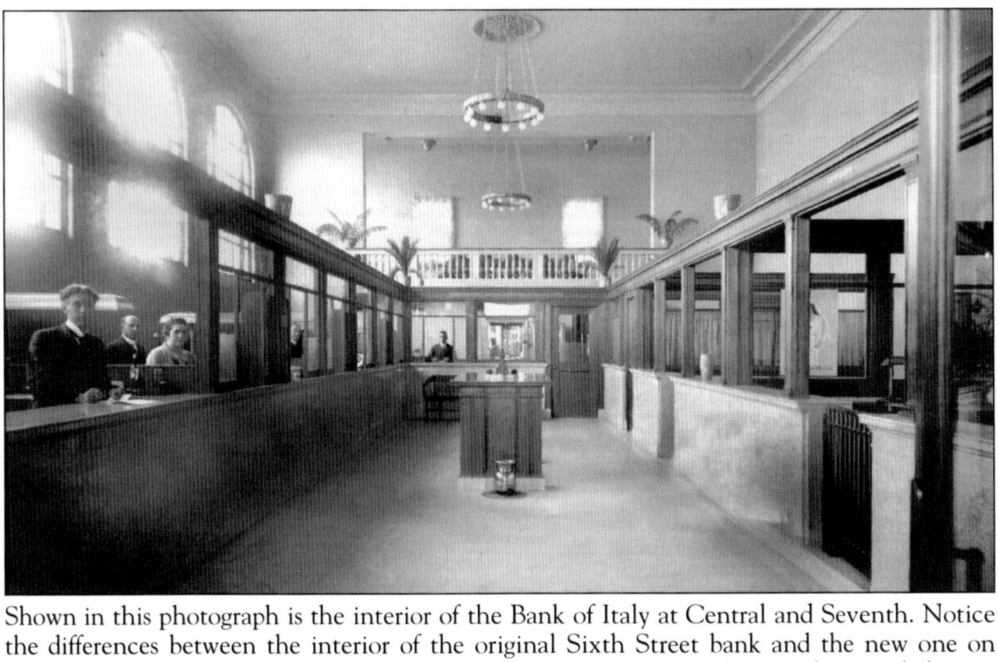

Shown in this photograph is the interior of the Bank of Italy at Central and Seventh. Notice the differences between the interior of the original Sixth Street bank and the new one on Central. This building is listed on the National Register of Historic Places and currently houses an office of the San Joaquin County District Attorney.

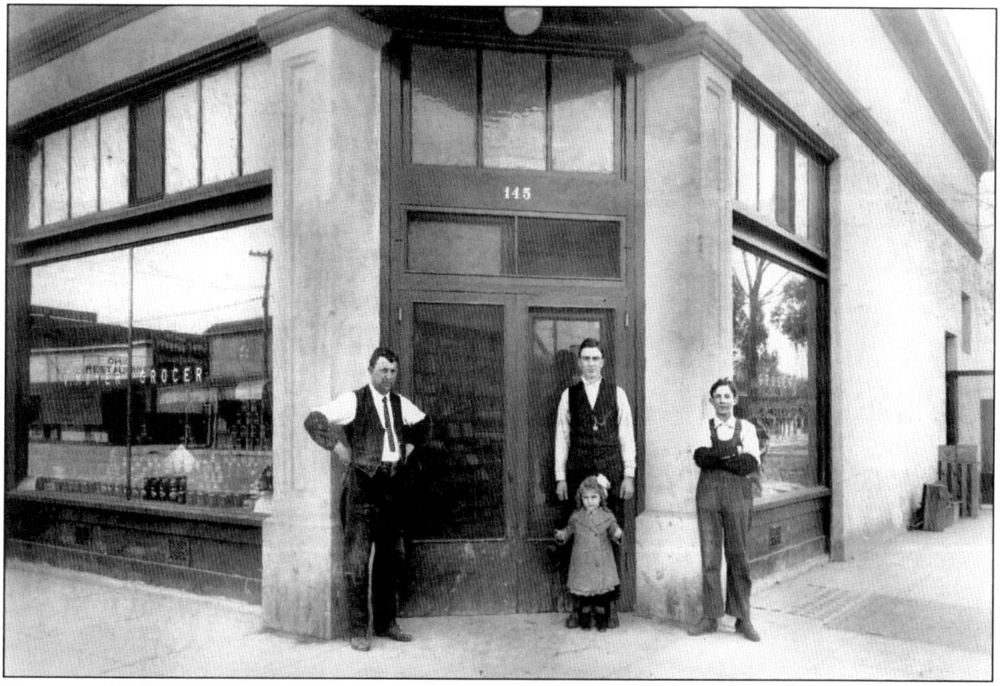

Photographed in 1917 Byers Cash Store, owned by E.R. "Ed" Byers, was on the northwest corner of Central Avenue and Eighth Street (currently the site of the West Side Market). For many years Beyers operated a profitable cash and carry grocery business, unlike the other local stores who allowed their customers to buy on credit.

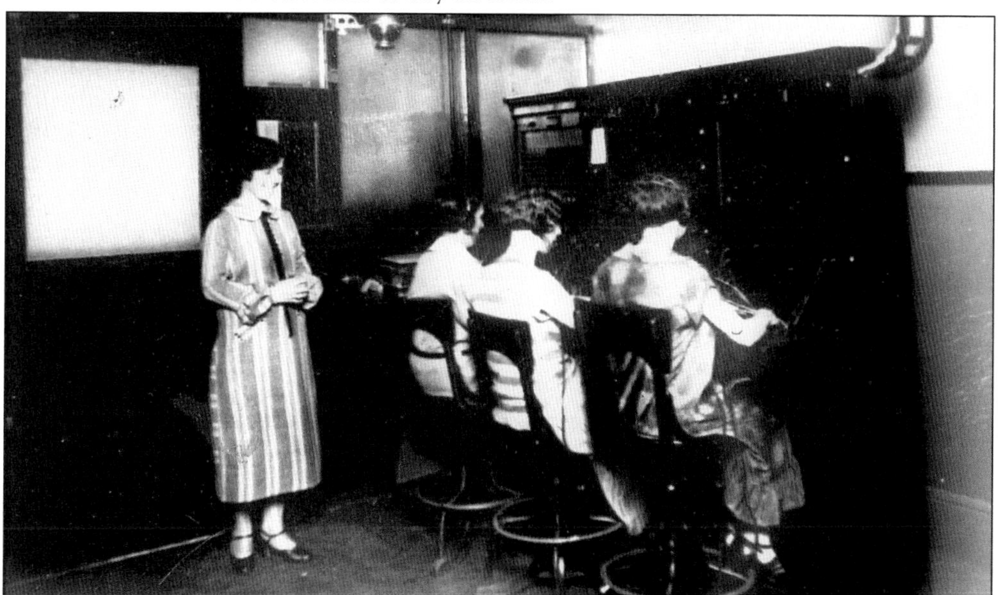

Photographed in 1924, the telephone office was next to the Bank of Italy on Central Avenue, between Sixth and Seventh Streets. Telephone operators, seated at a switchboard, answered the phones as soon as a caller picked up the telephone receiver from its cradle. Callers told the operator the number they wanted, and the operator made the connection for them.

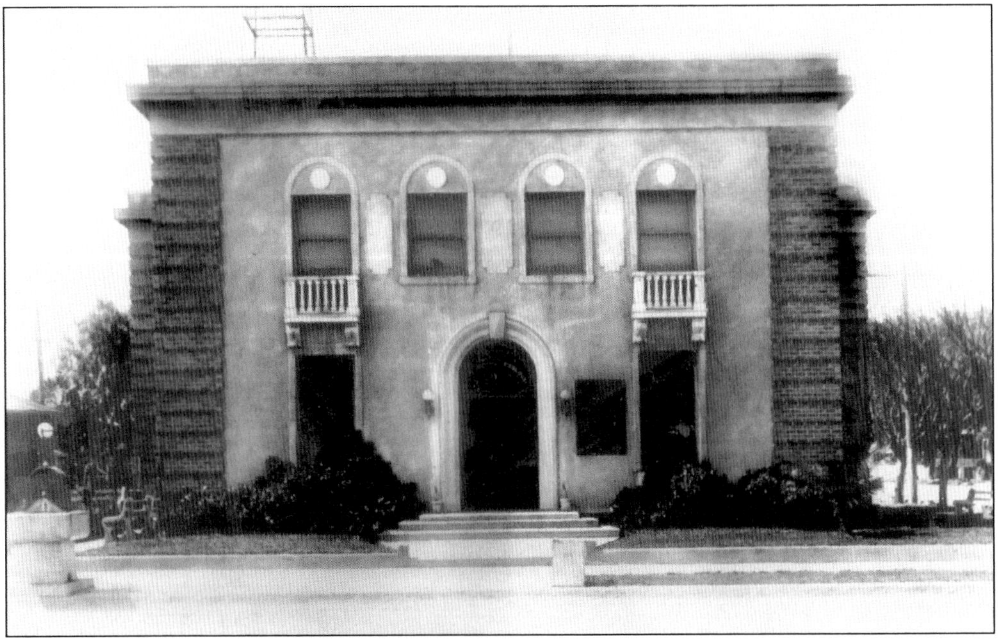

The two-story city hall building at the southwest corner of Central and Ninth Streets was dedicated on April 27, 1917. The city clerk's office, the police office, the Tracy Fire Department, the Tracy Library, and the city council chamber were all housed in this building. The city offices and the library moved to the old Central School building in 1947.

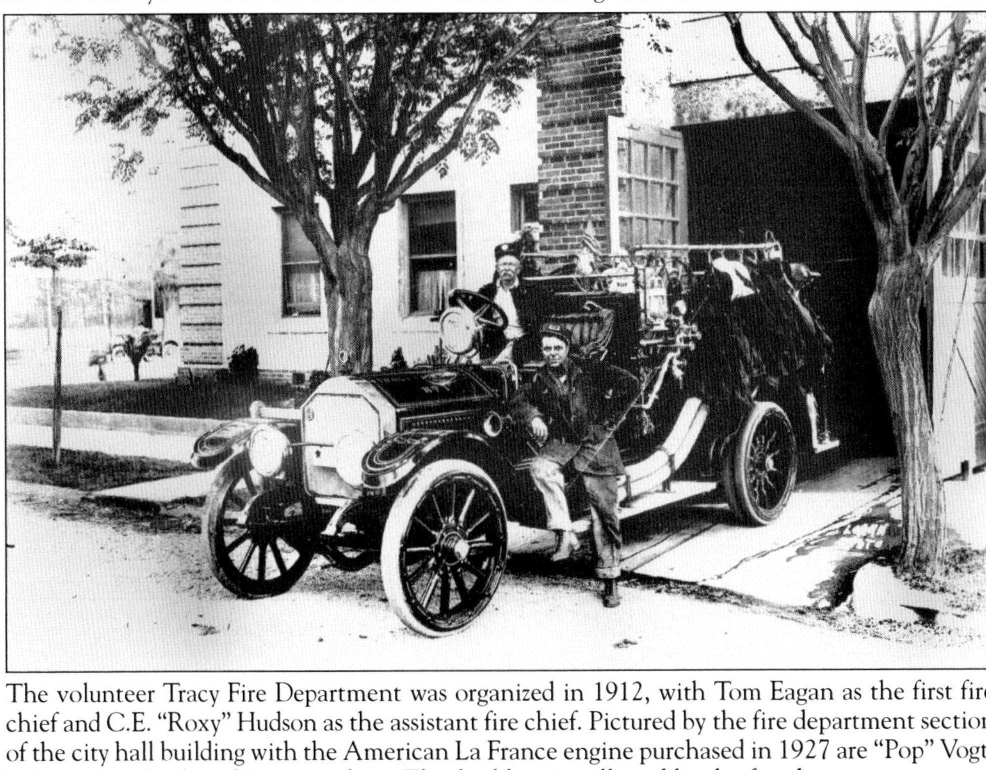

The volunteer Tracy Fire Department was organized in 1912, with Tom Eagan as the first fire chief and C.E. "Roxy" Hudson as the assistant fire chief. Pictured by the fire department section of the city hall building with the American La France engine purchased in 1927 are "Pop" Vogt, behind the wheel, and Roxy Hudson. This building is still used by the fire department.

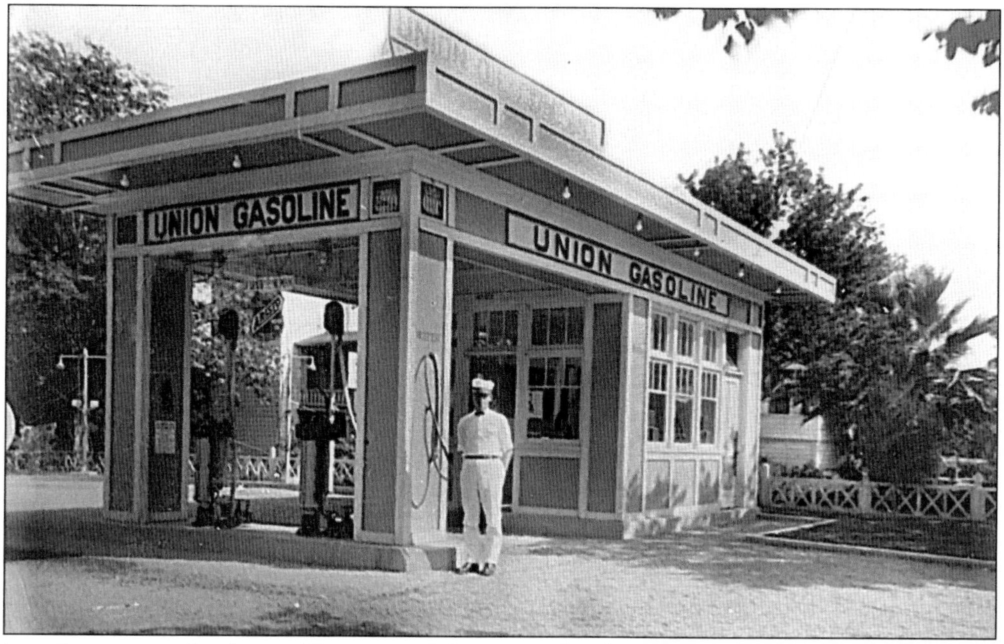

In order to meet the demand for automobile services by the traveling public, many gas stations and garages opened for business on Eleventh Street after it became part of the Lincoln Highway in 1914. One of those businesses was the Union Gasoline Station, located at the intersection of Eleventh Street and Central Avenue.

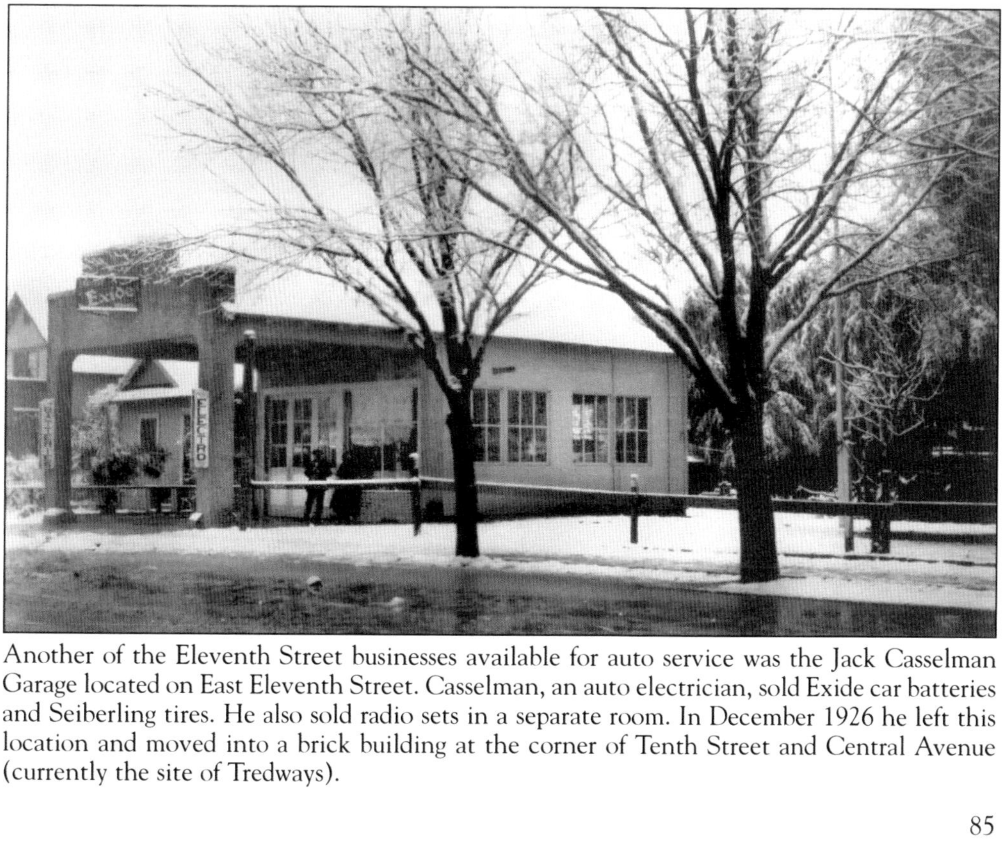

Another of the Eleventh Street businesses available for auto service was the Jack Casselman Garage located on East Eleventh Street. Casselman, an auto electrician, sold Exide car batteries and Seiberling tires. He also sold radio sets in a separate room. In December 1926 he left this location and moved into a brick building at the corner of Tenth Street and Central Avenue (currently the site of Tredways).

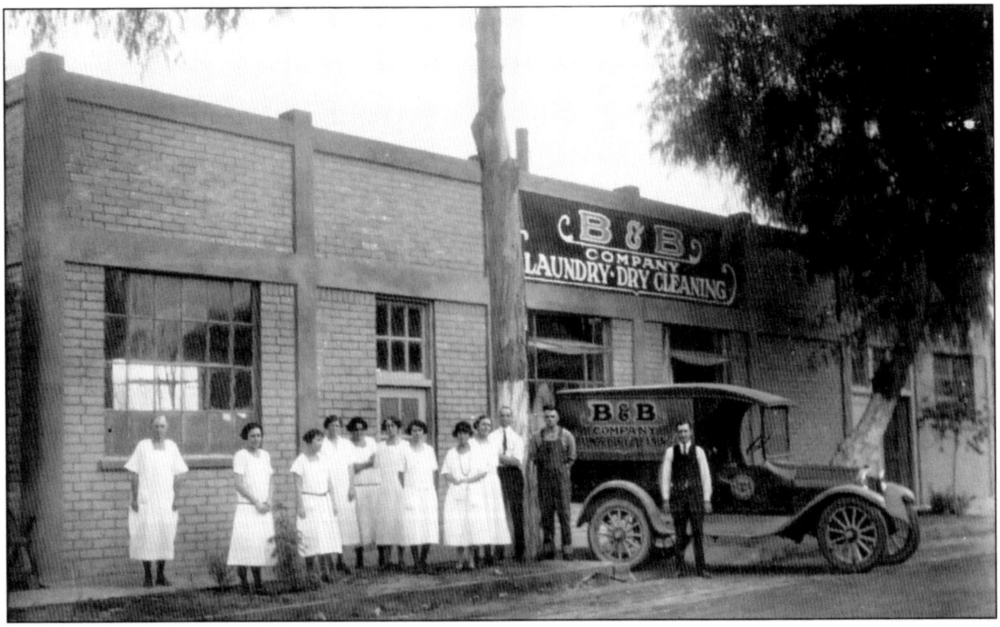

B and B Laundry Company, at 139 Central Avenue in 1928, was a laundry and dry cleaning business in Tracy. The earliest laundries in Tracy were Chinese laundries; the most well-known was operated by Hong Sing next to the Tracy Town Hall and Jail on West Seventh Street. Barbershops also provided laundry service; patrons could drop off their laundry to be sent to Stockton for laundering.

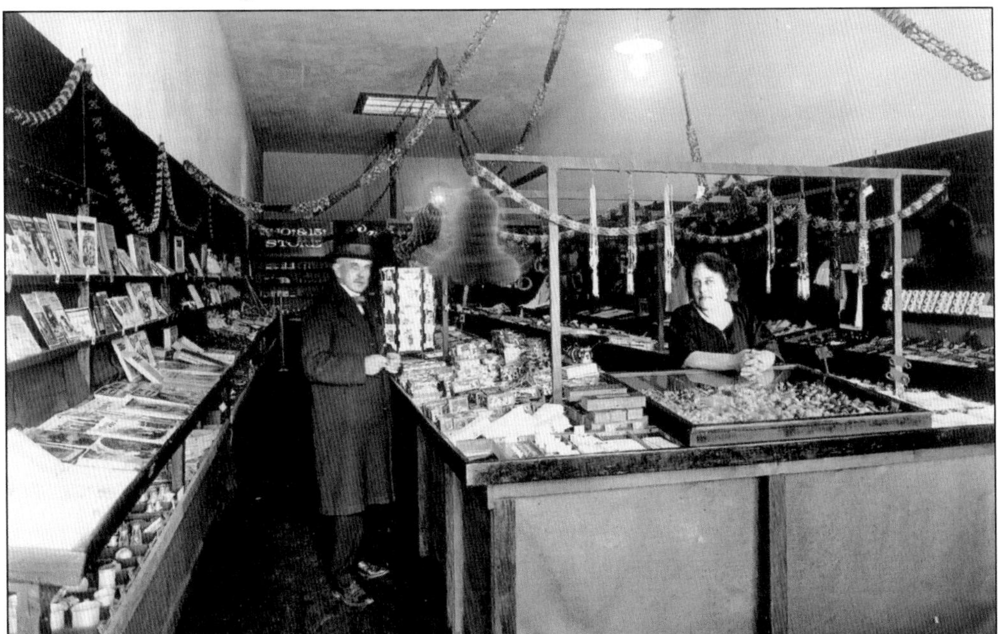

The Firth 5¢, 10¢, & 15¢ store, photographed in 1921, was typical of variety stores during that time period. Variety stores carried items such as toys; household items; jewelry; postcards; magazines; sewing notions; crochet, embroidery, and knitting supplies; knick-knacks; etc. Lighting in stores usually consisted of hanging light bulbs and skylights.

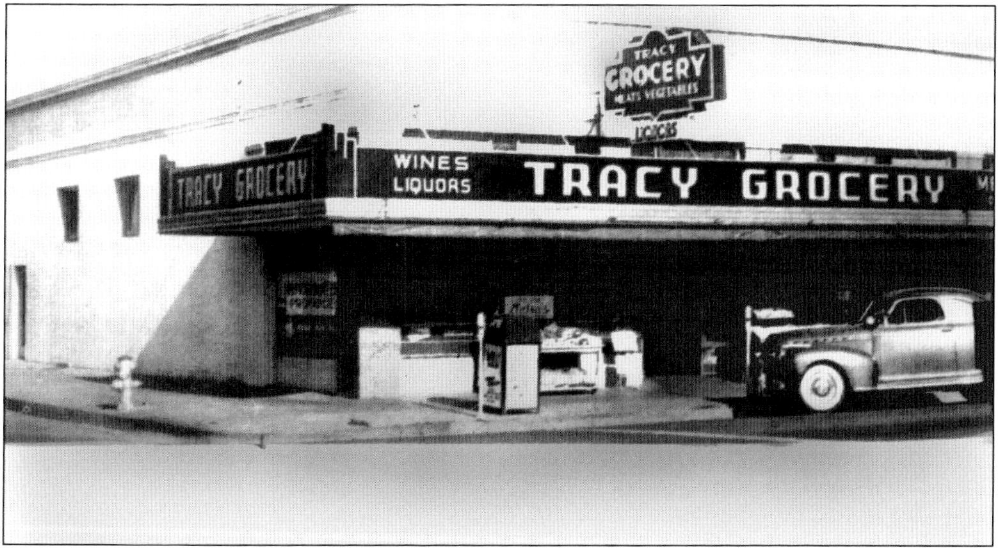

Frank Vellis came to Tracy in 1919 and bought a half interest in the Tracy Fruit Market at 128 Central Avenue. A year later he bought out his partner and changed the business into a full-fledged grocery store. Shown in this photograph is Tracy Grocery after it was moved in 1927 to a larger building at 238 Central Avenue.

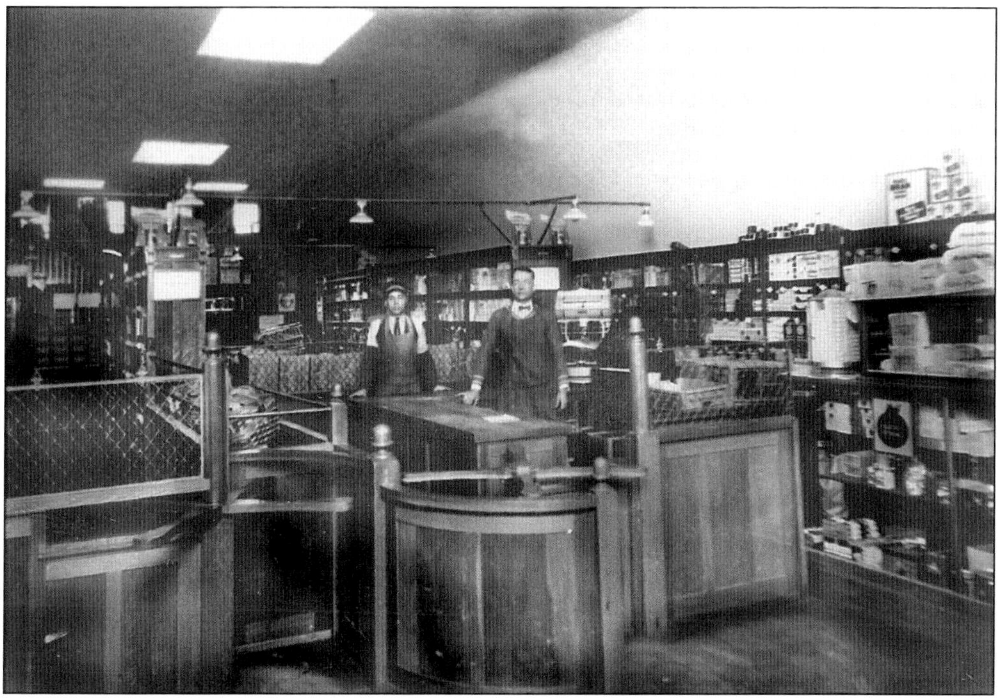

Piggly Wiggly, a national chain of self-serve grocery stores, opened a store in Tracy in December 1923 at 337 Central Avenue. This photograph, taken shortly after the store opened, shows the interior with its neatly stocked shelves and beautiful hardwood turnstiles and check-out stands. Store hours were from 7 a.m. until 6 p.m. daily, except Saturday, when it stayed open until 8 p.m.

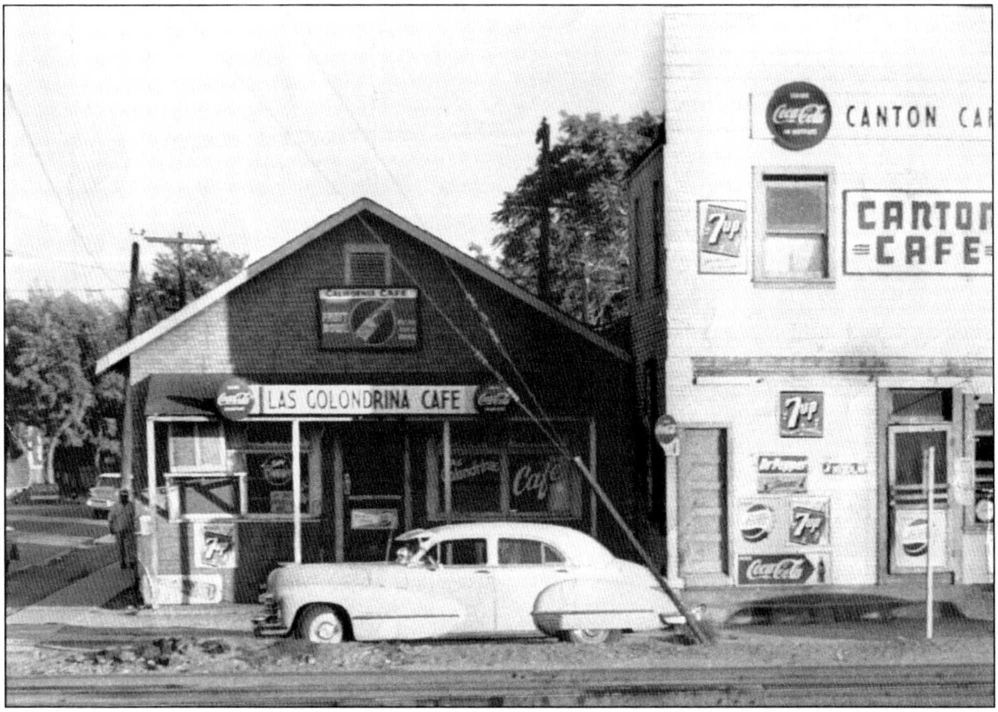

Fourth Street, the first street south of the railroad tracks, was the center of the business district on the South Side. Two businesses on Fourth near C Street, the Las Golondrinas Cafe and the Canton Cafe, reflect the cultural diversity of the South Side community, which included many first generation immigrants from Mexico, China, Japan, Portugal, Italy, Greece, and Croatia.

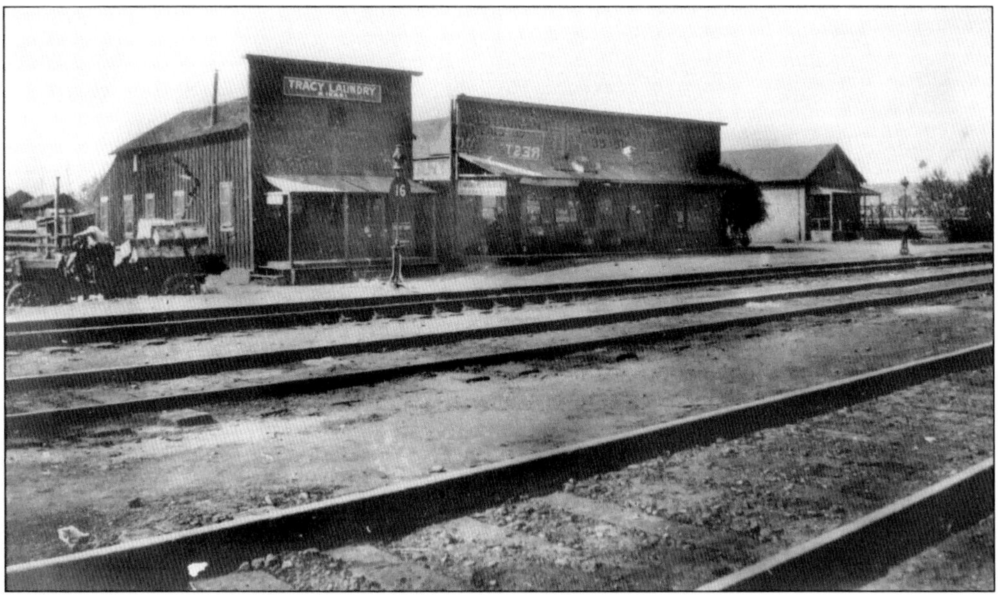

The area of Tracy south of the railroad tracks was where the railroad originally established section houses for the Chinese, Japanese, and Mexican laborers who worked for the railroad. Some of the businesses in the area along Fourth Street are shown in this photograph from 1914: N. Ikari's Tracy Laundry, a restaurant, and a lodging establishment.

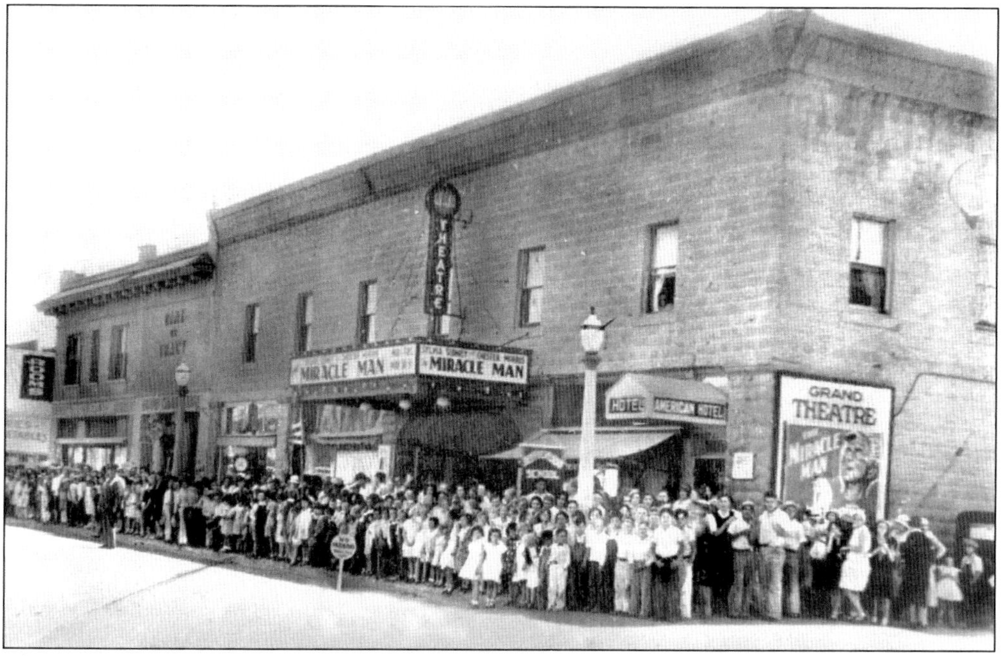

The Grand Theater, built by one of Tracy's early developers John C. Droge, opened for business on Central Avenue between Seventh and Eighth Streets on August 11, 1923. The theater, with seating for 835, replaced the Arlington as Tracy's vaudeville and silent movie theater. Sound equipment was added in 1929 when "talkies" were introduced.

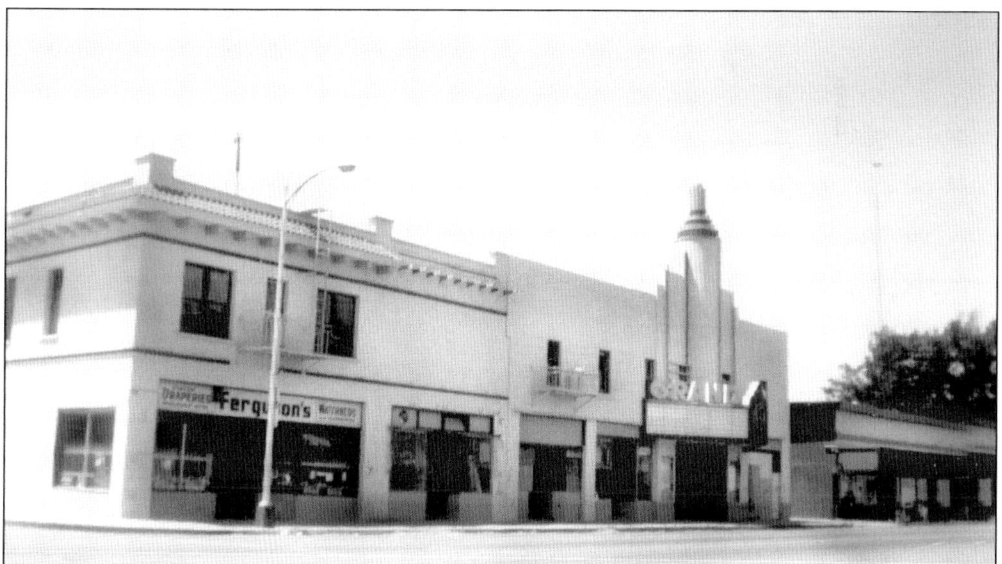

The Grand Theater, Tracy's main movie theater from 1923 to 1974, was remodeled in 1941. Added to the exterior of the building were a neon-framed tower and marquee and a ticket booth. Inside, the lobby was redecorated with new carpeting, new decorations, and a large mural titled *The Future of Tracy*. Robert H. "Bob" Allen was the manager at the time.

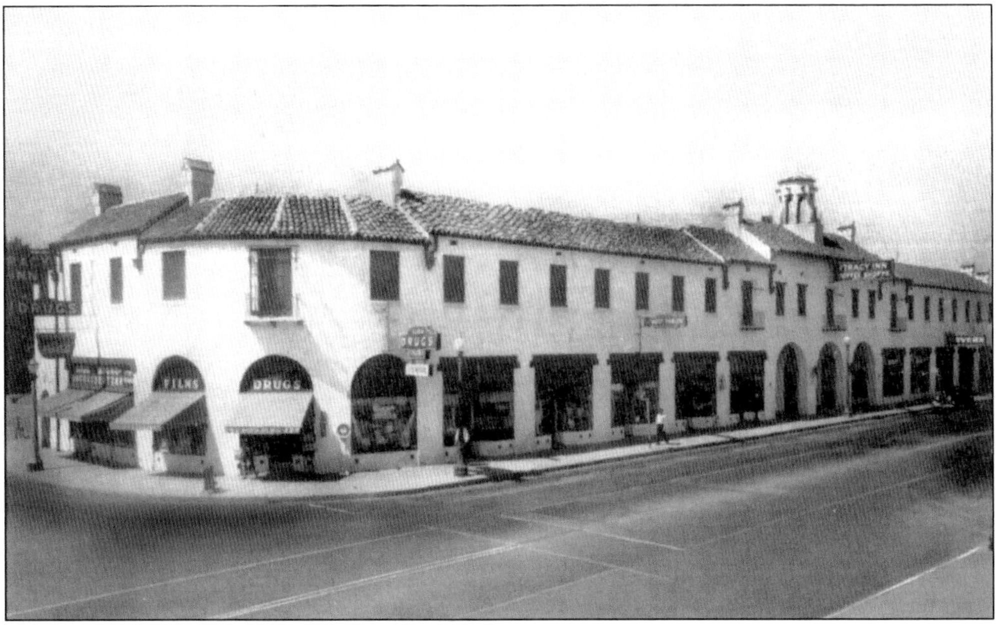

Construction of the Tracy Inn on the southwest corner of Eleventh Street and Central Avenue began in 1926. The building was financed by the sale of stock to local citizens and opened its doors for business in January 1927. A Tracy landmark for generations, it is listed on the National Register of Historic Places and still houses the Tracy Inn, as well as various businesses.

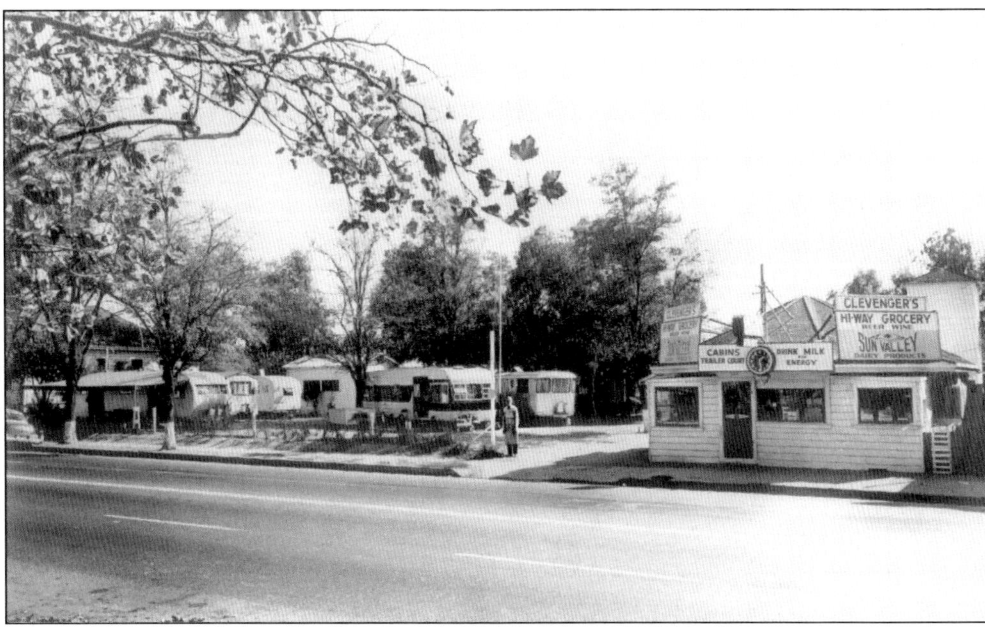

Clevenger's Hi-Way Grocery, located on the southeast corner of Eleventh Street and Taft Avenue (currently the Old River Veterinary Hospital), provided groceries along with cabins and a trailer park for travelers on the Lincoln Highway through Tracy. In its beginnings in the 1920s it was an "autocourt" where travelers could pull off the road for the night and rest in one-room cabins.

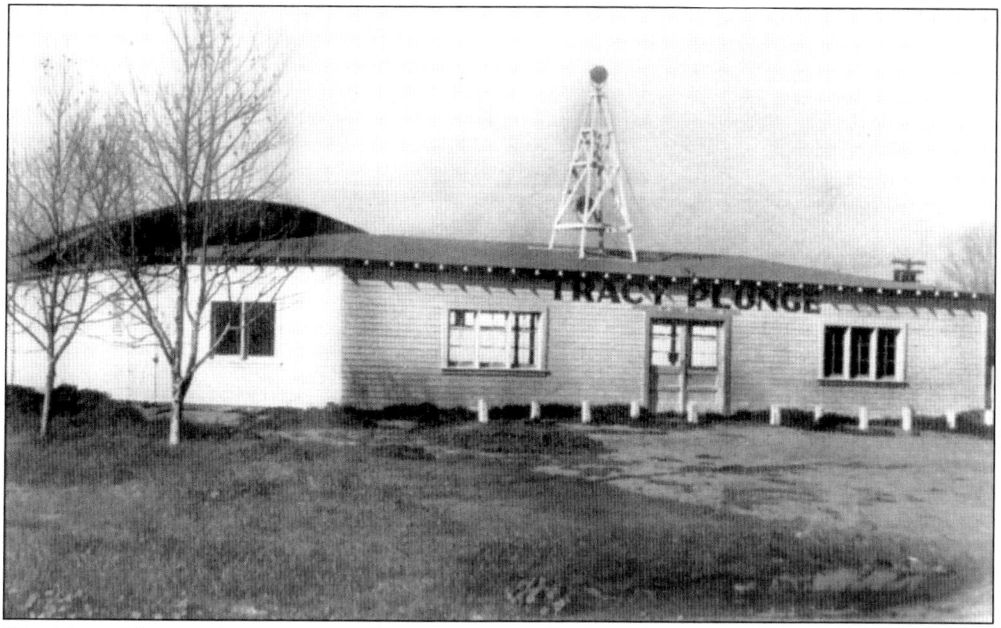

The Tracy Plunge, the community's swimming pool, was a wooden structure on Holly Drive built in 1931 as a business venture by C.B. Wightman of Byron. A few years later it was sold to the Tracy Elementary School District, and in 1952 the Tracy Recreation Commission took charge of its operation. The pool at Dr. Powers Park opened in 1986; the Plunge closed. The building burned down in 1998.

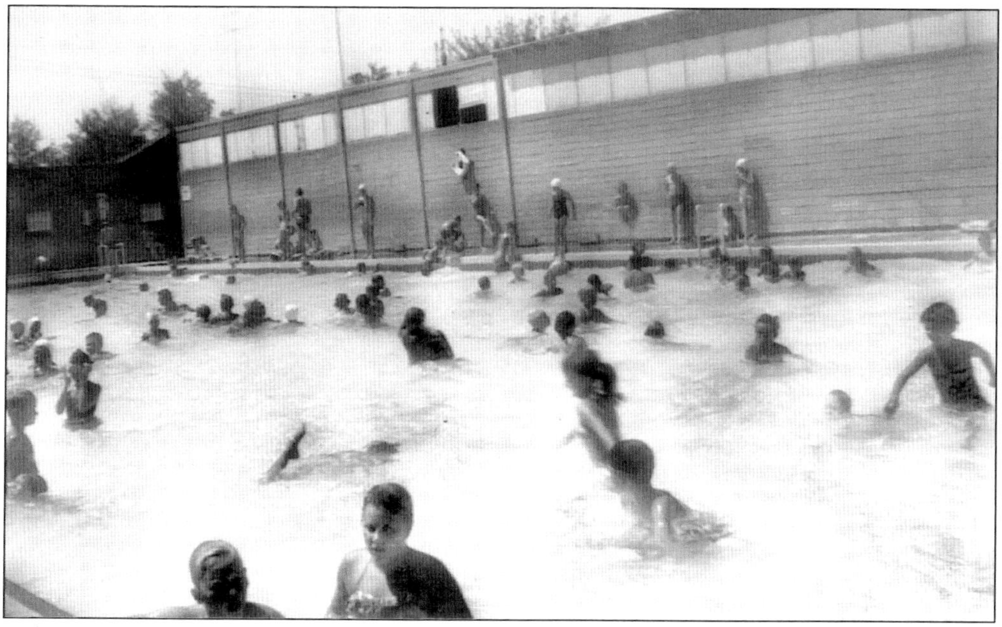

Before Tracy had a community swimming pool, irrigation ditches in town were often used for swimming during hot Tracy summers. When the Tracy Plunge opened, residents had a first-class pool, 45 feet by 125 feet in size, for swimming lessons and recreational swimming. This photo, taken by Ruth Maddix, shows the Plunge filled with kids on a hot summer day. (Courtesy of Dennis Maddix.)

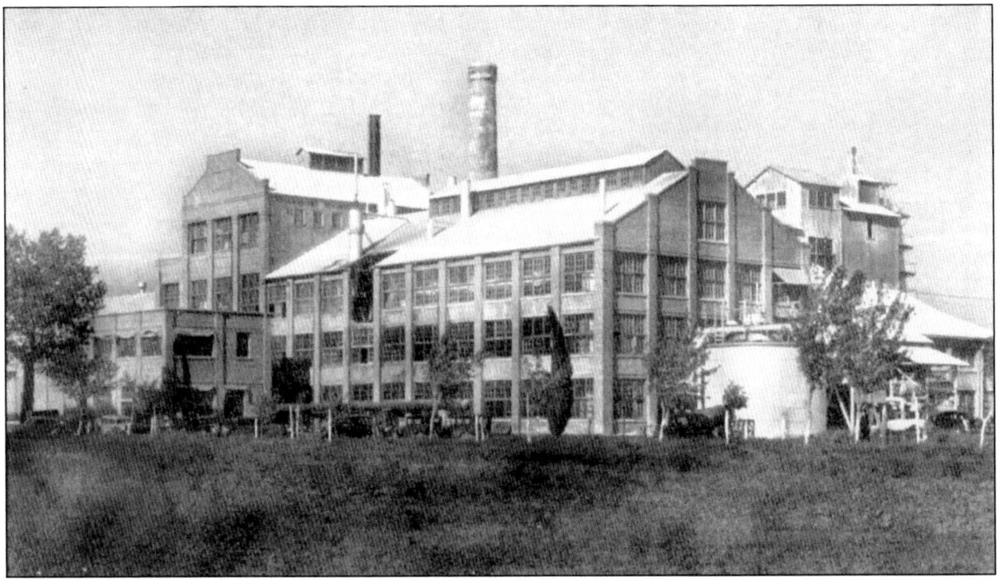

The Pacific Sugar Company, formed by backers of the Whitehall Estates farming operation, built a sugar plant north of Tracy in 1917. After several years of operational difficulties, the Holly Sugar Corporation took over operations in 1926 and became one of Tracy's major employers. The plant was sold to the Imperial Sugar Company in 1988 and ceased production in 2000.

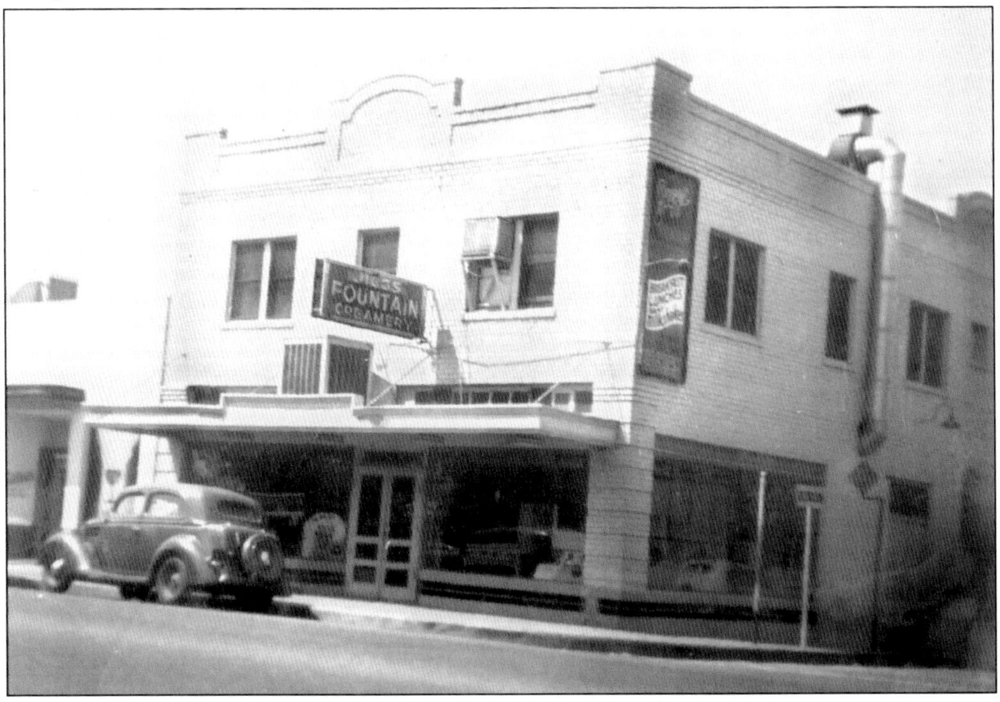

In January 1935 Leonard "Jiggs" Ackerman leased the front of Hughes Creamery and renamed it Jiggs Fountain Creamery. Prior to establishing Jiggs, Ackerman had worked in the L.O. Stark business located in the front area of the Peterson Creamery. Jiggs Fountain Creamery, at the corner of Eleventh and Walnut Streets (currently a parking lot), was in business for many years.

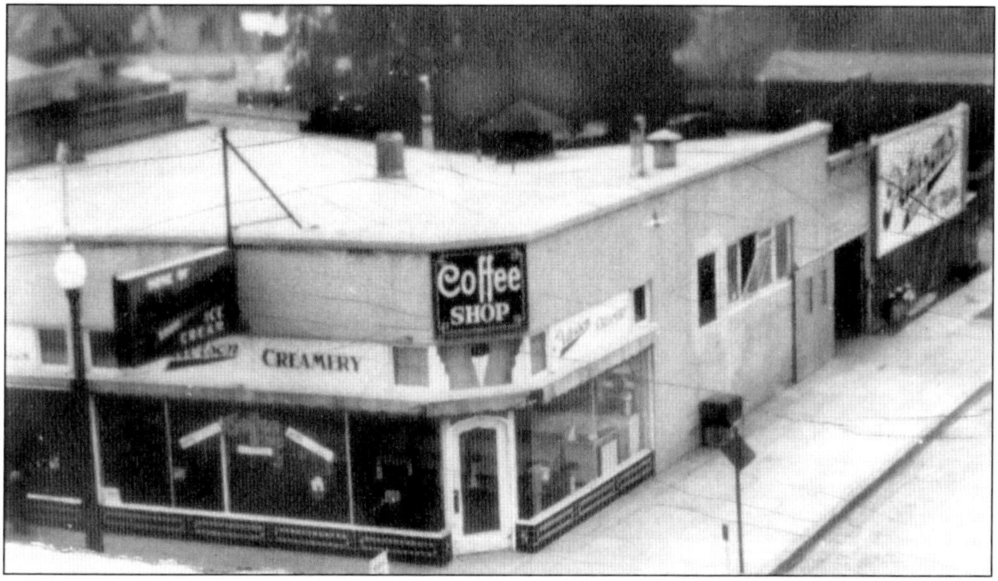

Peterson's Ice Cream Company, established by C.W. "Pete" Peterson in 1925, was on the southeast corner of Eleventh and B Streets (currently the location of the Little Flower Shop). The front portion of the building was a popular restaurant and ice cream fountain, and the ice cream manufacturing operations were in the back part of the building. The business was sold in 1953.

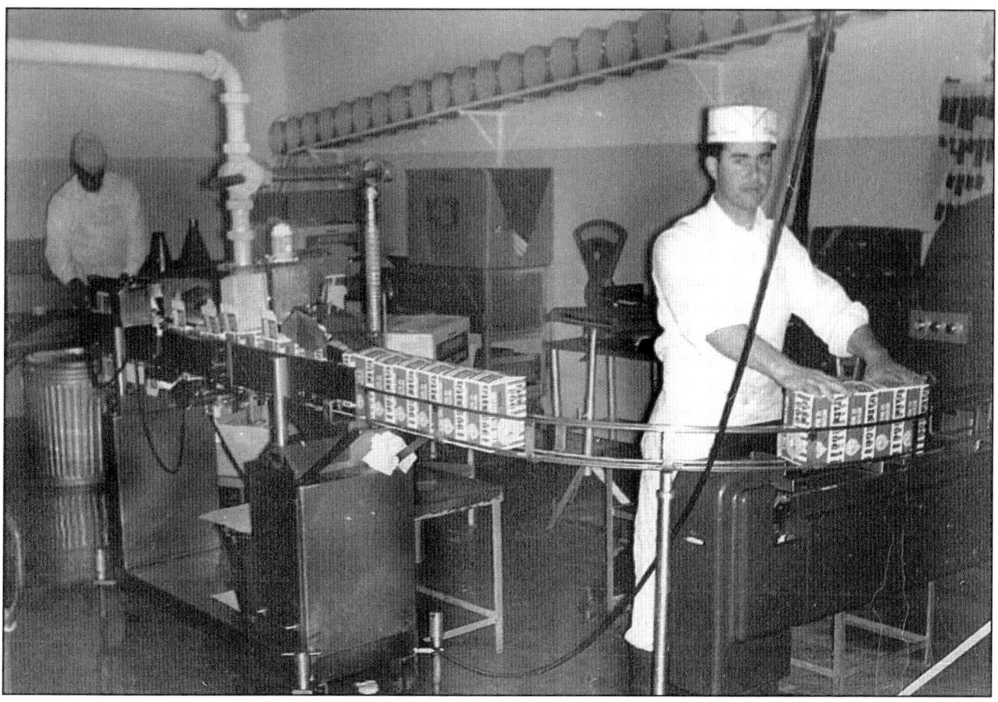

Local residents enjoyed the variety of flavors produced by Peterson's Ice Cream Company. Ice cream mix made in this plant was sold to businesses throughout northern California. Pictured here are unidentified workers employed in the plant. At one time Peterson's employed more people than any other locally owned business.

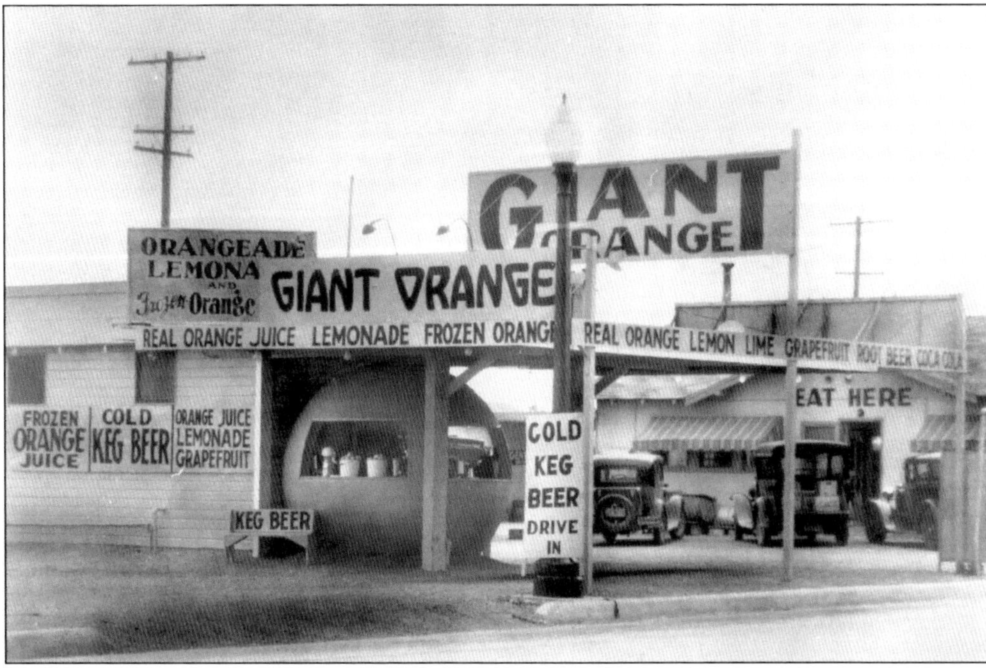

Travelers through Tracy enjoyed stopping for a refreshing drink of freshly squeezed orange juice served with special syrup and crushed ice at the Giant Orange, a distinctive orange-shaped stand at Eleventh and E Streets. Opened in 1926 by Frank "Pop" Pohl and his wife, Lora, this was the first stand of what later became a California sandwich, snack, and beverage chain.

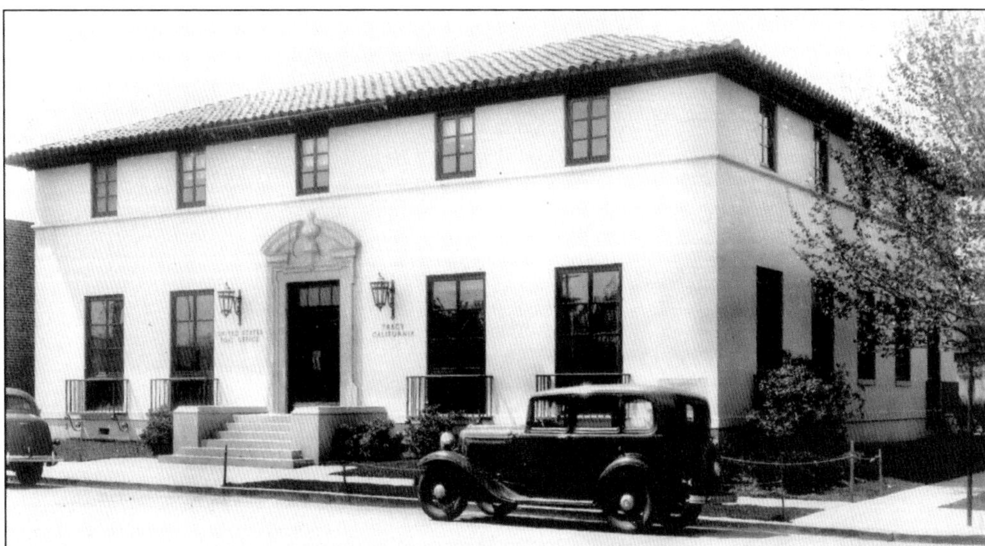

Built as part of the federal building program during the Great Depression, this building at the corner of Twelfth and Adam Streets housed the United States Post Office from 1937 until 1967. In 1968 the city bought the building, which became the Joe Wilson Recreation Center. In 2002, after renovation by the city, it became the home of the Tracy Historical Museum, operated by the West Side Pioneer Association.

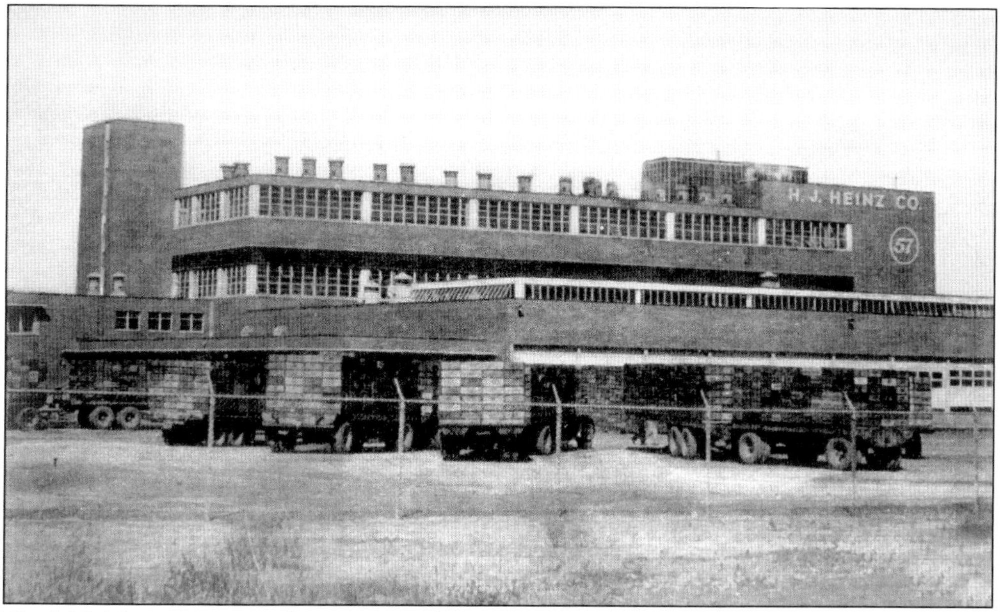

The H.J. Heinz Company factory opened on Eleventh Street on the eastern edge of Tracy in 1946. Many World War II veterans were hired to work in the plant, which became one of the major employers in Tracy. With the opening of the plant, which primarily produced tomato products such as tomato paste, ketchup, and juice, tomatoes became a major Tracy area crop.

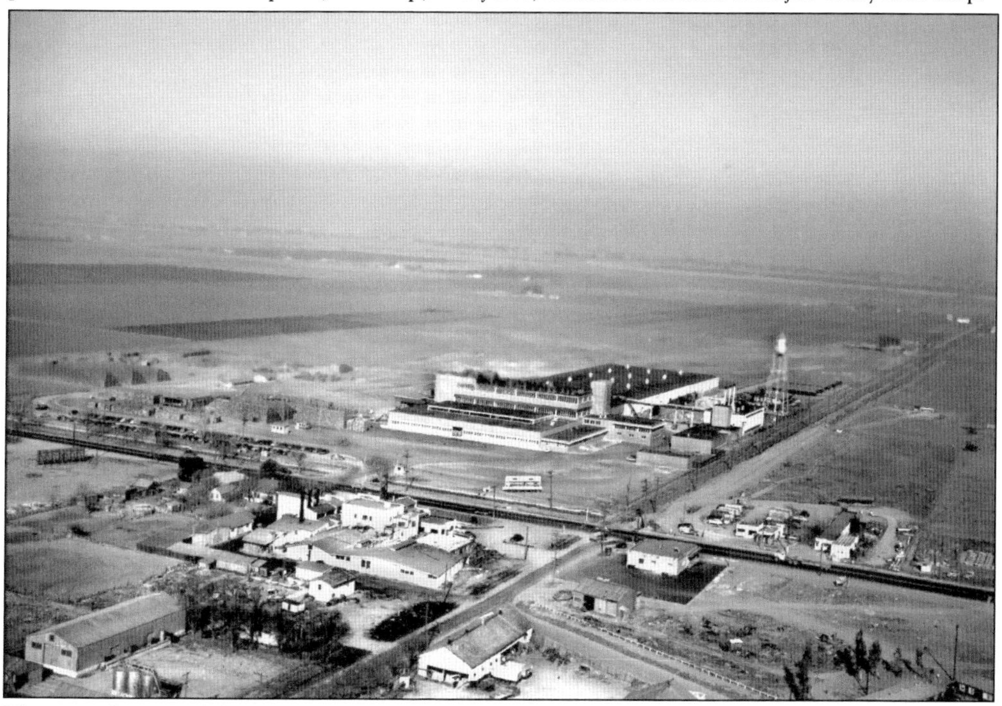
This aerial view of the Heinz plant was taken in 1946. The plant increased in size over the years and also served as the principal warehouse and distribution center for Heinz on the West Coast. Besides tomato products, some of the other items processed in the Tracy plant included baby foods, soup, pickles, and vinegar. The plant closed in 1998.

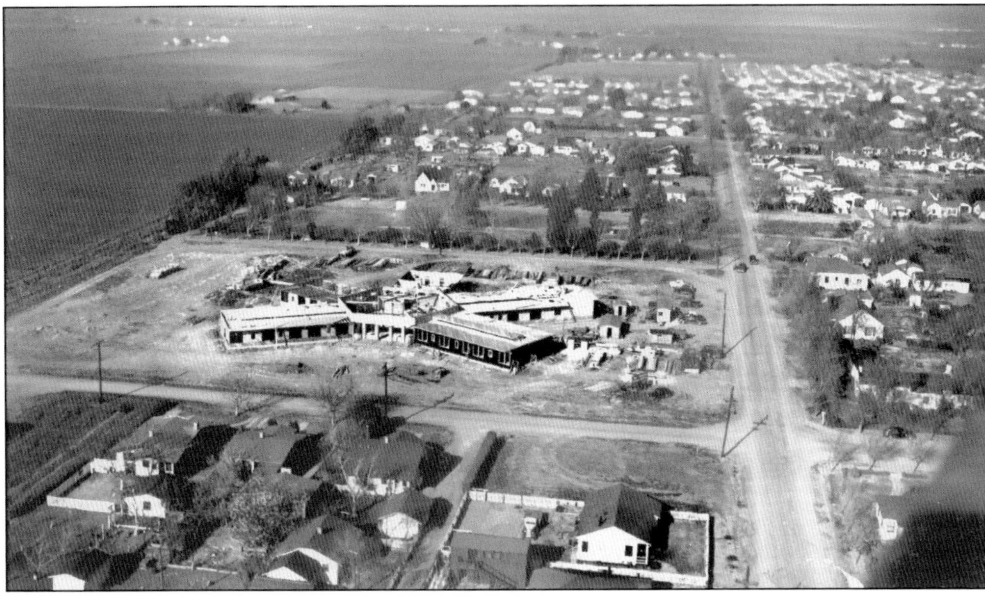

Tracy Community Memorial Hospital (now called Sutter Tracy Community Hospital) opened for business on December 12, 1948. Built with funds raised by local residents, the hospital, shown here during construction, had five wings coming out from a central hub. Prior to the hospital's opening, Tracy residents in need of full hospital services went to French Camp, Stockton, Oakland, or San Francisco.

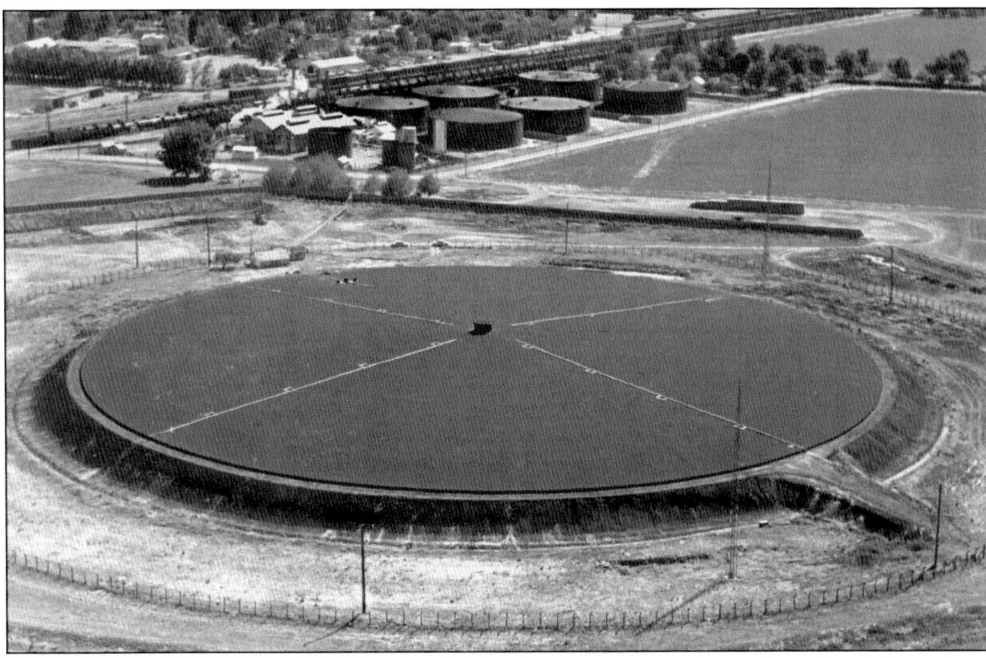

This oil storage tank, owned by the Standard Oil Company, was located south of the railroad tracks just west of what is now Tracy Boulevard. The tank, the largest in the world in the early 1940s, was removed in the 1950s. Standard Oil had a presence in Tracy beginning in 1903 when the first oil pipeline was laid. Kendall "Ken" Lowes and J.B. Stocking were long-time Standard Oil managers.

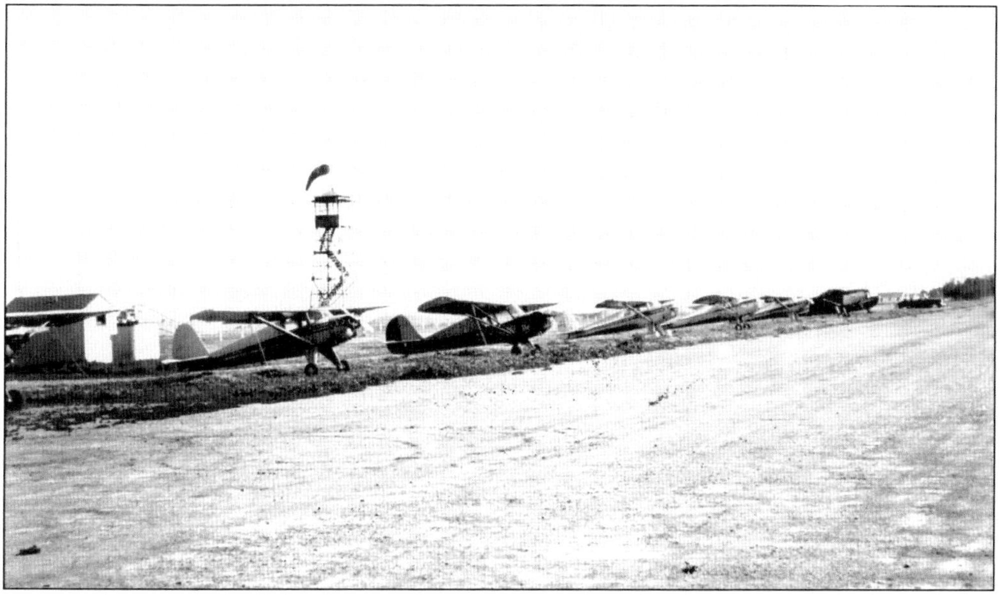

In September 1928 an agreement was reached between the James McDermott Post of the American Legion and the Tracy City Council to create an airport in Tracy. Persuaded by American Legion members, the city agreed to purchase the 160-acre site, which had been part of the Alfred Pereira farm south of Tracy. In return, the American Legion agreed to develop the runways, build hangars, and lease the airport for three years.

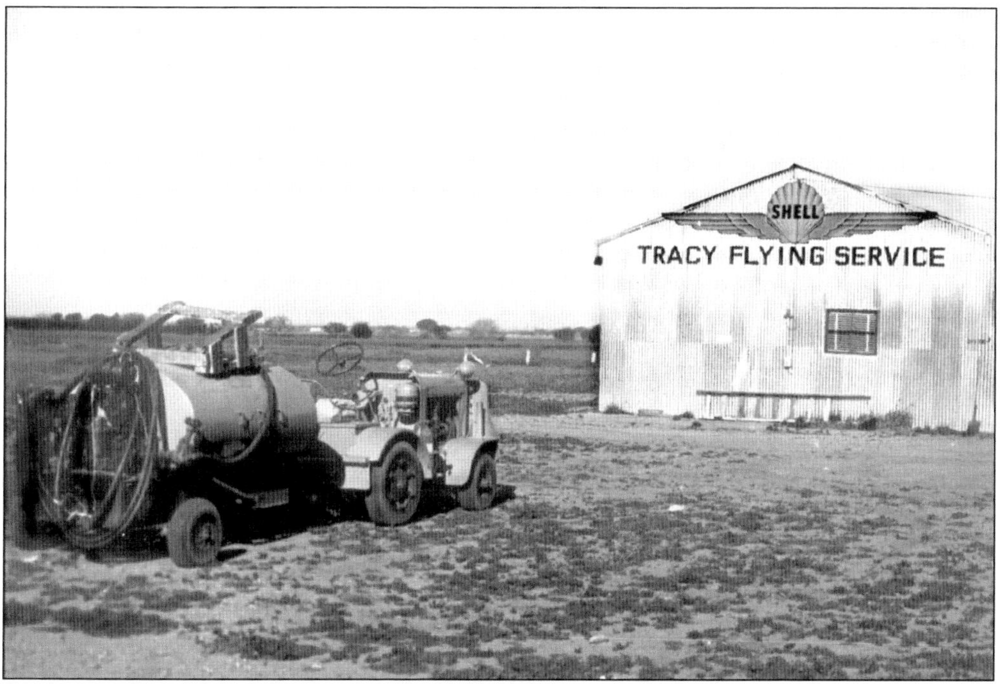

The efforts of the American Legion members and the Tracy City Council culminated in an air show that lasted three days, April 26–28, 1929, to mark the dedication of the American Legion Airport (now Tracy Municipal Airport). The small town of Tracy, with a population under 5,000, was inundated with people when over 40,000 visitors attended the activities.

One of the more unusual aspects of the airport dedication ceremonies was a special stamp cancellation created by the U.S. Post Office. Thousands of airmail letters were sent to all parts of the United States through the Tracy Post Office to receive the special cancellation during the dedication. The cancelled envelope shown here is on display at the Tracy Historical Museum.

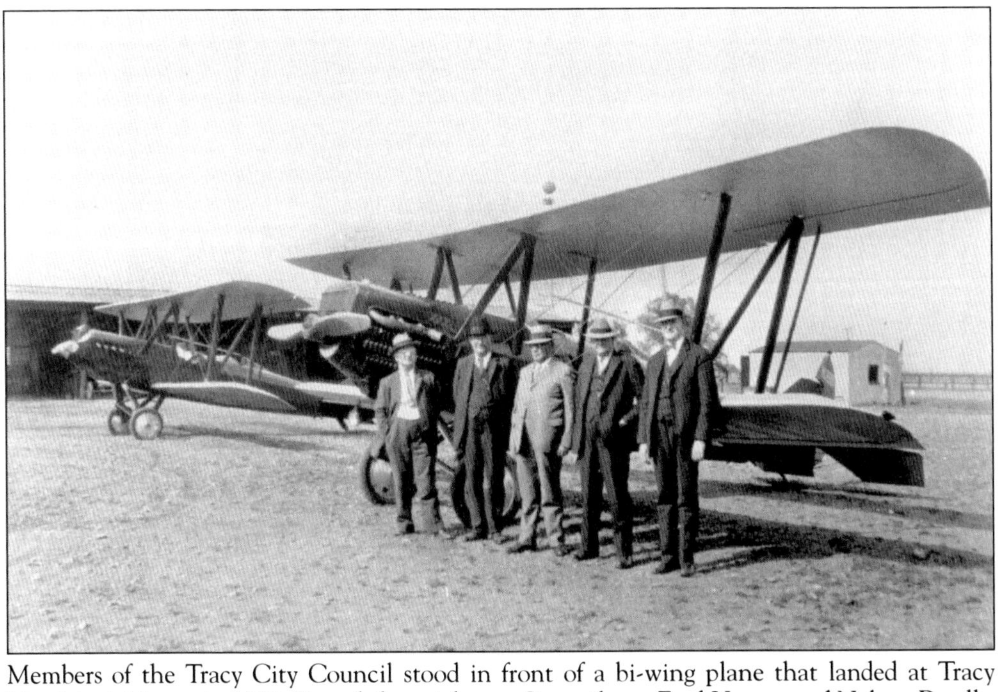

Members of the Tracy City Council stood in front of a bi-wing plane that landed at Tracy Municipal Airport in 1931. From left to right are Councilmen Fred Herzog and Nelson Dwelly, Mayor John Ranley, and Councilmen Robert G. Harvey and Charles L. Sheppard. Operation of the airport was turned over to the city after the American Legion's three-year lease came to an end in 1932.

Seven

STREETS

According to the first map of the Town of Tracy, the boundaries of the town were West Street on the west, South Street on the south, East Street on the east, and the County Road (later renamed Eleventh Street) on the north. The earliest businesses were established near the railroad tracks, which ran between Fourth and Sixth Streets. Sixth Street (also known as Front Street), on the north side of the tracks, was the center of the early business district. On the south side of the tracks businesses concentrated on Fourth Street. Residences were established close to the business districts on both sides of the tracks. Development spread north up Central and along the side streets, eventually crossing Eleventh Street when it became part of the Lincoln Highway. Early development on the south side was along Fourth and Third Streets and Central Avenue.

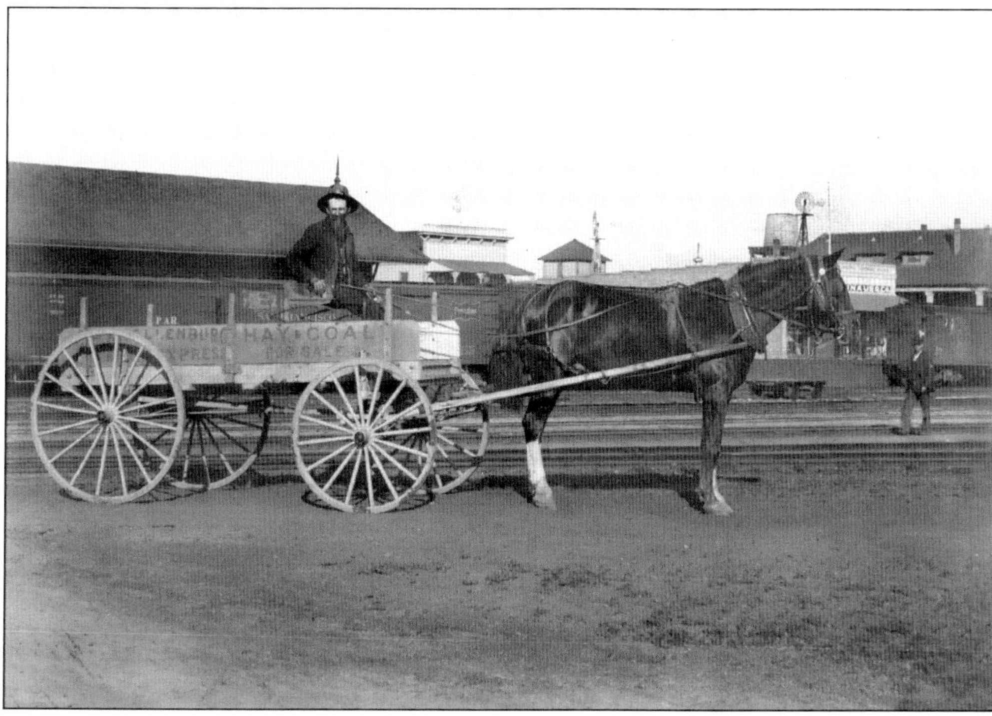

Peter Knollenburg, who operated the Tracy Express for many years, was photographed near the freight shed in the Southern Pacific Yard south of West Sixth (Front) Street in 1902. The horse-drawn wagon from his drayage business was a familiar sight on the streets of Tracy.

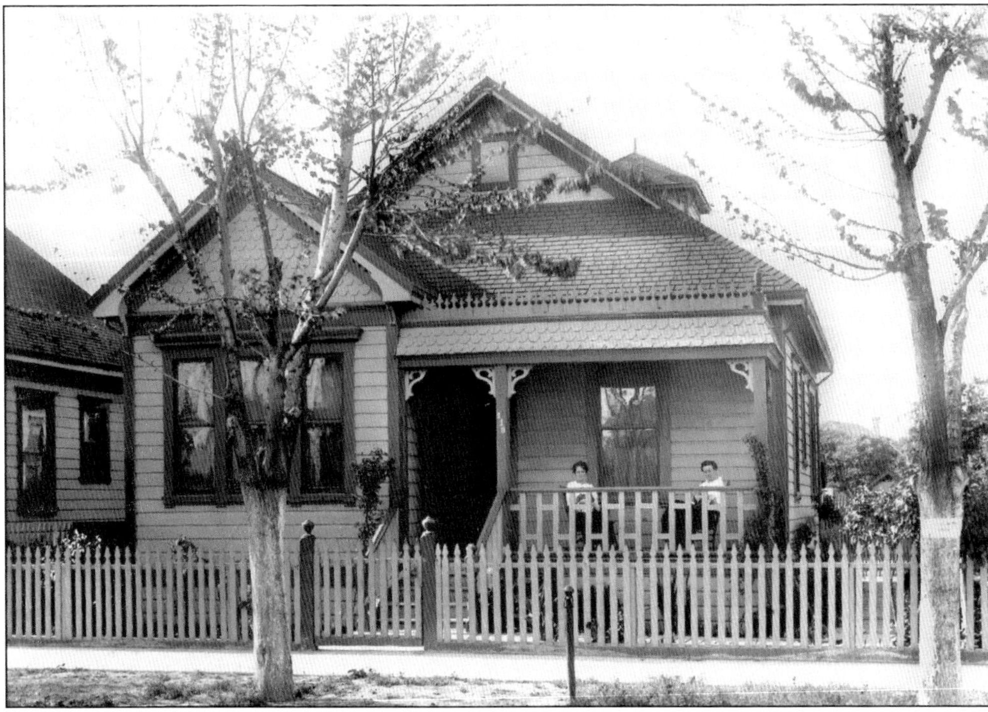

Mrs. Rhinehart, on the left, and another woman, probably Mrs. McKeany, are visiting on the front porch of a home on West Eighth Street in this 1915 photograph. A typical, late Victorian home built in Tracy in the 1890s, this home and others like it usually had two bedrooms, a small dining area, a parlor, and a kitchen. Many of these homes still exist in Tracy.

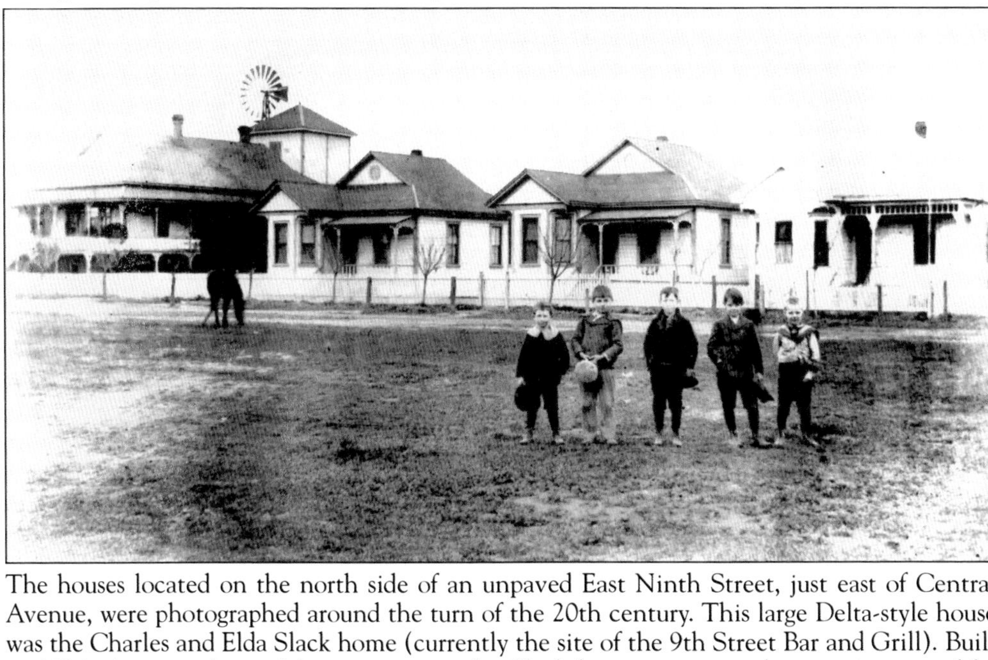

The houses located on the north side of an unpaved East Ninth Street, just east of Central Avenue, were photographed around the turn of the 20th century. This large Delta-style house was the Charles and Elda Slack home (currently the site of the 9th Street Bar and Grill). Built in 1896, the two identical houses next to the Slack home were rental properties owned by the Slacks.

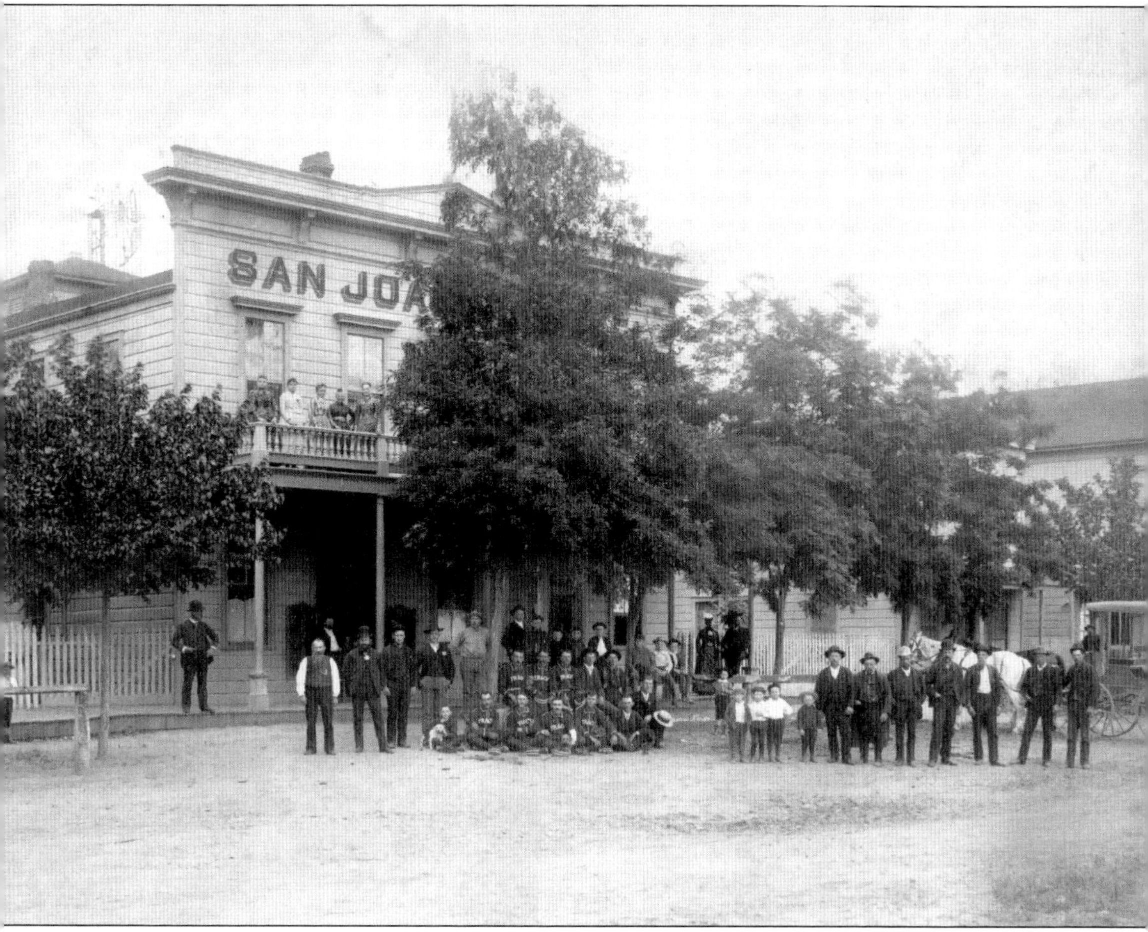

This street scene photographed in 1889 in front of the San Joaquin Hotel on East Sixth Street north of the railroad tracks was typical of Tracy streets in the late 1800s. Trees had been planted to break the force of the winds coming through the Altamont Pass and to provide needed shade from the summer heat. Wooden sidewalks lined the unpaved street. This photo was taken during the summer months when the streets were dry and not muddy, as they often became during the wet winter months. Many Tracy residents gathered to participate in the photograph, including members of the Tracy baseball team, members of the Ludwig family who ran the hotel, and other unidentified folks. One little fellow even brought his dog to be included in the photograph. The ladies assembled on the balcony.

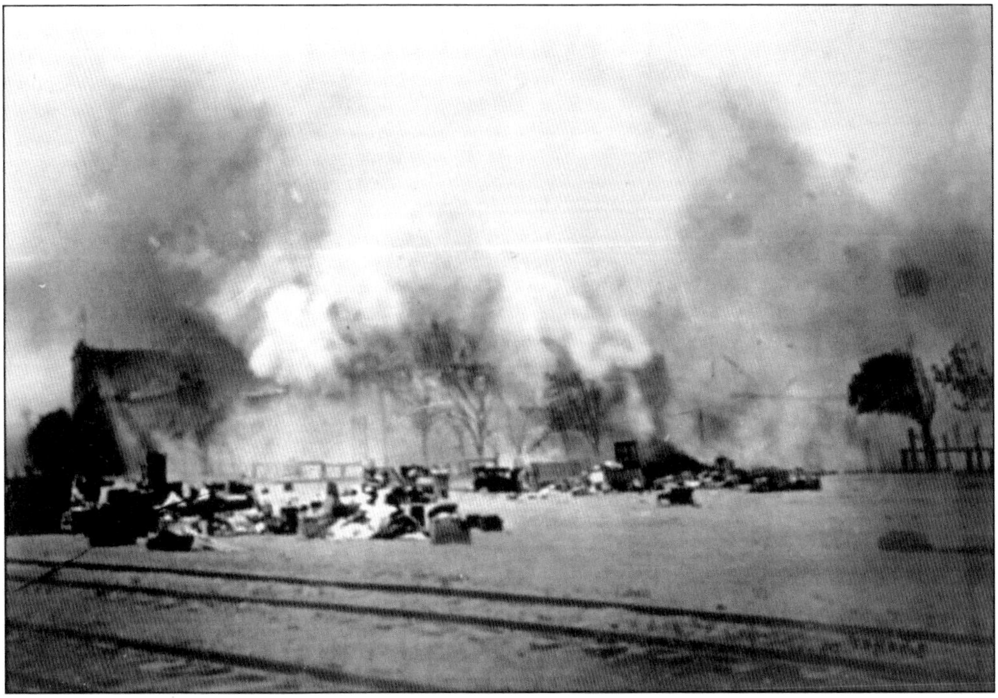

Smoke hung over the town of Tracy from the fire of June 19, 1898. The fire began in Mrs. Mary Mannis's restaurant at the corner of Front and C Streets that Sunday morning and, driven by the wind, consumed all the buildings, including the business district and several houses, in a four-block path as it quickly swept down Front Street.

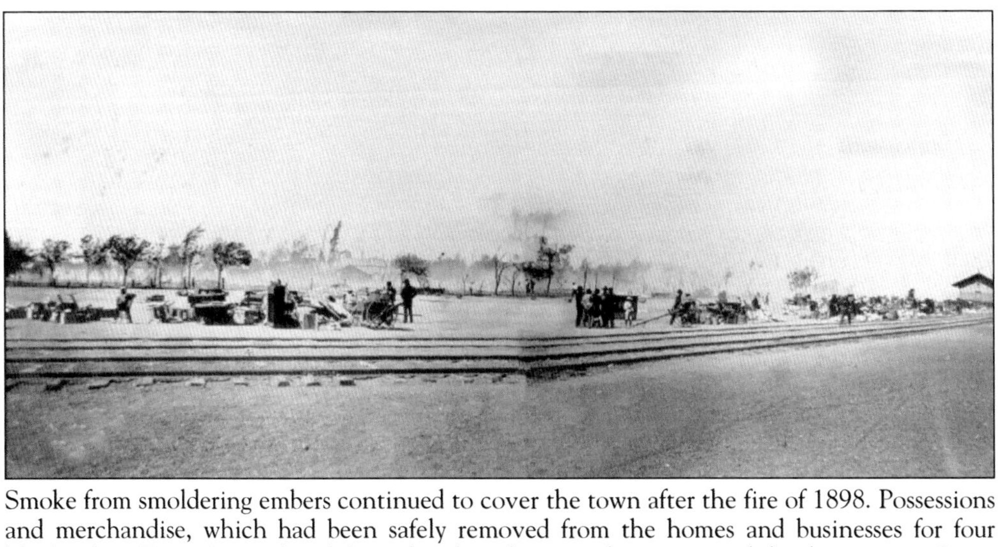

Smoke from smoldering embers continued to cover the town after the fire of 1898. Possessions and merchandise, which had been safely removed from the homes and businesses for four blocks along Front Street, lined the railroad tracks as residents surveyed the devastation. Some business owners rebuilt immediately, while other lots remained empty for several years.

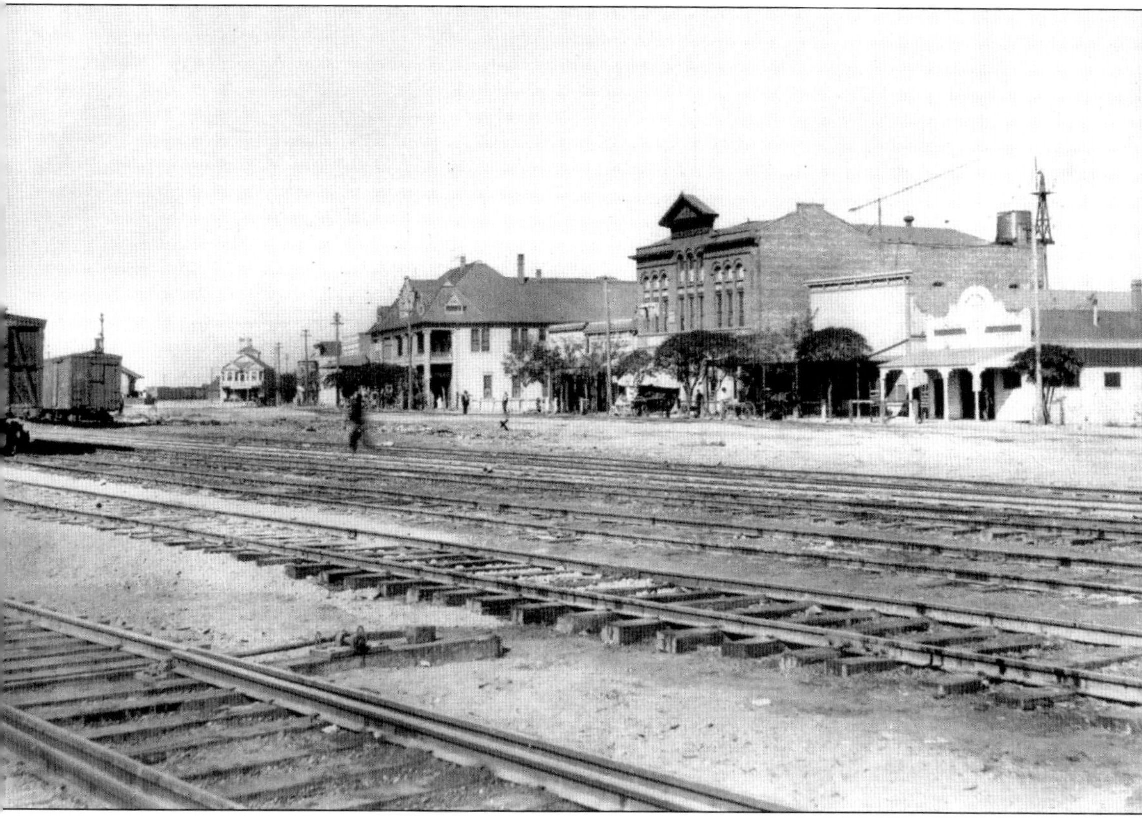

This 1904 photograph, looking west along Front Street (now called Sixth Street), offers viewers a sense of the importance of the railroad to the community. Front Street, just north of the railroad tracks, became the heart of Tracy's business district in the early years. Passengers arriving in Tracy by train could find several hotels, saloons, pool halls, and stores right across the street from the depot. Front Street was unpaved, and in the rainy season was quite muddy, making it difficult for passengers, especially women in their long skirts, to cross the tracks to the business district. The large three-story brick building is the IOOF building, which is the only building in this photograph still standing today. The large building to the left of the IOOF building was the Tracy Hotel at the corner of Front Street and Central Avenue. The building to the far left in the picture was the Golden State Hotel.

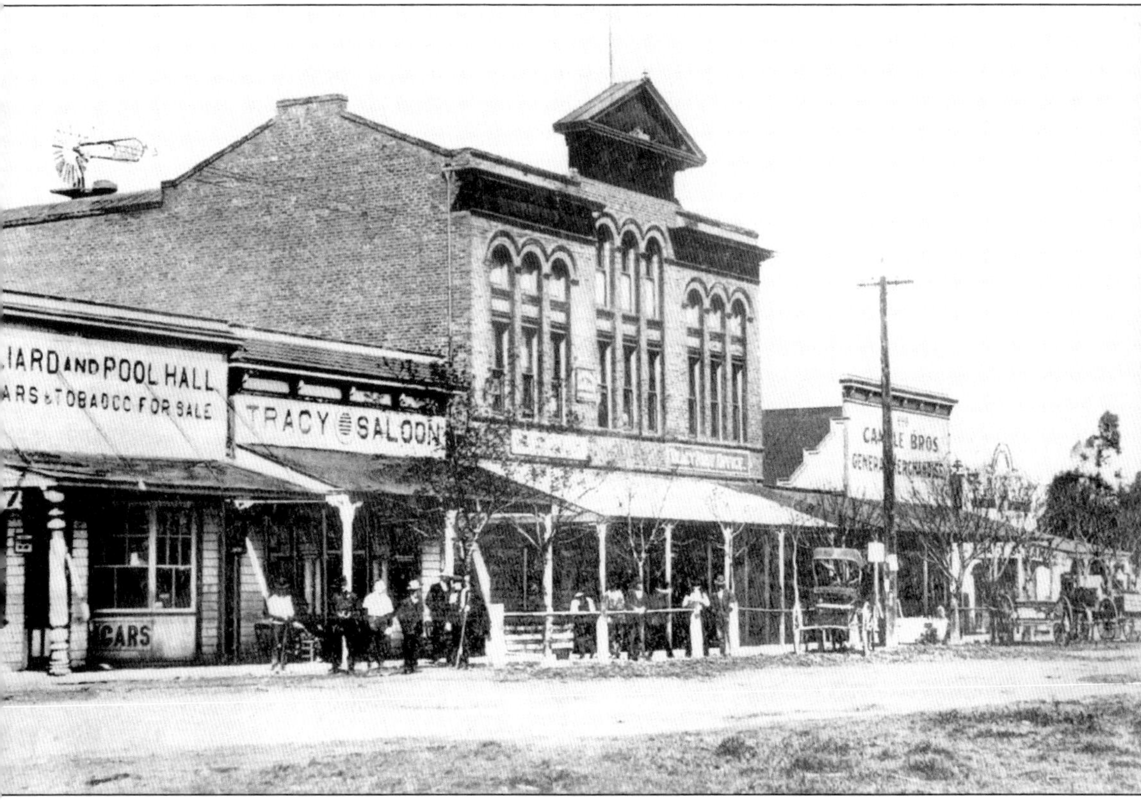

This photograph, looking east along Front Street (now called Sixth Street), shows part of Tracy's main street in 1907. The large, three-story, brick IOOF building dominated this end of Front Street and was surrounded by some of the numerous saloons that lined both East and West Front Street, such as the Tracy Saloon, Billiard and Pool Hall, the Gilt Edge Saloon inside the IOOF building, and the White Front Saloon to the right of Canale Brothers General Merchandise store. Trees had been planted to provide some cooling shade during the hot summers, but the tree-lined street was unpaved. Aside from the train, horses and buggies were the primary mode of transportation in the early 1900s, and hitching posts, such as those shown in front of Canale Brothers General Merchandise Store and the post office on the first floor of the IOOF building, were provided all along the street.

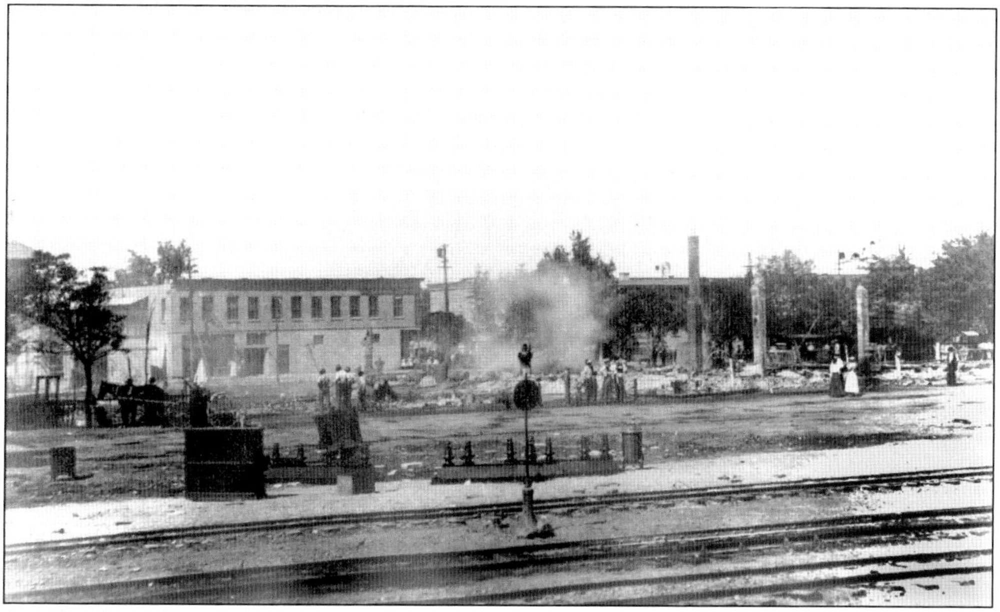

Another large fire, this one on August 11, 1911, changed the look of Front Street again. The fire began in the chimney of the stately Tracy Hotel on the corner of Front and Central and consumed all of the wooden buildings east of the hotel. The fire was stopped at the brick IOOF building. After this fire, most of the buildings erected on Front Street were made of brick.

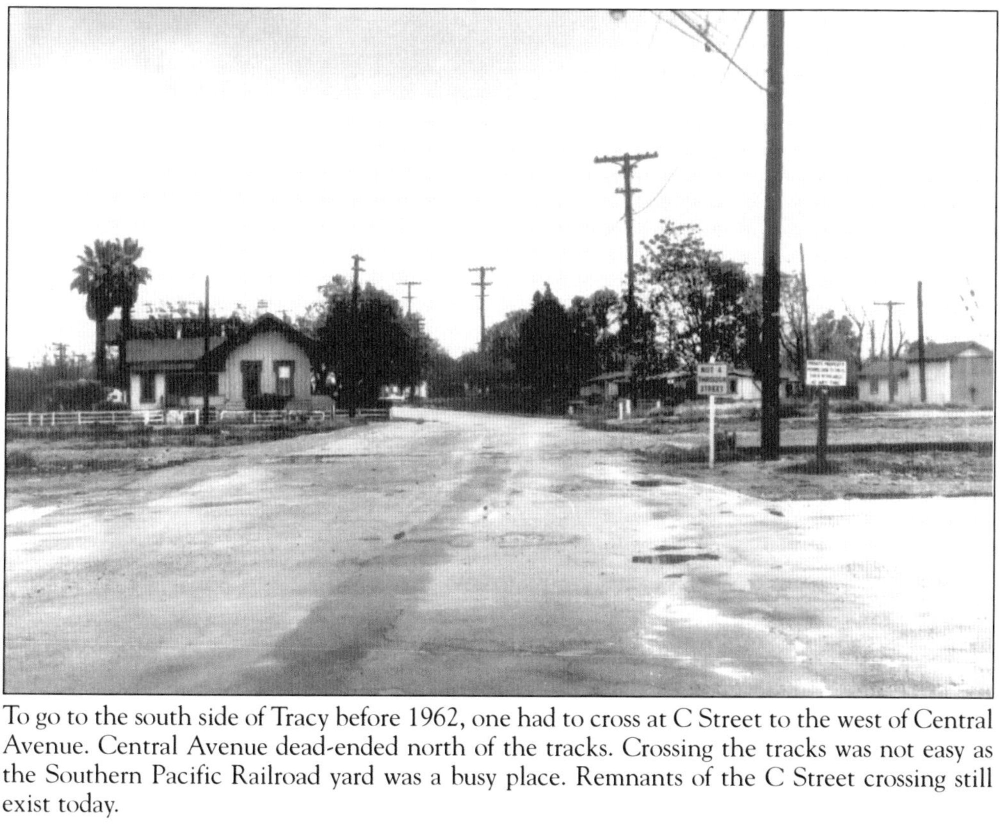

To go to the south side of Tracy before 1962, one had to cross at C Street to the west of Central Avenue. Central Avenue dead-ended north of the tracks. Crossing the tracks was not easy as the Southern Pacific Railroad yard was a busy place. Remnants of the C Street crossing still exist today.

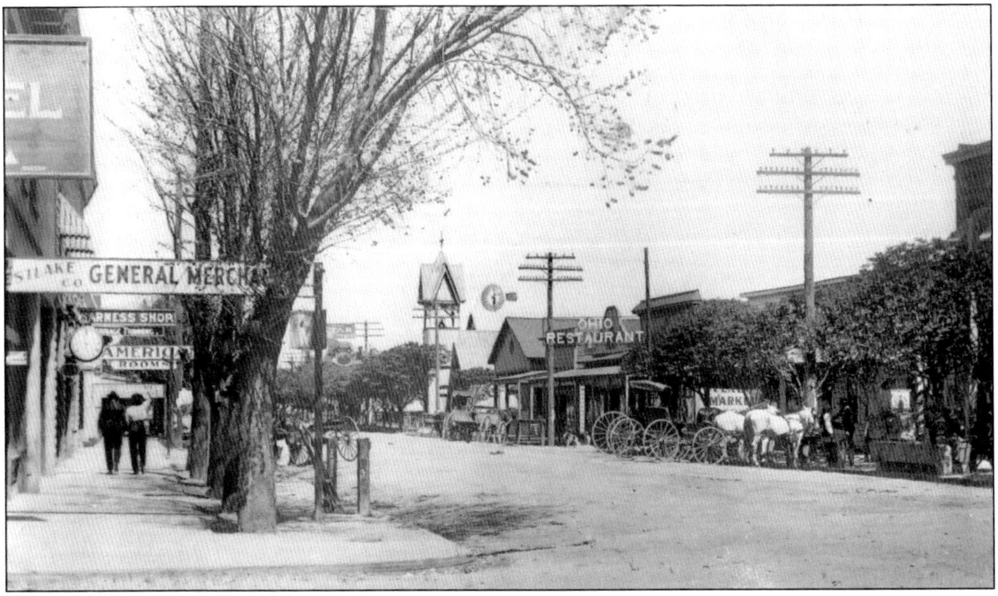

Looking north from Seventh Street up Central Avenue, this 1908 photo shows the business district beginning to develop up Central from Front Street. The steeple of the original Catholic church building at Eighth and Central and a windmill stand out amid the many businesses along the street. Water tanks and windmills, providing needed water for businesses and homes, were prominent in all street scenes of that era.

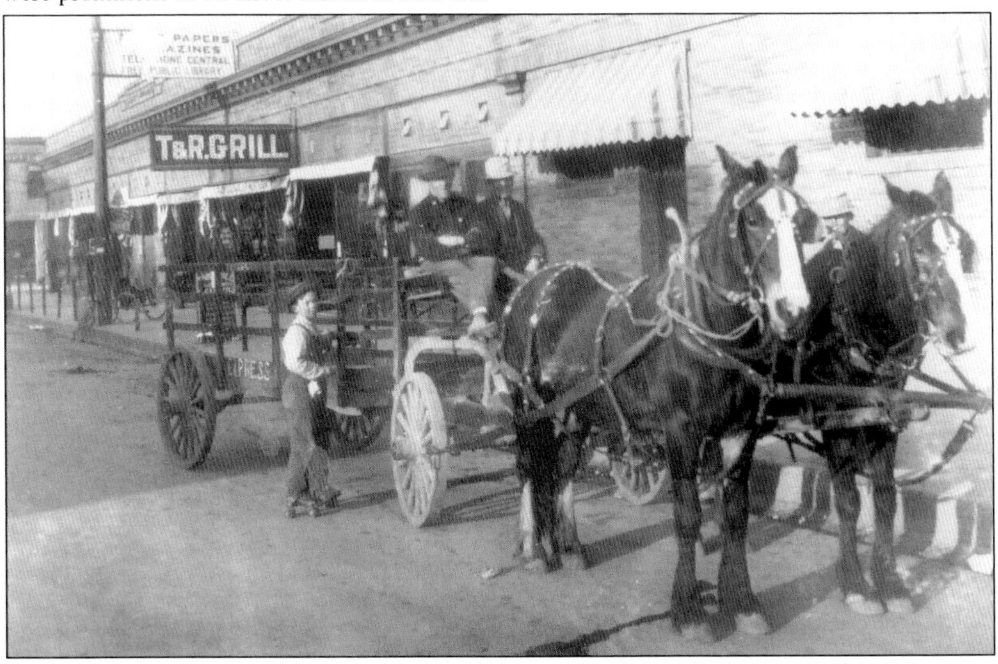

This photograph, taken in 1913 along Central Avenue by the T&R Grill in the block between Sixth and Seventh Streets, shows a mode of transportation, the horse and wagon, which was beginning to be replaced by the automobile. Driven by Frank Penney, this team belonged to Mike Obad. Note the window awnings, which provided some relief from the heat in the days before air conditioning.

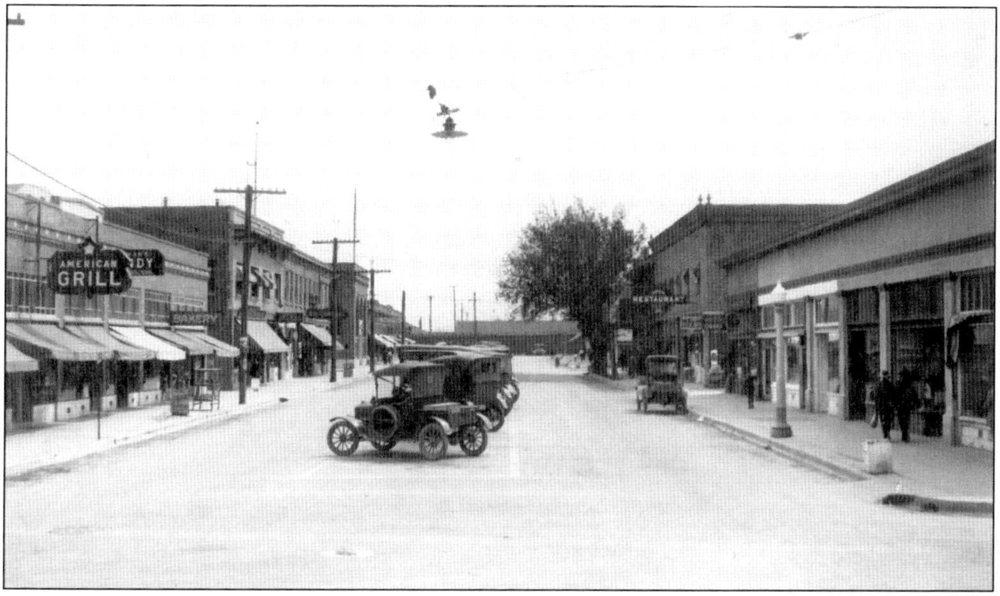

Looking south from Eighth Street, this photograph of Central Avenue from the early 1920s shows that substantial brick buildings had replaced the wood-frame buildings seen in the earlier 1908 image. Automobiles had replaced horses, and the hitching posts were gone. Parking in the center of the street was allowed, as well as parking along the curbs. In 1924 the city trustees banned parking in the center of the street.

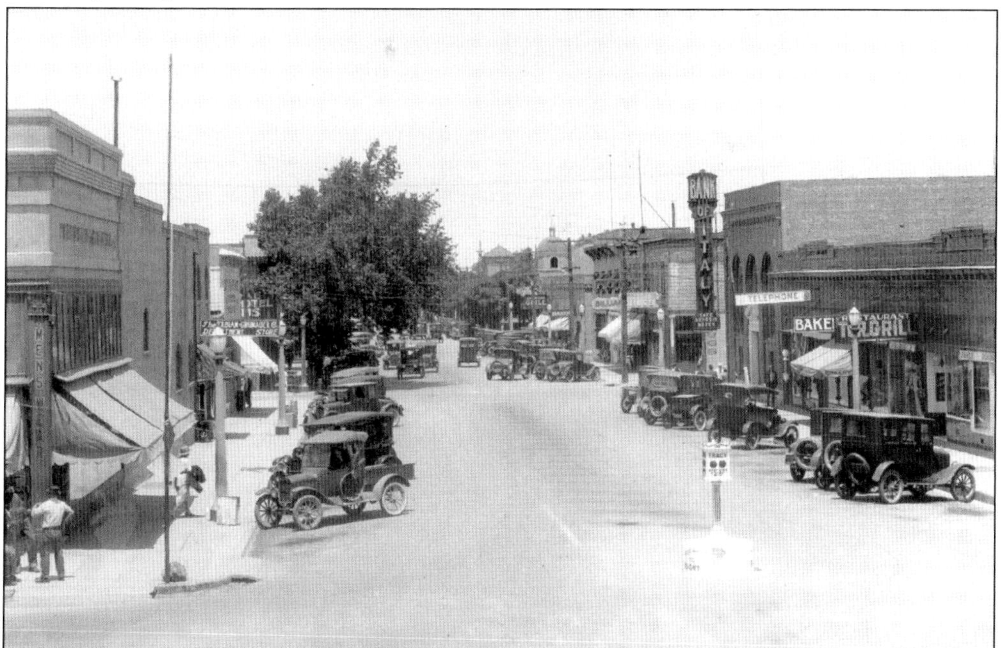

Tracy had a population of 2,460 by 1920 and a thriving business community. By the time this photograph of Central Avenue, looking north from Sixth Street, was taken in the mid-1920s, cars had replaced horses and Central Avenue had replaced Sixth Street as the center of Tracy's business community.

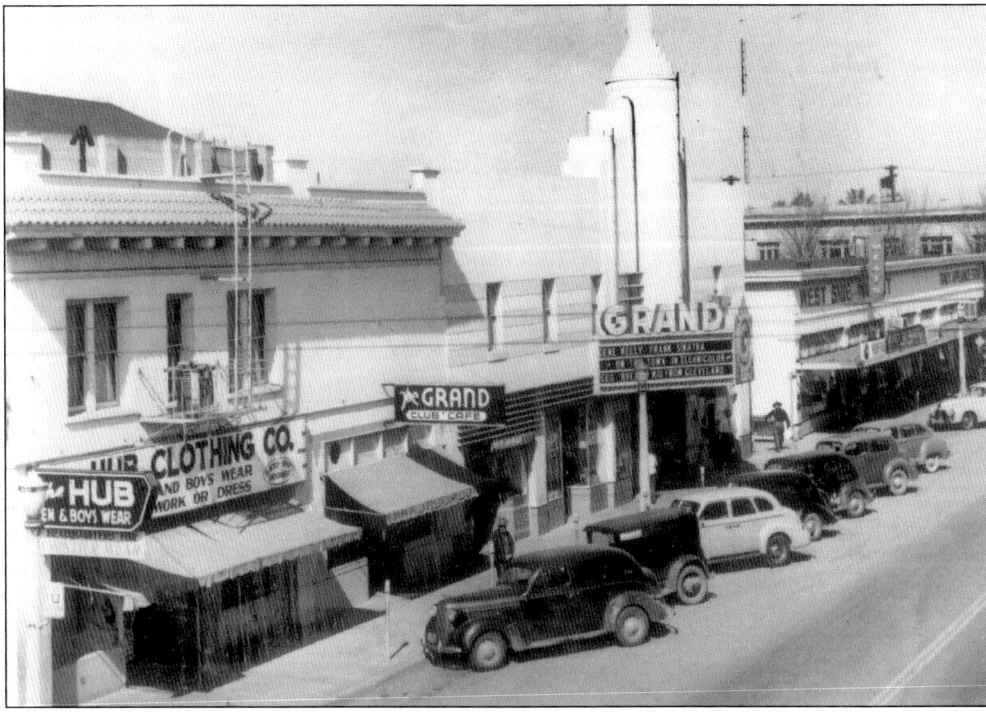

Shown in this photograph, taken after the marquee was added to the Grand Theater in 1941, are several of the businesses that lined the west side of Central Avenue: The Hub Clothing Company selling men and boy's wear, the Grand Club Café, the Grand Theater, and the West Side Market.

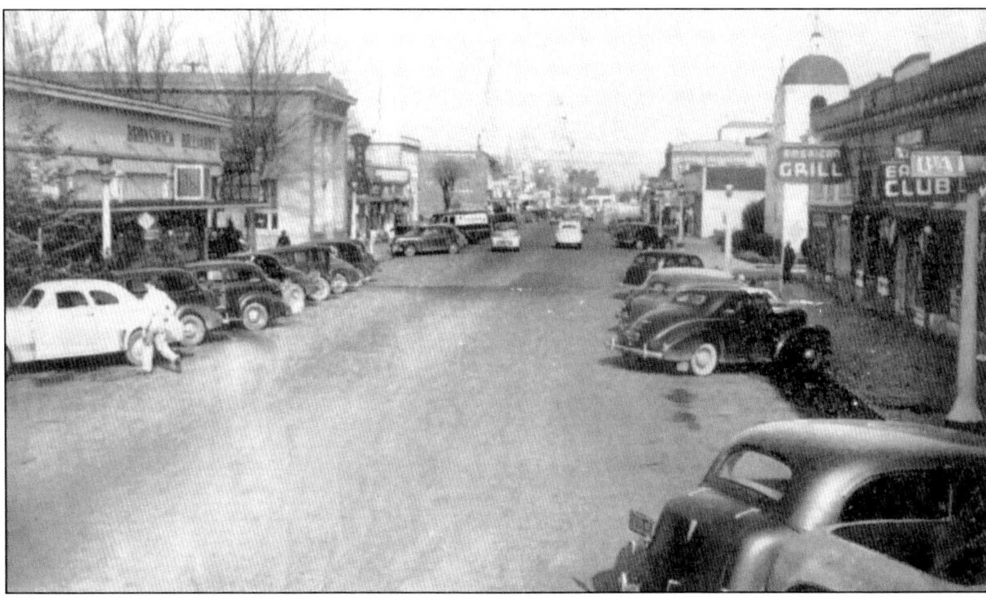

Looking north on Central Avenue during World War II in 1944, from the block between Seventh and Eighth Streets, this photograph shows the development of the business district up to Eleventh Street. The American Trust Bank on the left and the Catholic church on the right dominate this street scene.

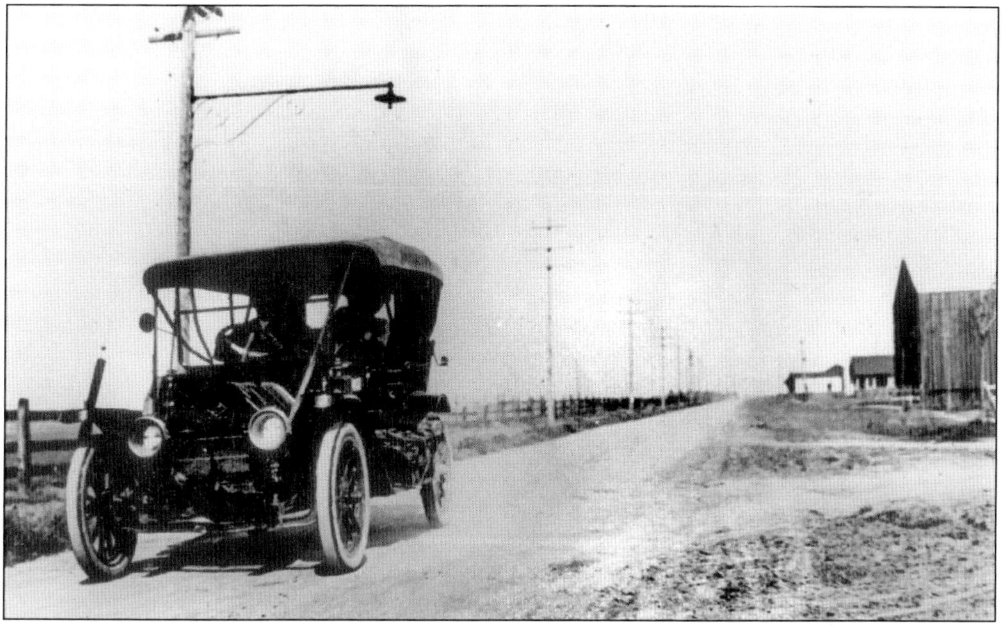

The County Road, which marked the north side of Tracy in its early days, was renamed Eleventh Street as development moved northward from the railroad tracks. This automobile on Eleventh in 1912 was near the intersection of what is now called Bessie Avenue. Even though it was part of the City of Tracy, Eleventh Street was a gravel road and appeared to be in the country.

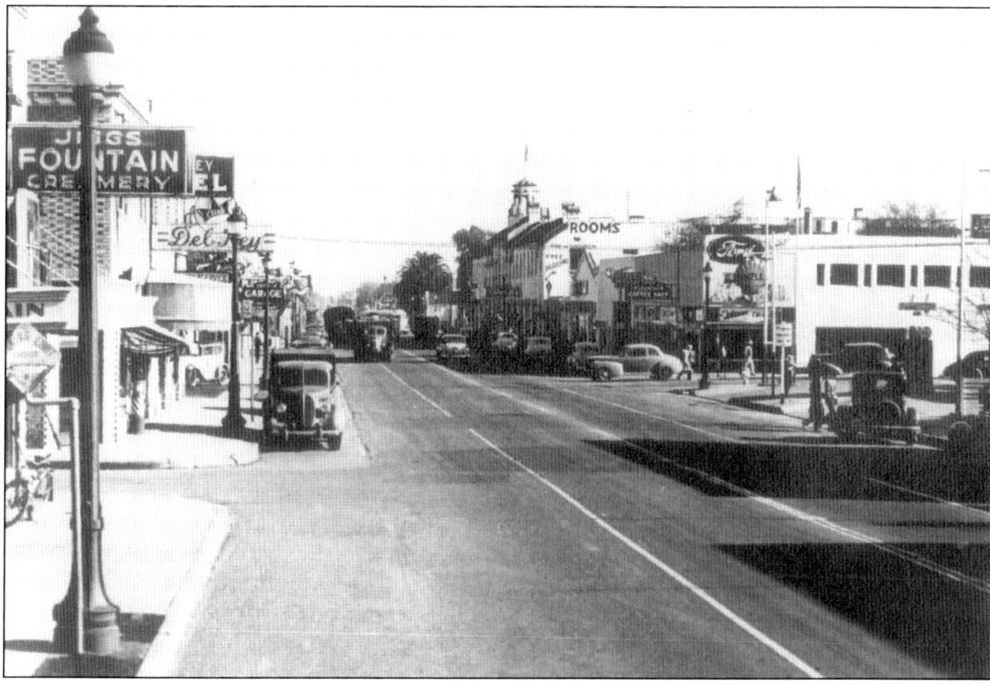

After Eleventh Street became part of the Lincoln Highway in 1914, the street was eventually paved and widened as automobile traffic increased. This photograph, looking east from the corner of Eleventh and Walnut Streets in the late 1940s, shows how the street had changed from a quiet country road into a busy highway lined with restaurants, service stations, and hotels.

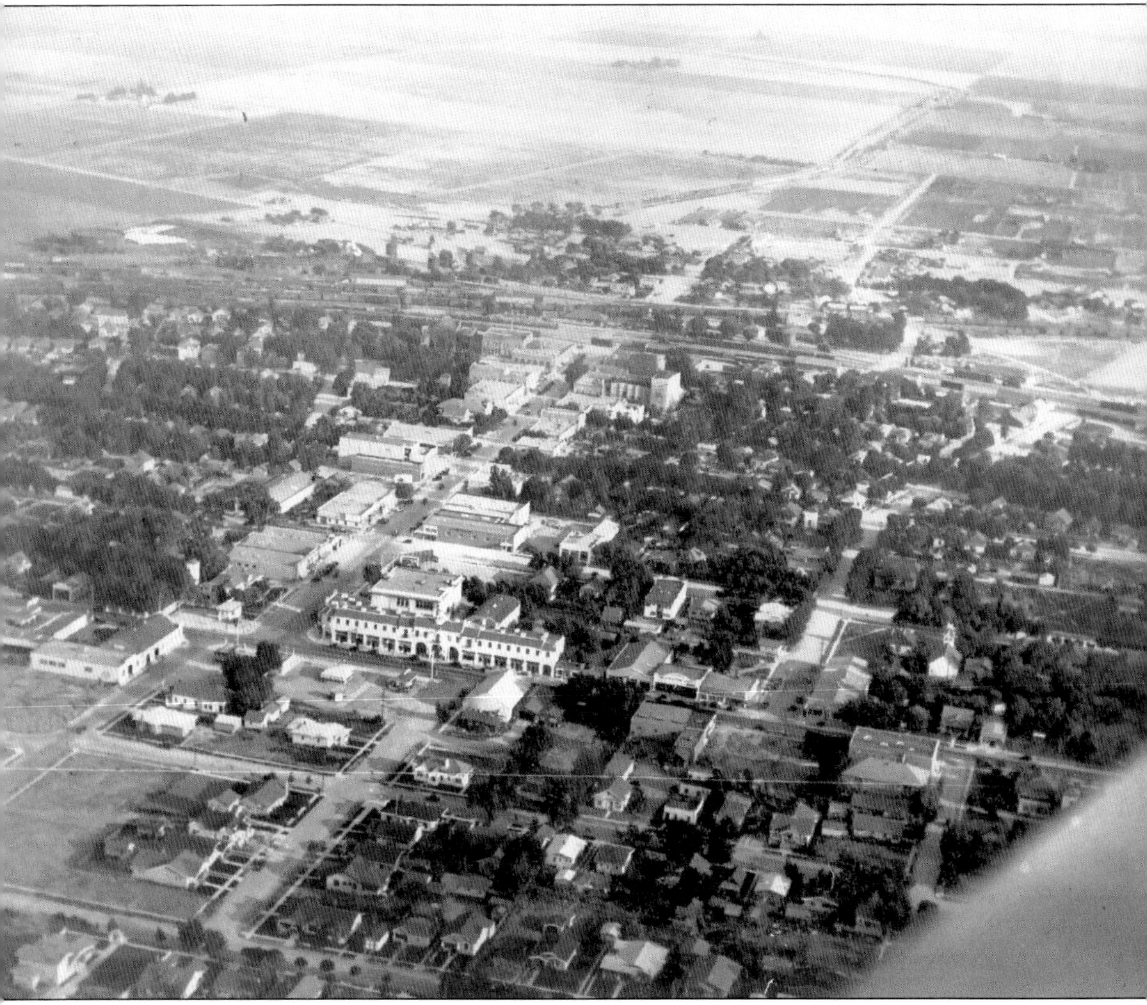

This aerial view of Tracy in 1934 shows the growth of the town and its business district from its original location along the railroad tracks along Sixth Street (shown at the top of the photo), north on Central Avenue to Eleventh Street. The Tracy Inn at Eleventh and Central and the original Central School on Central Avenue are prominent in the photo. By 1934, with the introduction of the automobile and the establishment of the Lincoln Highway through Tracy, Eleventh Street had become the major street through town. In the upper left corner of the photograph is the Tracy Public Cemetery, which was started in 1880 on land donated by the Central Pacific Railroad. By 1934 the town, which started out with wooden buildings and no trees, had turned into an attractive community with brick and concrete buildings in the business district and tree-lined streets in the residential areas.

Eight

PEOPLE

The earliest inhabitants of the Tracy area were the Yokut Indians, followed by Spanish explorers, rancho owners, and their workers. After California became a state and the United States government opened the land for settlement, the population of the area steadily increased. Settlers came from numerous countries and from other areas in the United States, all looking to make a new life in golden California. Many immigrants from Germany and the Canadian province of Nova Scotia were among the early pioneers. The building of the railroads brought workers from China, Japan, Ireland, and Mexico. This influx of people from so many different cultural and economic backgrounds made for an interesting mix of languages and customs among the residents of the Tracy area. Photographs in this chapter represent Tracy area citizens from all "walks of life."

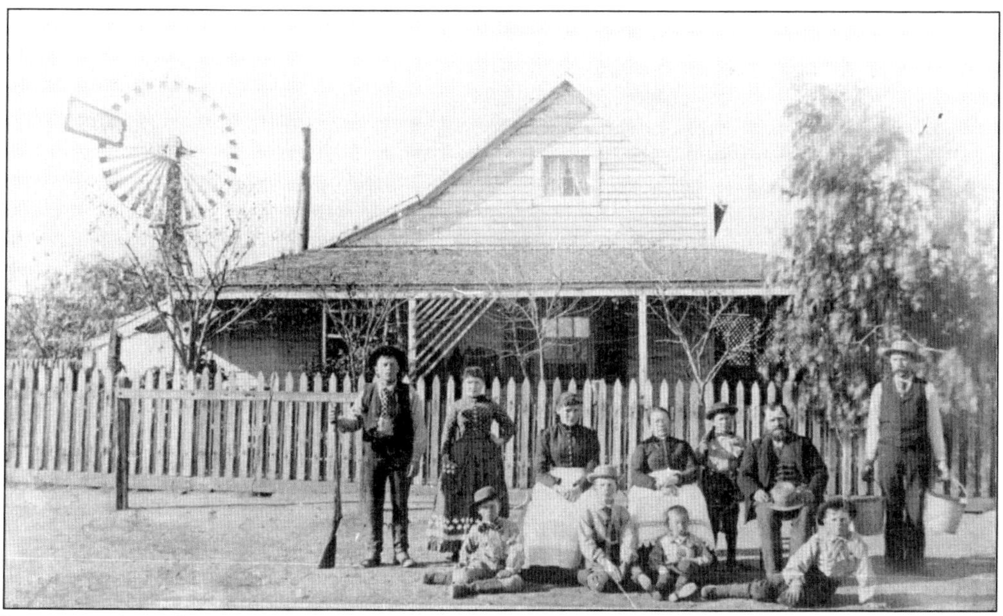

In 1900 when this unidentified Tracy family was photographed in front of their home, the population of Tracy was approximately 700 people. Photographs of families taken in front of their homes with some of their prized possessions were often taken and sent to relatives "back home" to show how well they were doing in their new homes.

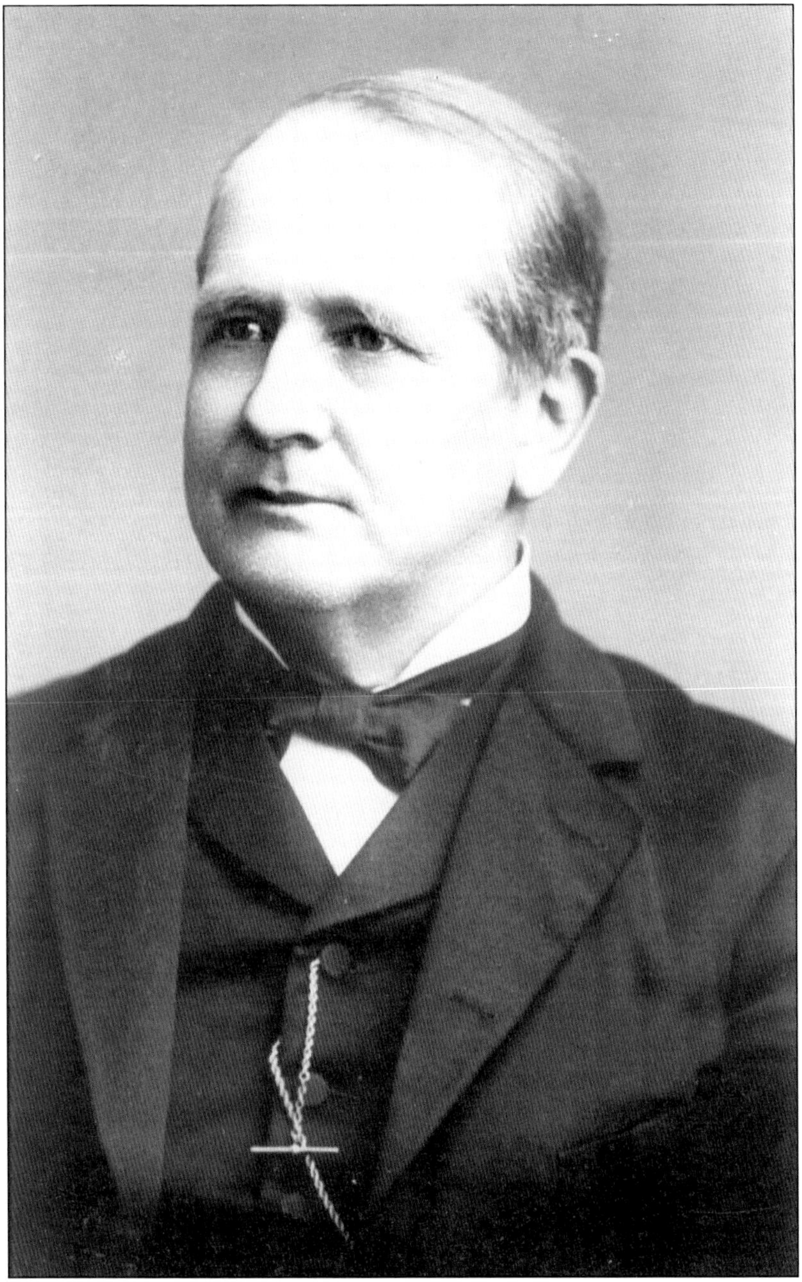

Lathrop Josiah Tracy, for whom Tracy was named in 1878, was a grain merchant in Mansfield, Ohio, and was also a member of the board of directors of the Sandusky, Mansfield & Newark Railroad in Ohio. J.H. Stewart, the superintendent for laying the tracks of the San Pablo & Tulare Railroad line from Martinez to Tracy in 1878, had worked for the Ohio railroad, admired Mr. Tracy, and honored his former employer by naming the town created at the junction of the new line with the Central Pacific's Altamont line for him. Lathrop J. Tracy, who never saw the town named for him in California, died on September 24, 1897 in Alliance, Ohio. His son Rufus A. Tracy did visit Tracy in 1918, however, and a grandson Rufus A. Tracy II, came here from Carmel Valley in 1978 to help celebrate the Tracy centennial.

James Eagan and his wife, Mary, natives of County Mayo, Ireland, were married in Stockton on January 31, 1875, and were probably Tracy's first residents. James worked for the Central Pacific Railroad at Ellis and became the section foreman at the new junction called Tracy. After retirement, he tended his cows on a little farm behind their home on East Sixth Street. James died in 1922. (Courtesy of Kate DeLap.)

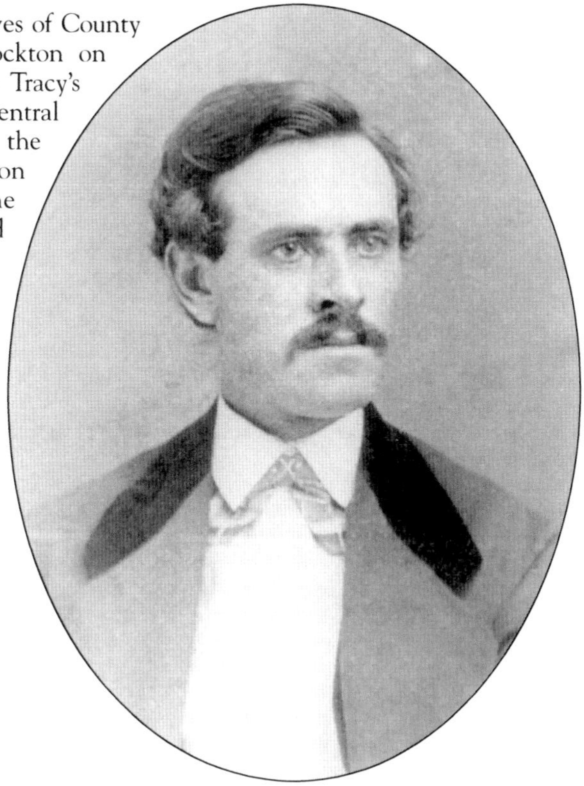

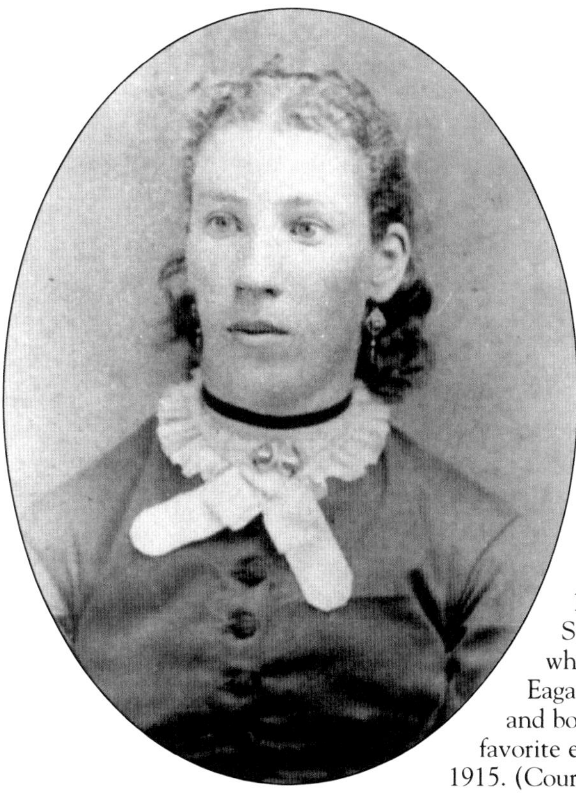

James and Mary (McAllen) Eagan moved to the new town of Tracy in 1878 where they purchased lots on East Sixth Street and built a large house in which they raised eight children. Mrs. Eagan's home, which was also a rooming and boarding house for railroad workers, was a favorite eating place for the "rails." Mary died in 1915. (Courtesy of Kate DeLap.)

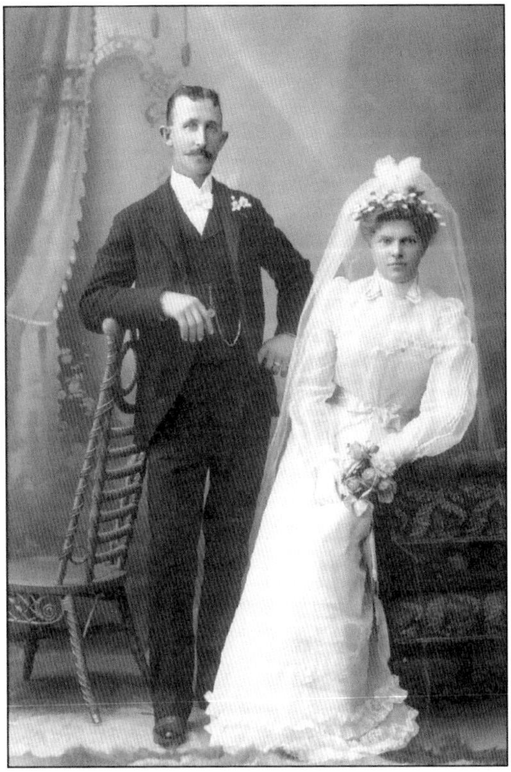

This photograph shows the clothing style popular for weddings in the early 1900s. Frenz W. "Frank" Huck, the son of Frenz and Margaretta (Warch) Huck, and Anna Marie Thoming, the daughter of Jurgen "George" and Lena (Mashoff) Thoming, all residents of Tulare Township, were married on April 8, 1901. The Hucks raised three children—Frances, Lester, and Lao—on their farm southeast of Tracy.

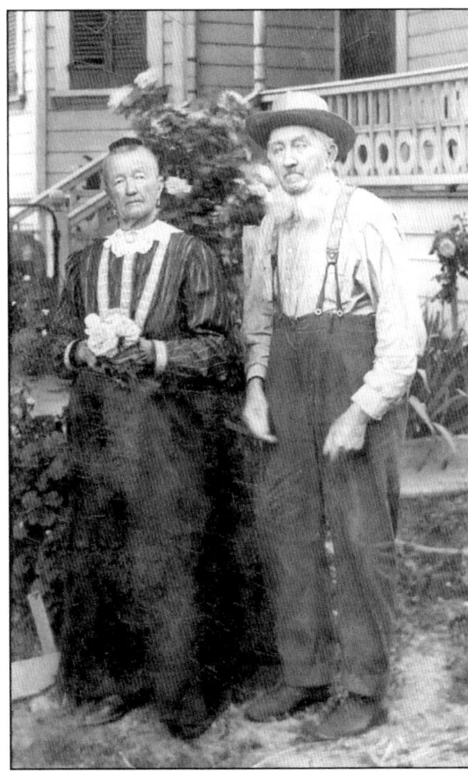

Pictured are a beloved Tracy couple, Anna and Wilhelm Pruser. Wilhelm Pruser settled on a farm in the Tracy area in 1867. Anna (formerly Mrs. Henry Freie) was his second wife. They married in 1895 and retired from farming around 1906. The Pruser home was known for its warm hospitality, and guests looked forward to any event held in their home.

These two unidentified children photographed by Batchelder, 183 El Dorado in Stockton, is a striking example of the "Sunday-best" clothing and high-buttoned shoes worn by children around the turn of the 20th century. Both the boy and girl are holding dolls typical of the time period.

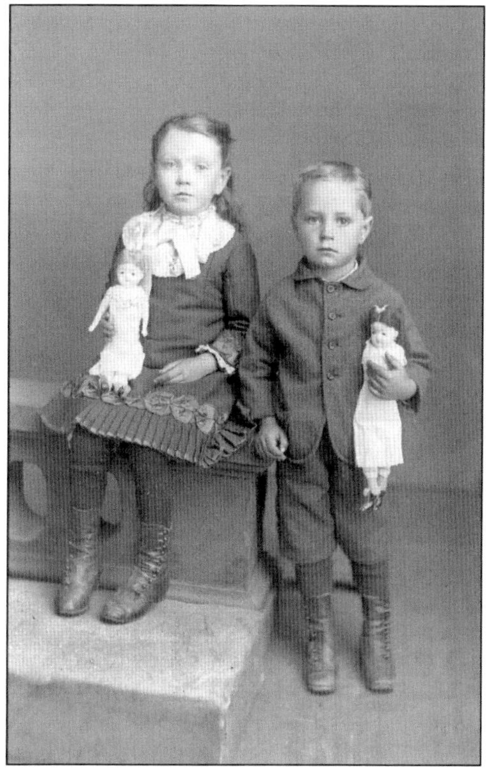

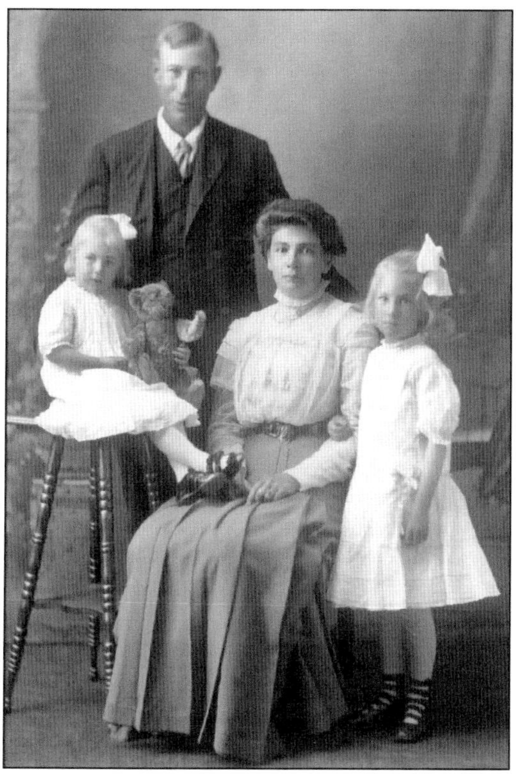

Charles Brandemann of San Francisco and Anna Steinmetz of Banta were married in San Francisco on November 14, 1900. They moved from San Francisco to a ranch south of Tracy in the Carbona area in the fall of 1909 and raised their two daughters on the ranch. Pictured, from left to right, in this family portrait are Mae, Charles, Anna, and Georgia Brandemann.

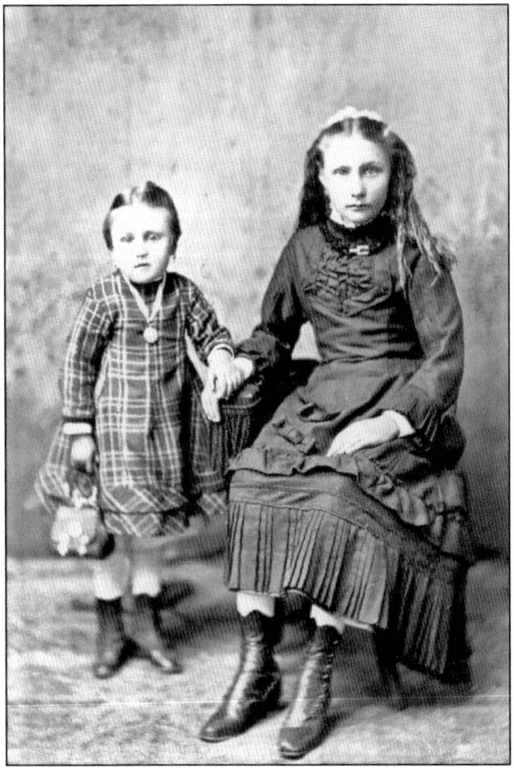

Pictured in the late 1800s, from left to right, are Annie Gesena "Sena" and Matilda Lammers, daughters of Diedrich and Dorathea (Hemsen) Lammers, wearing girls' clothing of the period, including high-button shoes. Matilda married George J. Luhrsen, a farmer in the Lammersville district, in 1894, and Sena married Frank O. Housken, Tracy's first city attorney, in 1901.

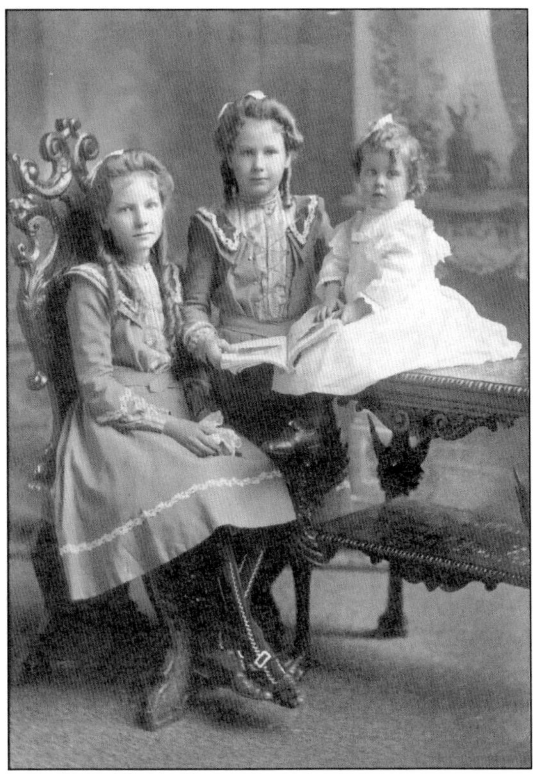

Pictured *c.* 1901 in their best dresses and curls are, from left to right, Violet, Olive, and Lily, the daughters of Claus and Marie Josephine "Josie" (Mohr) Schlichtmann. The Schlichtmanns farmed in the Lammersville/Bethany area until 1896, when they moved to Bethany to operate the general store, blacksmith shop, and post office.

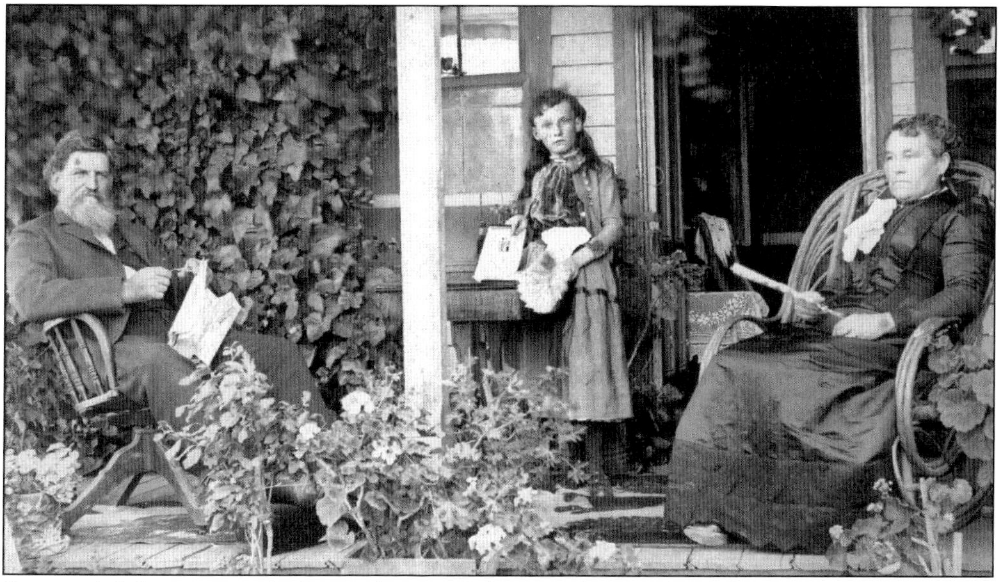

Surrounded by vines and planter boxes of flowers, the Stocking family spends some time together on their pleasant front porch. Front porches were wonderful places to sit and visit after supper, to read the daily newspaper, to greet neighbors, and to escape the heat of the house on hot summer days.

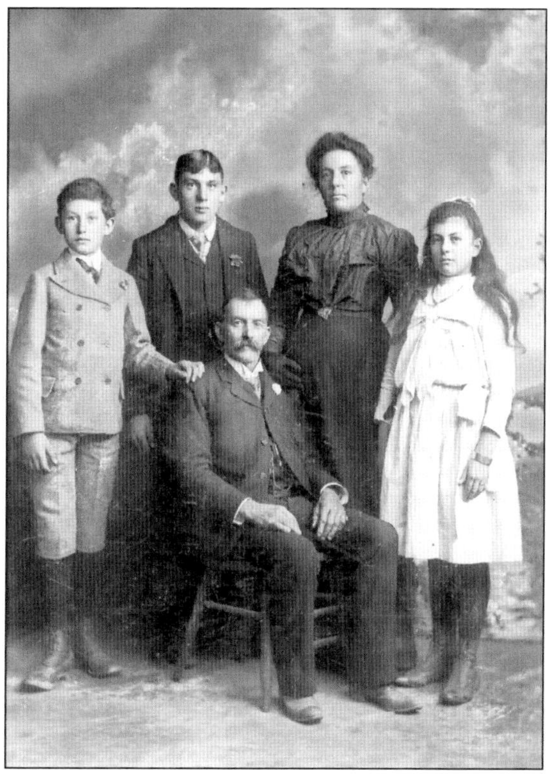

G. Joseph Brichetto opened a general merchandise store in Banta in 1872 and married Luigia Canale in 1879. The Brichettos farmed many sections of land around Banta and Tracy, including the land donated for the Tracy Golf and Country Club on Chrisman Road. Family members seen here are, from left to right, Joseph, John, Mr. and Mrs. Brichetto, and Molly. Not pictured are daughters Irene and Minnie.

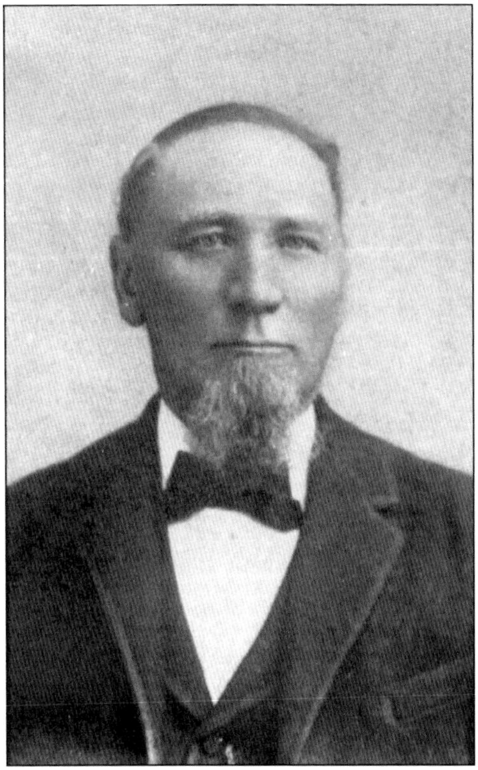

Martin Lammers and his wife, Dorothea, both natives of Germany, established a major farming operation in the area known as Lammersville and on the banks of Old River. They had no children of their own, but over the years they raised over a half dozen children who needed homes. Martin was elected to the California General Assembly in 1876 and authored the West Side Irrigation bill. He died in 1909.

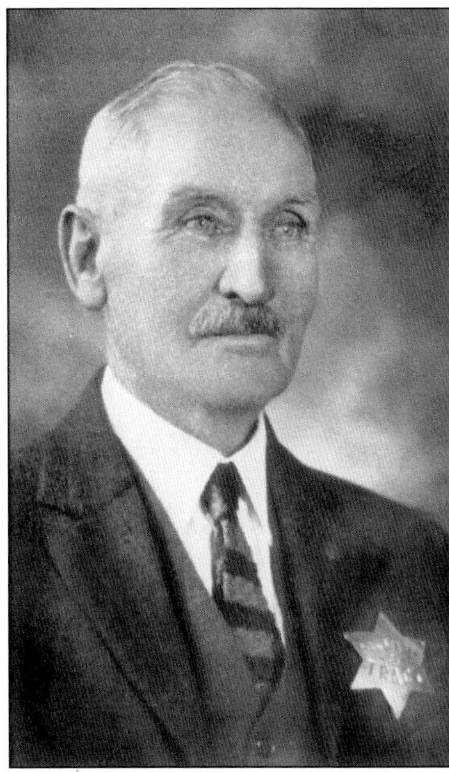

Ernest A. "Pop" Gieseke began his life in the Tracy area as a farmer specializing in thoroughbred stock. Moving to Tracy in 1878, he established Pacific Stables and ran a livery business. Elected constable of Tulare Township in 1886, he held that position until his death in 1933. Part of the time he was also town marshal. Ernest and Margaret (Yost) Gieseke were the parents of three children.

Pearl (Gieseke) Lamb, a daughter of Ernest and Margaret (Yost) Gieseke, was born in 1891 in Tracy and married James N. Lamb in 1908. They had one son, Norman. A very active woman in many aspects of community life, Pearl Lamb served as grand president of California's Native Daughters of the Golden West in 1927. She died in 1967.

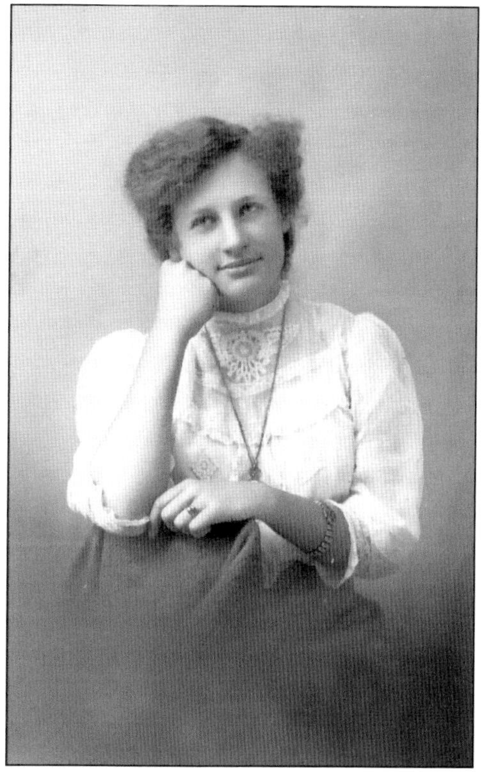

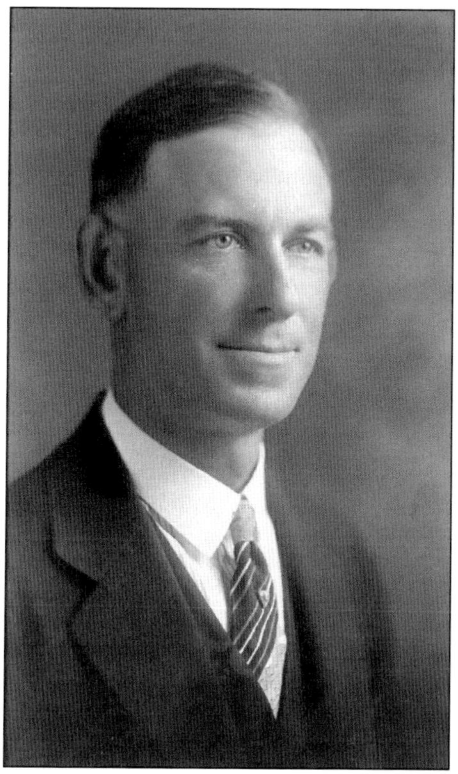

James N. "Jim" Lamb came to Tracy in the early 1900s from Livermore with his family. Along with his father and brother, he operated the Tracy Bottling Works on West Sixth Street. They also sold ice, wood, and coal. He served as a member of Tracy's first city council in 1910 and as mayor from 1926 to 1930 and 1938 to 1942. He died in 1952.

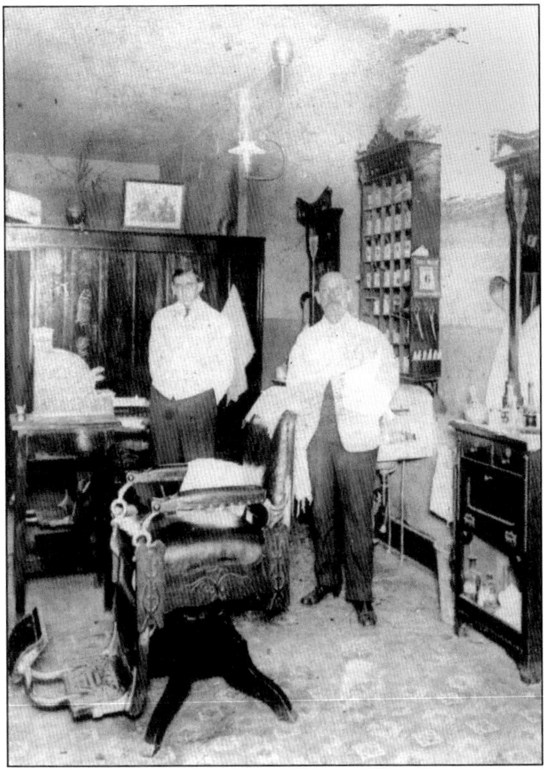

William H. "Billie" May, the proprietor of the Bank Barber Shop, which was located next to the Bank of Italy on Central Avenue between Sixth and Seventh Streets, was photographed inside his barbershop in 1909 with Ira Hutchinson. The barbershop also provided hot and cold baths and served as an agent for the New Method Laundry of Stockton.

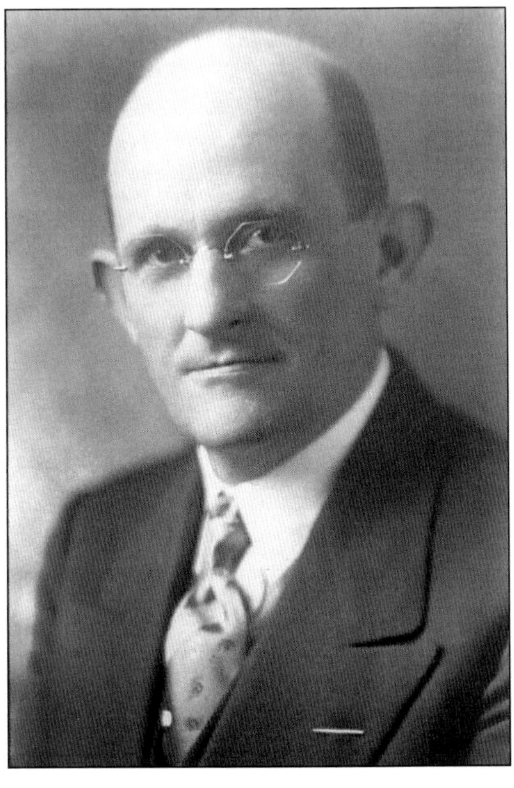

After becoming a lawyer, Bradford S. Crittenden came to Tracy in 1915 and set up a law firm that represented local irrigation districts. In 1920 he was elected to the state assembly and in 1930 to the state senate. He fathered the State Water Resources Act of 1945, which established the Department of Water Resources, leading to the creation of the federal Central Valley Project. (Courtesy of the *Tracy Press*.)

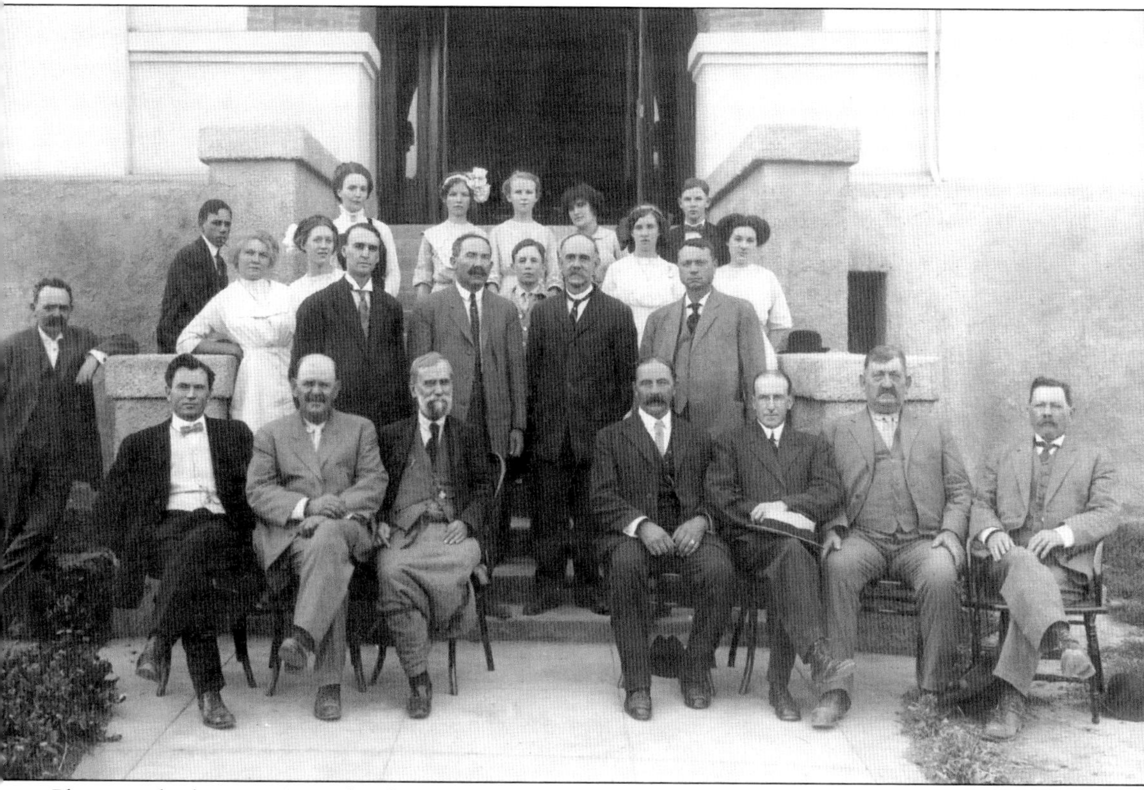

Photographed in 1913 on the front steps of the Tracy Grammar School were the first high school students at West Side Union High School, which met in second-floor classrooms at the school on Central Avenue. Also pictured are the two teachers, members of the board of trustees, and other community leaders. From left to right are (front row) Reverend MacArthur, trustee George Luhrsen, clerk of the trustees Dr. Joseph S. West, president of the trustees William Schlossman, O.H. Root (cashier at the Bank of Tracy), trustee William Schmidt, and physician Dr. J.G. Murrell; (second row) physician Dr. Kass, Myrtle Frerichs (Fisk), *Tracy Press* editor Warren Henshaw, Mayor Abe Grunauer, principal and professor A.D. Tenney, and unidentified; (third row) students Joe DeLamater, Viola Sehrt, Lyle McKeany, Gladys Westlake, and Gladys Powell (Burt); (back row) teacher Mary Acheson, and students Millie Schmidt, Eva Schmidt (Cooper), Vesta Ludwig, and Harry Hicks.

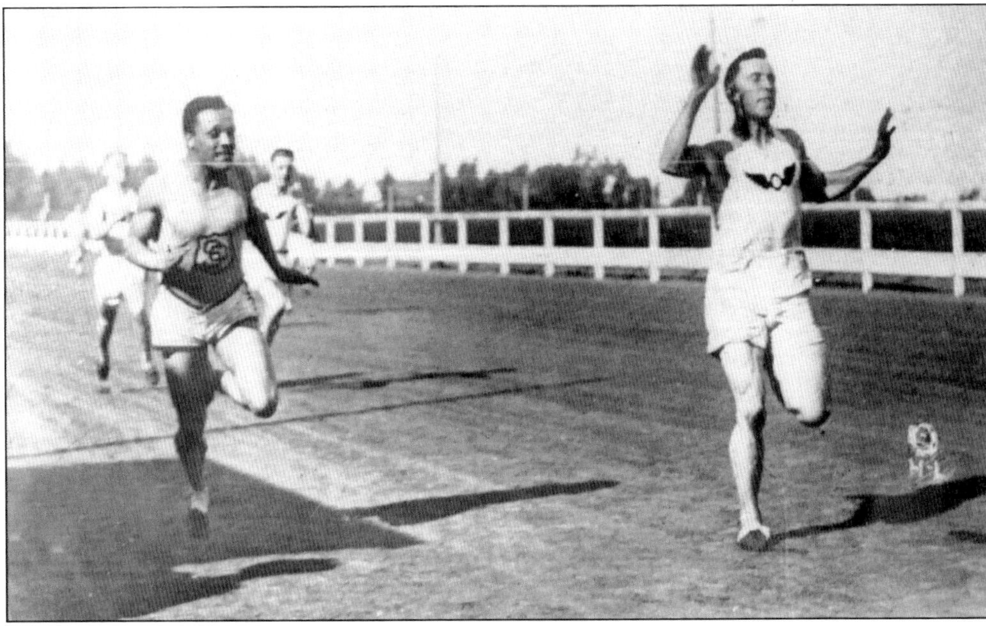

George L. Parker defeated Howard Drew in the 220-yard dash in a world record time of 21.2 seconds on October 2, 1914. A Tracy farm boy, George began his track career at Stockton High School before Tracy had a high school. Tracy's first nationally known sports figure, he was unable to participate in the Olympics in 1916 because the games were canceled due to World War I.

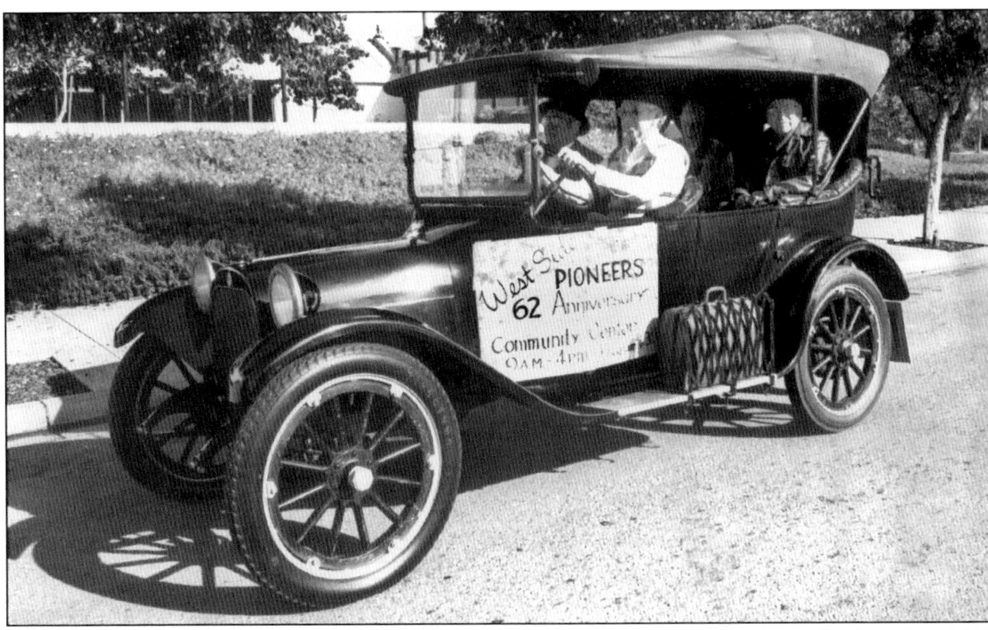

John Thompson, a former Dodge-Plymouth dealer in Tracy, was photographed in his 1915 Dodge touring car in a parade with Melvin Routt in front and Louie Villalovoz in back. John ran the Dodge-Plymouth dealership, which was originally operated by his father, George E. Thompson. G.E. Thompson & Son was located on the southwest corner of Eleventh Street at F Street (currently a car wash).

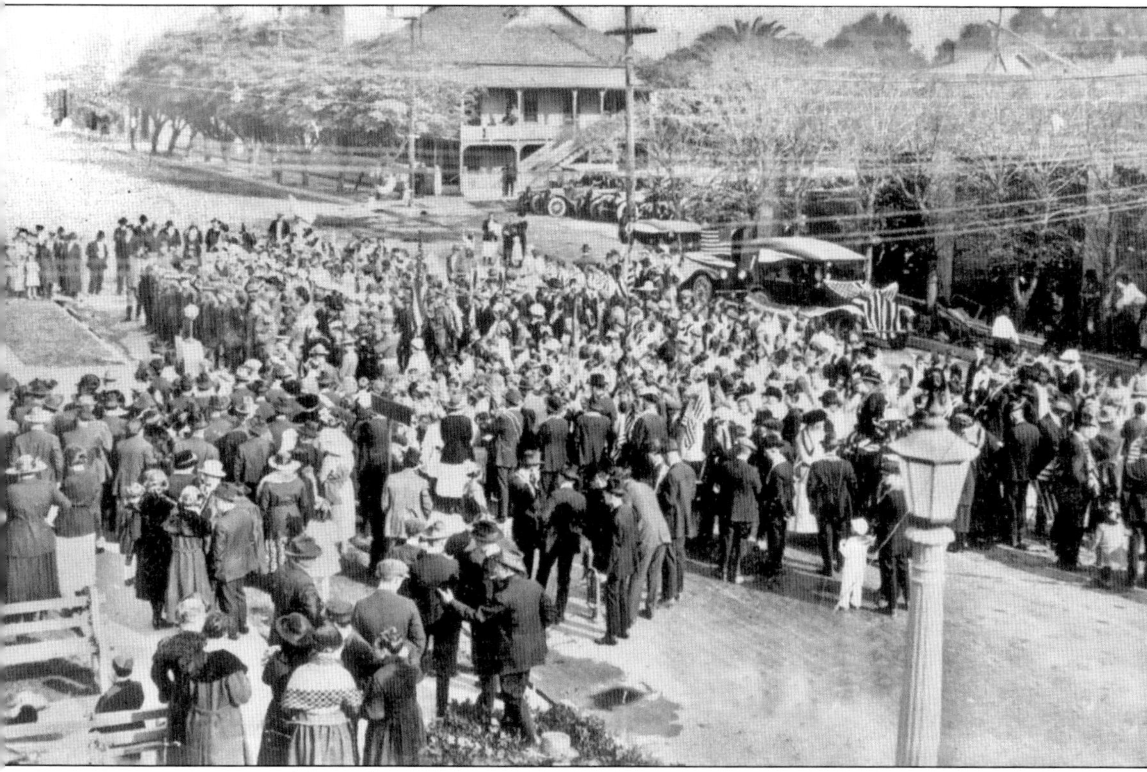

Armistice Day was celebrated on November 11, 1921, in front of Tracy City Hall at Ninth Street and Central Avenue, three years after the end of World War I. The observance was opened with a parade from the Odd Fellows Hall on East Sixth Street to City Hall. The Tracy Band led the procession, followed by the veterans, in whose honor the parade was held. Many members of community organizations and students from both the high school and grammar schools followed the veterans. So many citizens, in fact, participated in the parade that the "line of spectators was quite thin." At City Hall, Assemblyman Bradford S. Crittenden of Tracy gave a spirited speech in celebration of the war victory and also spoke of the need for legislation to assist the disabled veterans. Afterwards, veterans of "the war to end all wars" were treated to a Thanksgiving feast of turkey, mince pies, and all the trimmings in the patriotically decorated IOOF Hall.

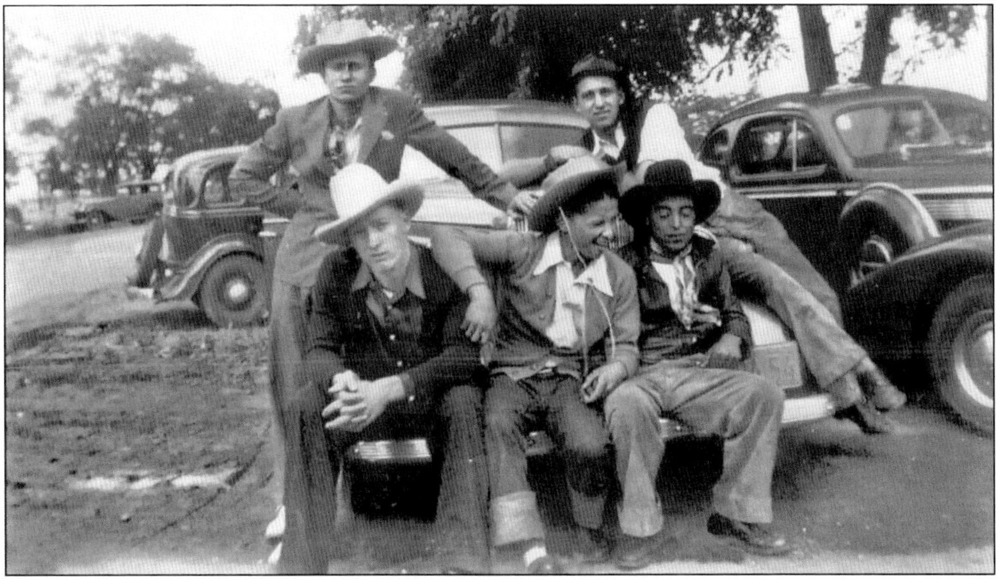

Friends from Tracy's South Side were decked out in cowboy gear in 1939 to participate in Tracy's first Frontier Days. Seated on the bumper, from left to right, are Al Salice, "Foo," and Al Gomez. Leaning on the hood, from left to right, are Al and Mario Rinaldo. Frontier Days were celebrated in 1939 and 1940 and for three years after World War II. (Courtesy of Al Rinaldo.)

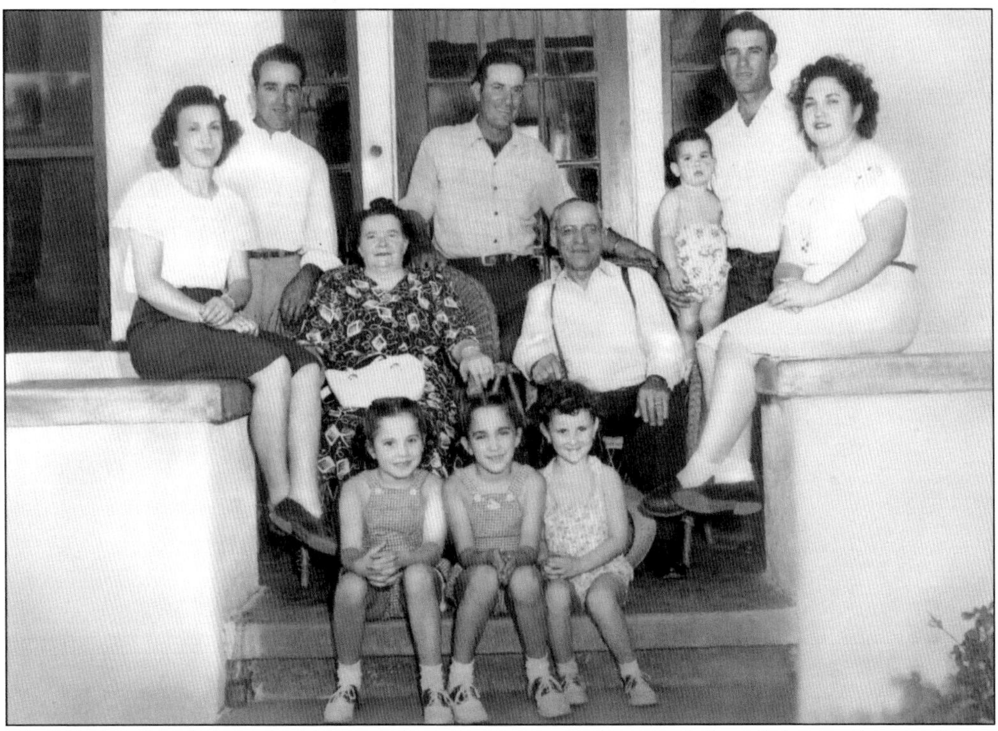

The Alvarez family came to Tracy in the 1930s. Pictured in 1946, from left to right, are (front row) Marijane, Marielena, and Cathy Alvarez, daughters of Gabe and Stephanie Alvarez; (middle row) Jose and Lorenza Alvarez, parents of the three sons pictured; (back row) Bre and Joe Alvarez, Pete Alvarez, and Gabe and Stephanie Alvarez with their son Gregory.

Fire Chief Roxy Hudson presents a certificate of appreciation to George E. Thompson, Tracy Dodge-Plymouth dealer, for his support of Tracy Fire Department projects in 1948. After World War II, when equipment was difficult to obtain, Thompson was able to provide through his dealership the chassis needed to build two fire trucks for the Tracy Fire Department. At right is Fire Capt. Nick Canale.

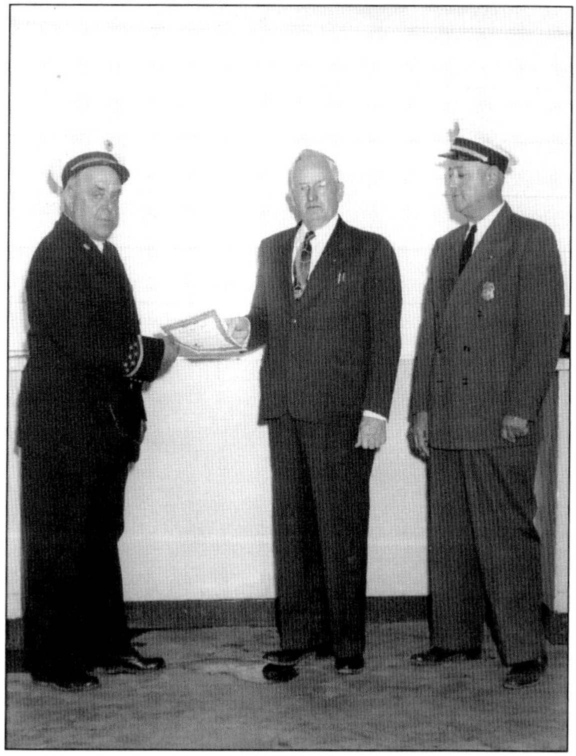

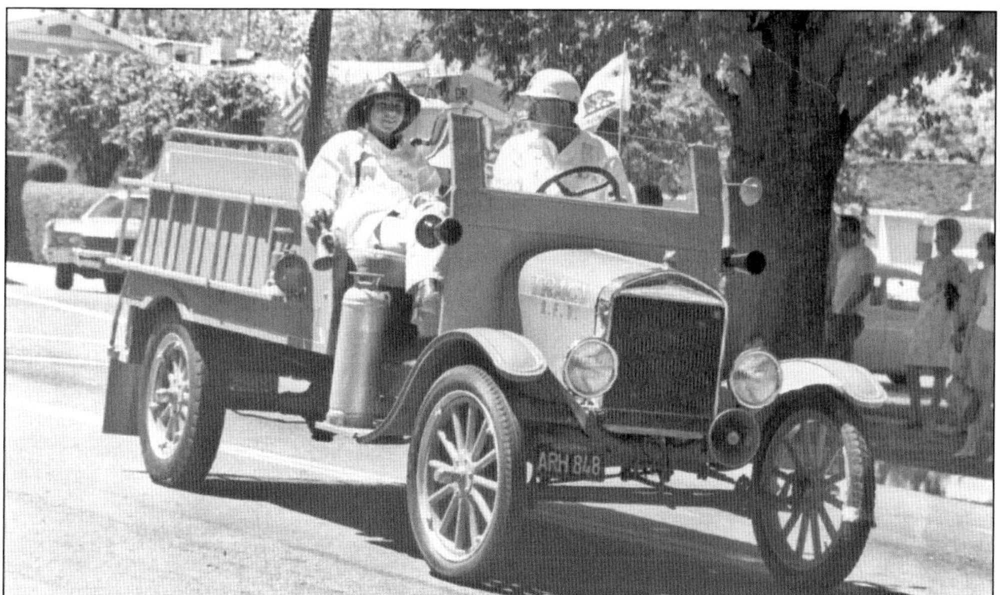

Al Ekenberg, a volunteer with the Tracy Rural Fire Department, drives a simulated fire truck in a Tracy parade. Connie Maciel is his passenger. Ekenberg was the custodian and bus driver at New Jerusalem School for 38 years before he retired in 1972. He and his wife, Bertha, were community leaders for the New Jerusalem 4-H Club for 55 years. Bertha died in 2000, and Al died in 2002.

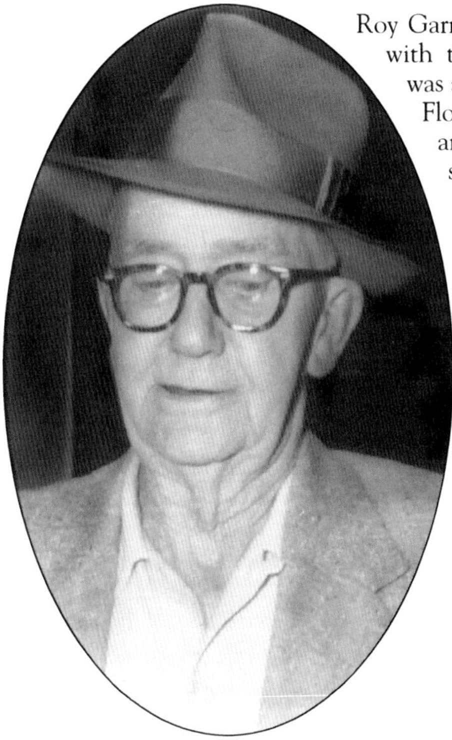

Roy Garrison, a Nebraska native, was a longtime engineer with the Southern Pacific Railroad. After retiring, he was a regular at the Old Timers Club. Roy and his wife, Florence, had two sons—Fred Garrison of Sebastopol and Duane Garrison, who operated a sporting goods store in Tracy and was a longtime columnist for the *Tracy Press*.

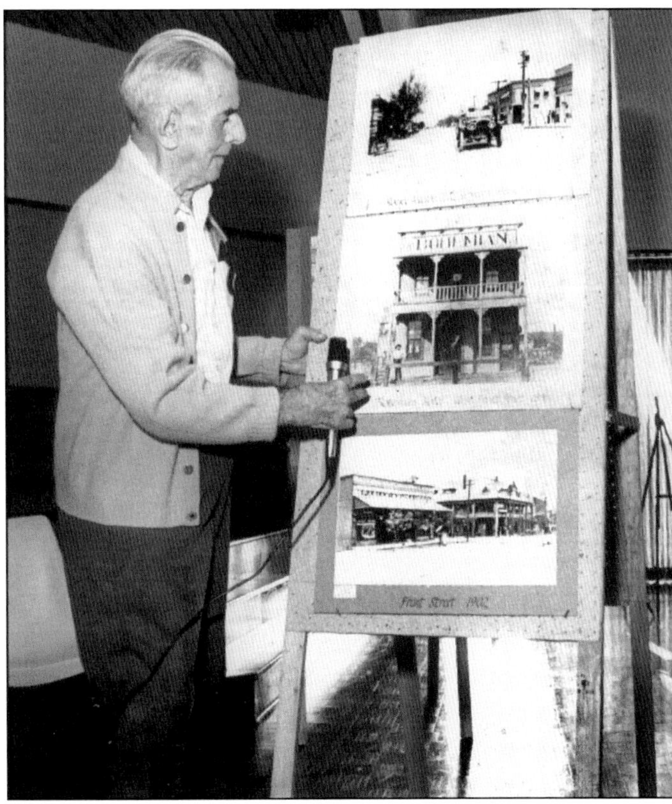

Many of the early Tracy photographs in this book were part of the Waldo Stevens collection. Waldo, a member of the pioneer Ebe family, is shown here in 1982 displaying part of his collection, which was later donated to the West Side Pioneer Association, of which he was an active member. He died in 1983.

Emma M. Baumgardner, an educational and cultural force in Tracy for 60 years, taught English and drama at Tracy High School and challenged students to "read, think, and act." After retiring in 1954, she taught at the University of the Pacific and at Ewha University in Seoul, Korea. "Mrs. B" also directed theater productions in Tracy. The Emma Baumgardner Theater at Tracy High is named in her honor.

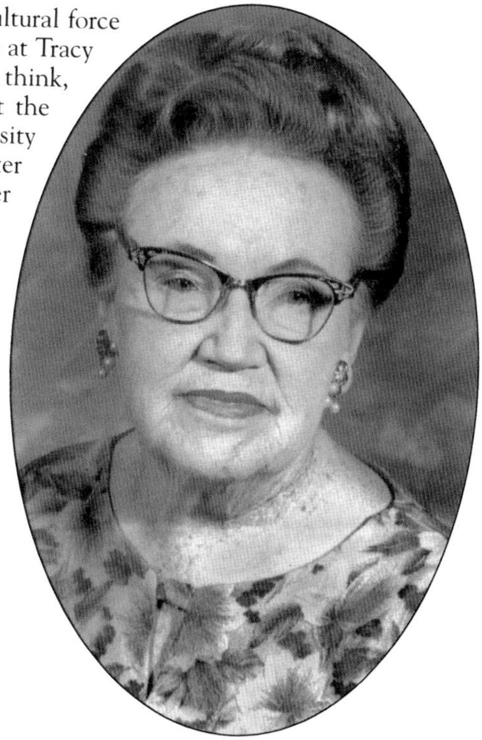

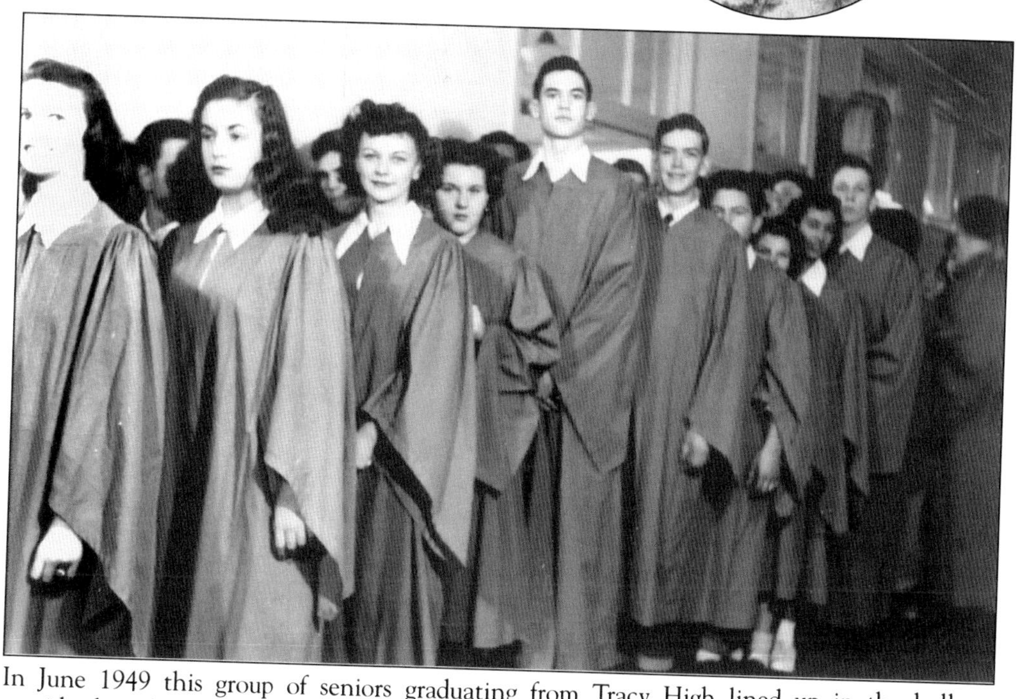

In June 1949 this group of seniors graduating from Tracy High lined up in the hallway outside the school auditorium before commencement exercises began. The first five students are, from left to right, Robbie Couch, Mary Serpa, Onalee Lowes, Margaret Saling, and Tom Matthews. One of the graduates, Onalee Lowes Koster, currently directs the operation of the Tracy Historical Museum.

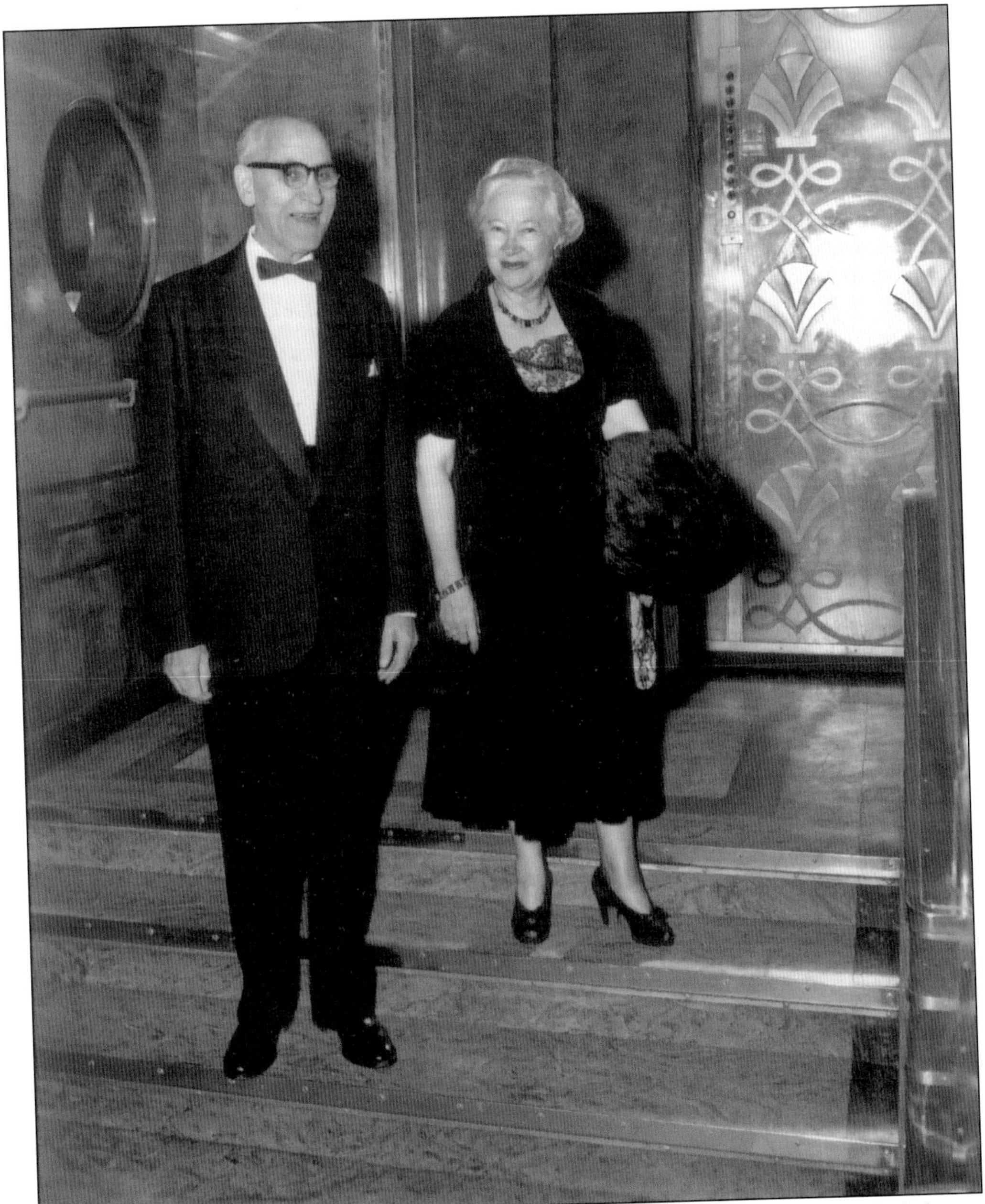

George and Marguerite Wadsworth were photographed aboard the liner *Queen Elizabeth* during a journey across the Atlantic. George Wadsworth, a graduate of the University of Chicago, came to Tracy from Idaho in 1917 to become principal of West Side Union High School (later Tracy Union High School). Several years later he completed his study of law and passed the state bar examination. He became Tracy's city attorney and also was an attorney for the West Side Irrigation District. Marguerite was an English teacher at the high school. In 1960, after the deaths of Mr. and Mrs. Wadsworth, the city of Tracy received $100,000 in stock from their estate to build what became the Wadsworth Memorial Library in Lincoln Park. The library, opened in 1961, was enlarged in 1987 and renamed Tracy Branch Library. The meeting room is now named the Wadsworth Room, in honor of George and Marguerite Wadsworth.